RE-CLAIMING
THE BIBLE
FOR A
NON-RELIGIOUS
WORLD

BOOKS BY JOHN SHELBY SPONG

Honest Prayer

Dialogue in Search of Jewish-Christian Understanding
(with Rabbi Jack Daniel Spiro)

Christpower (compiled and edited by Lucy Newton Boswell)

Life Approaches Death: A Dialogue in Medical
Ethics (with Dr. Daniel Gregory)

The Living Commandments

The Easter Moment

Into the Whirlwind: The Future of the Church

Beyond Moralism (with the Venerable Denise Haines)

Survival and Consciousness: An Interdisciplinary Inquiry into
the Possibility of Life Beyond Biological Death (editor)

Living in Sin? A Bishop Rethinks Human Sexuality

Rescuing the Bible from Fundamentalism:
A Bishop Rethinks the Meaning of Scripture

Born of a Woman: A Bishop Rethinks the Virgin Birth and
the Role of Women in a Male-Dominated Church

This Hebrew Lord: A Bishop's Search for the Authentic Jesus

Resurrection: Myth or Reality? A Bishop Rethinks the Meaning of Easter

Liberating the Gospels: Reading the Bible with Jewish Eyes

Why Christianity Must Change or Die:
A Bishop Speaks to Believers in Exile

The Bishop's Voice: Selected Essays (1979–1999)
(compiled and edited by Christine Mary Spong)

Here I Stand: My Struggle for a Christianity
of Integrity, Love, and Equality

A New Christianity for a New World: Why Traditional
Faith Is Dying and How a New Faith Is Being Born

The Sins of Scripture: Exposing the Bible's Texts
of Hate to Reveal the God of Love

Jesus for the Non-Religious: Recovering the
Divine at the Heart of the Human

Eternal Life: A New Vision—Beyond Religion,
Beyond Theism, Beyond Heaven and Hell

RE-CLAIMING
THE BIBLE
FOR A
NON-RELIGIOUS
WORLD

John Shelby Spong

HarperOne

An Imprint of HarperCollins*Publishers*

HarperOne

RE-CLAIMING THE BIBLE FOR A NON-RELIGIOUS WORLD. Copyright © 2011 by John Shelby Spong. All rights reserved. Printed in the United States of America. No part of this book may be used or reproduced in any manner whatsoever without written permission except in the case of brief quotations embodied in critical articles and reviews. For information address HarperCollins Publishers, 10 East 53rd Street, New York, NY 10022.

HarperCollins books may be purchased for educational, business, or sales promotional use. For information please e-mail the Special Markets Department at SPsales@harpercollins.com.

HarperCollins website: http://www.harpercollins.com

HarperCollins®, ®, and HarperOne™ are trademarks of HarperCollins Publishers.

FIRST HARPERCOLLINS PAPERBACK EDITION PUBLISHED IN 2013

Library of Congress Cataloging-in-Publication Data is available upon request.

ISBN 978-0-06-201129-9

13 14 15 16 17 RRD(H) 10 9 8 7 6 5 4 3 2 1

Dedicated to
Mike Keriakas
Mark Tauber
Ben Wolin
the founders of Agoramedia.com, which evolved into
Waterfrontmedia.com and finally into EverydayHealth.com,
who invited me to become a weekly columnist, a role that
I have now filled for nine years—
and to
Mark Roberts
Mekado Murphy
Tony Brancato
Roseanne Henry
Sarah Hutter
Daniela Descano
who worked with me on this column during the years of our association.
I am grateful to them all.

CONTENTS

Preface   xi

PART I
SETTING THE STAGE: POSING THE PROBLEM

1 Examining the Bible's Mystique   3

PART II
THE FORMATION OF THE TORAH

2 Breaking Open the Books of Moses   21
3 The Yahwist Document: The Original Narrative   29
4 The Elohist Document: The Torah Expands   37
5 The Deuteronomic Writers:
   The Third Strand of the Torah   45
6 The Priestly Document:
   The Fourth Strand of the Torah   51

PART III
THE RISE OF THE PROPHETS

7 The Transitional Books: Joshua, Judges and Samuel   63
8 The Story of Nathan: All Are Subject to the Law   71

9 I and II Kings, Elijah and Elisha:
   Step Two in the Prophetic Tradition   77

PART IV
INTRODUCING THE WRITING PROPHETS

10 The Prophetic Principle: Ancient and Modern   85
11 The Isaiahs I, II and III   91
12 Jeremiah: Prophet of Doom   105
13 Ezekiel: Prophet of the Exile   111
14 Daniel: Misplaced but Potent   117

PART V
THE MINOR PROPHETS: THE BOOK OF THE TWELVE

15 Hosea: The Prophet Who Changed
    God's Name to Love   125
16 Amos: The Prophet Who Changed
    God's Name to Justice   131
17 Micah: The Prophet Who Turned Liturgy into Life   137
18 Jonah: Definer of Prejudice   143
19 I and II Zechariah: Shapers of the Jesus Story   149
20 Malachi: The Dawn of Universalism   155

PART VI
THE BIBLE'S PROTEST LITERATURE

21 Job: Icon of a New Consciousness   163
22 Ruth: The Myth of Racial Purity   169

PART VII
LITURGICAL BOOKS AND WISDOM LITERATURE

23 The Book of Psalms   177
24 Wisdom Literature: Proverbs, Ecclesiastes
    and the Song of Solomon   183

25 Lamentations and Esther:
Books Designed for Liturgical Observances 189
26 The Chronicler, Ezra and Nehemiah:
National Mythmakers 195

PART VIII
INTRODUCING THE CHRISTIAN SCRIPTURES,
COMMONLY CALLED THE NEW TESTAMENT

27 A New Beginning—An Old Theme 203
28 Dating the Historical Jesus 209
29 Dating the New Testament in Relation
to the Life of Jesus 215
30 The Oral Period 221

PART IX
PAUL: THE FIRST NEW TESTAMENT WRITER

31 The Witness of Paul 229
32 Paul's Secret Thorn 235
33 Paul's Early Epistles: I Thessalonians and Galatians 241
34 The Corinthian Letters 247
35 Resurrection According to Paul 253
36 Resurrection Through Jewish Eyes 259
37 Romans: The Gospel of Paul 265
38 The Theology of Paul as Revealed in Romans 271
39 Who Is Christ for Paul? The Gospel in Romans 277
40 The Elder Paul: Philemon and Philippians 283
41 Post-Pauline Epistles:
II Thessalonians, Colossians and Ephesians 289

PART X
THE SYNOPTIC GOSPELS

42 Exploring Mark: The Original Gospel 297
43 Mark's Use of Synagogue Worship Patterns 303

44 Mark's First Narrative of the Crucifixion:
     A Passover Format   309
45 Matthew: The Most Jewish Gospel   317
46 Matthew's Interpretive Secret   323
47 Matthew and the Liturgical Year of the Synagogue   329
48 Luke: Moving Toward the Gentile World   333
49 Luke's Vision of Universalism   339
50 Acts: The Spirit That Embraces the
     World and Drives Toward Wholeness   347
51 Paul and Early Christians as Viewed Through Acts   353

PART XI
THE PASTORAL EPISTLES, HEBREWS
AND THE GENERAL EPISTLES

52 I and II Timothy and Titus: "We Have the Truth!"   361
53 The Epistle to the Hebrews   367
54 The General Epistles: James, I and II Peter and Jude 373

PART XII
THE JOHANNINE CORPUS

55 Introducing the Johannine Material   381
56 The Gospel of John: Not a Literal Book   387
57 The Raising of Lazarus and
     the Identity of the Beloved Disciple   393
58 The Epilogue of John   399
59 The Johannine Epistles and the Book of Revelation   405

    Bibliography   411

The idea for this book was born in 2006 in a summer retirement community in Highlands, North Carolina. Highlands is a small town nestled in the beautiful mountains of Macon County, about an hour's drive southwest of Asheville. During the height of the summer season the permanent residents, eager to enhance the attractiveness of this area to tourists, together with some summer-only residents, organize events to engage and entertain the hundreds and even thousands of vacationers seeking to escape the heat of the South in the cooler temperatures of the North Carolina mountains. These summer activities have two primary foci. First these Highlanders plan for and carry out a schedule of magnificent concerts, involving visiting artists, vocalists and string and chamber groups who perform until early August. To head up this activity there is a governing board and designated leaders, but when I talk to the musicians it is clear that they believe that Mark and Kathy Whitehead, he a retired urologist and she a retired nurse, are the soul of this activity. A major resource available to the Whiteheads and their fellow planners is that these mountains attract each summer a number of musicians who are in residence, including some who are part of the Atlanta Symphony. One of them, William Ransom, a pianist of uncommon talent, not only directs these events, but also performs in them as an artist. Every one of these concerts seems to be a sellout, and a gala celebration dinner at the end of the summer season is the high social point of the year.

The second summer offering is sponsored by an organization known as HIARPT, which stands for the Highlands Institute for American Religion, Philosophy and Theology. This organization sponsors a weekly summer lecture series. HIARPT's founder and president, a man named Creighton Peden, was formerly the Calloway Professor of Philosophy at Augusta State University. He is ably assisted in this activity by Everett J. Tarbox and his wife, Nancy, he a retired university professor and she a student of religion. Obviously others also assist in this process. Many of the residents and vacationers are people who have had distinguished careers in academia, business, law and medicine, primarily across the South. The leaders of HIARPT are dedicated to their goal of guaranteeing that the intellectual life of this summer community will always be stretching. Toward that end, in this lecture series they bring to Highlands philosophers and theologians to be guest lecturers throughout the summer. I have been privileged to be one of these since 2003. For me this has meant that on Monday and Tuesday evenings for two, three or four weeks each summer, I have addressed this audience as a teacher. My subject has always been some aspect of the Bible, demonstrating my conviction that if the Bible is taught to laypeople in the same way that it is taught in academic centers like Union Theological Seminary in New York or Harvard Divinity School in Cambridge, Massachusetts, with no attempt to protect the fairly juvenile Sunday school knowledge to which so many otherwise learned people still cling, there will be a significant response. I have never believed that the Bible needs to be protected either from critical biblical scholarship, or from the insights that come from astrophysics, astronomy, biology, psychology or any other source.

As part of this HIARPT program in the summer of 2006 I began a series of lectures on how the various books of the Bible came to be written and then how these writings later came to be regarded as "sacred scripture." I think it is fair to say that my audience had lived generally within the cultural framework of the evangelical religion that seems native to the South, but can be found anywhere in the Christian world and is today particularly noted as the form of Christianity present and growing in the Third World. In this religious expression the tendency is to treat the Bible in a more or less literal way. The unspoken assumption for some is that the Bible dropped from heaven fully written, divided into chapters and verses and, if they are English-speaking people, in the King James Version! I discovered, however, in the course of my presentations over the next five summers that most of these people did not really believe these things about the Bible at all. They only pretended that they did, because they thought that this was what Christianity and their evangelical, religious culture required them to believe. Perhaps an even greater factor sustaining this childlike belief system was that they knew of no other way to engage the Bible, or indeed that there even was another way! When they began to understand that a literal view of the Bible was not what Christian scholars had believed for almost two hundred years, they responded with great enthusiasm. Far from experiencing from this audience the sense of threat and fear that so many evangelicals manifest, I found in them a sense of freedom and an eagerness to know more. Seldom was there an empty seat available over the summers. Indeed, the venue had to be moved to a larger space just to accommodate the crowds.

What I hoped to do in these lectures was to discover a way to introduce competent biblical scholarship to the people who sit in the pews of our churches. It was fascinating for me to see them engage the Bible in a way none of them had ever imagined doing so before. They quickly escaped the well-known religious anxiety which suggests that if the Bible is not believed literally it will not be believed at all. The question period that followed each lecture was animated and open with many of the members of my audience raising questions publicly that they had long harbored privately.

I was so encouraged by the response of these people to this public exploration into the Bible that I decided to introduce this material to a much wider and more diverse audience through the medium of my weekly column, which was published at that time by an Internet company known as WaterfrontMedia. That company, which has now changed its name to EverydayHealth, marketed this column across this nation and around the world, reaching a readership that in some weeks topped one hundred thousand people. The excitement I had experienced in my live audience each week in Highlands was now replicated in the response I received to my column over the next five years, a time-span that allowed me to be much more thorough and substantive than I could be in four to eight lectures each summer. In the column I went into the origins, the background and the essential meaning of each of the sixty-six books in the Bible. To my knowledge this was the first serious week-by-week study of the Bible from an academic perspective that had ever been tried on the Internet. By the time the series was concluded in 2010, the enthusiasm of my readers across America and around the world indicated to me that there was a vast audience of religiously hungry people eager to explore a meaningful journey into the Bible. It was then that my publisher, HarperOne, asked me to examine the possibility of turning these columns into a book on both the origins of the Bible and the essential message of each of its books, specifically aimed at inquisitive and educated laypeople for whom their familiar Sunday school stories still provided the substance of most of their biblical knowledge. My conviction was and is that what people learn in a typical Sunday school will never be adequate to sustain a believable faith for educated, questioning people living in the twenty-first century.

The purpose of these columns was not to be exhaustive so much as it was to be introductory. I deliberately did not seek to engage my readers in the debates over minutia, such as how many different strands make up the Elohist document in the formation of the Old Testament, or which of the words attributed to Jesus are authentic. Those are quite valid debates among biblical scholars, but they are outside the purview of this book. I have frequently participated in exactly those kinds of debates as a fellow of the Jesus Seminar, and I have found them both worthwhile and stimulating. My experience has been, however, that such debates are beyond the interest level of most people except for those who live in the academic community. My audience rather wanted to know the background, the context, the level of authenticity and even the trustworthiness of the message found in the various books now making up the Bible. They were aware that the Bible has been a major force in shaping the Western world, and they wanted to understand that impact and, in some cases, even wanted to see if they could find a way back into a realistic faith system.

I have sought, therefore, to introduce people to the themes and messages of the various books of the Bible by examining the sweep of history in which these books were originally written. What was the situation that compelled this or that particular writing? What was the message the author sought to convey, and what part of that message still has universal applications? I wanted to help my readers understand why these particular books, written between two and three thousand years ago, came to be regarded as authoritative and thus worthy of being preserved as sacred. I also wanted to trace the pathway that biblical religion traveled as it evolved over the centuries and how the human need to control behavior within the boundaries of what the community could tolerate in its struggle to survive shaped these texts. Above all, I wanted to watch how the sense of God found in the lives of our ancestors grew and developed over these centuries, as it illumined the mundanities of their lives and sustained them through the specific crises of their history. I wanted it to become crystal clear that anyone who thinks of the Bible as an unchanging book has never read it. The image of God, for example, begins in the Bible as a rather traditional dictatorial figure. This God was tribal in nature and, as such and very conveniently, this God hated all the enemies of the people who believed themselves to be God's chosen. Yet, if we continue to read the Bible we watch this idea of God evolve and change, becoming newly redefined as love, justice and a universal moral presence. Ultimately in this same book we hear this God enjoin us to love our enemies and even to let our enemies love us. I also wanted to reclaim not the literal power, but the essential meaning of the Bible in and for the non-religious world we inhabit. It was and is a "heady" task. For some of my more traditional religious readers I am certain that this book will be an uncomfortable, maybe even a shattering experience, should they bother to read it. Some will even perceive this book as an attack on the Bible itself. They will be wrong. I happen to love the Bible very deeply. That will certainly become obvious as the pages are turned.

My readers will find the format and style of this book to be somewhat different from what they might expect. The book inevitably reflects the fact that its various segments were originally written week by week in the format of a fifteen-hundred-word essay. Each essay could be read in ten to fifteen minutes at most. That fifteen-hundred-word boundary was necessary to meet the space requirements of my column. In preparing this material for a book I was able to expand many of these columns with new data, some additional stories and more enhancing illustrations, but this volume's pages continue to reveal short, complete segments. I did not want to change this format too dramatically, since I recognized that it will lend itself to use by study groups in a variety of church settings, and it will give to those who engage it the sense of having completed a major university course on the Bible. From that vantage point they will surely discover the fact that I have a profound respect for the Bible and that my goal is to build a similar respect in my readers.

For the help given to me in preparing this book I thank first my friends in Highlands (as well as in the neighboring communities of Cashiers, Sapphire, Franklin and Seneca). In addition to the Highlands people that I have already mentioned, I want to express my gratitude to Diane and Ray McPhail, Peggy Smith, Becky and Will McKee, Susan Davis, Nell and Bill Martin, Joan and Buster Bailey, Wanda and Bill Glover and a host of others too numerous to list.

Next I thank the founders of EverydayHealth, Ben Wolin, Mike Keriakas and Mark Tauber, to whom this book is dedicated. They helped me to create an audience for progressive Christian dialogue more extensive than anything I had seen before. Emerging out of the first Internet efforts of religious programming called Beliefnet.com, they managed to build a company that was successful beyond their wildest imagination. They have expanded from three employees in two rooms in Brooklyn to a company of more than three hundred employees occupying an entire building in Manhattan. I have now written over five hundred columns for them, some of which were picked up and rerun in a variety of print media forms, from op-ed pieces in daily newspapers to reprints in blogs and house organs of various sorts, which circulated my words to quite literally millions of people. One column, entitled "My Manifesto," on the struggle for justice for homosexual people, was passed and copied more than a million times and indeed is still circling the globe.

At HarperCollins I express my gratitude to Mark Tauber, who left Agoramedia to return to Harper to serve as publisher at HarperOne, along with Mickey Maudlin, my editor; Emily Grandstaff, my publicist; Lisa Zuniga, my production editor, and Kathy Reigstad, my copyeditor. I am also grateful to Kelly Hughes of the public relations firm of DeChant and Hughes in Chicago, who has been hired by Harper to launch almost all of my recent books. Kelly does this with an incredible professionalism and obvious competence that is deeply appreciated and with a friendship that is enduring. Playing the same launching role for me in Canada is Lindsey Love of HarperCollins in Toronto, and in Australia it is Christine Farmer at HarperCollins in Sydney.

Finally I express my love and appreciation to the members of my family: my wife Christine, who is a companion in all phases of my life beyond anything I ever dreamed possible. To say I love her sounds so inadequate, but it is deeply and profoundly true. She is also the best editor with whom I have ever worked, and she spent untold hours on this manuscript. Then there are my three wonderful daughters, Ellen, Katharine and Jaquelin, each now well established in successful careers in banking, law and science respectively. They are the children of my first wife, Joan, who died in 1988, and they are closer to me, I'm sure, because we walked through the pain and grief of my wife and their mother's death together. When Christine and I got married in 1990 I gained a wonderful first son, Brian Barney, and a wonderful fourth daughter, Rachel Barney. Our children's partners in life, Gus Epps, Jack Catlett, Virgil Speriosu and Julieann Barney, have also expanded our lives. Our grandchildren: Shelby and Jay Catlett, John and Lydia Hylton, and Katherine and Colin Barney, who range in age from twenty-three to nine, have kept us in touch with generations beyond our own. I salute them all and express my overwhelming love and admiration for each of them.

> John Shelby Spong
> Morris Plains, New Jersey
> September 2011

PART I

Setting the Stage: Posing the Problem

CHAPTER 1

Examining the Bible's Mystique

In the southern culture in which I was raised a special reverence was accorded to the book we called the "Holy Bible." For good reason this region of the country was and is called the "Bible Belt." Few homes would be without a family Bible as part of their permanent furnishings. In my childhood home that Bible was always prominently displayed on the coffee table in our living room, where no one could miss seeing it. I do not recall, however, that it was ever read, either silently or out loud. Its primary function seemed to be little more than a volume in which special moments in life's transitions were recorded.

We opened that Bible to fill in baptism, confirmation, marriage and burial dates. It was the repository of our family history. That alone appeared to be enough to endow this book with a sense of sanctity. There was, however, far more than this attached to the Bible in the life of our culture, and all of us breathed much of that "more" daily into our psyches. This book was called "God's Word." It was meant to be revered. No object could ever be placed on top of this book. Such behavior would constitute nothing less than a sacrilege. The place where this book had a unique position of honor, however, was inside the familiar institution called "the church."

I also cannot remember a time in my life when I did not regularly attend Sunday school, so it was there, not in our family, that
my siblings and I began to learn the content of the Bible. Sunday
school did not, however, give us anything close to an ordered kind
of learning. We certainly got the message that all of the Bible's
content was terribly important, although we were never introduced to most of that content. We concentrated primarily on the
familiar stories to which we could relate. The birth of Jesus was
first and foremost in importance, probably because Christmas
was by far the most popular holiday. So we knew about the star
in the east, the magi, the angels and the shepherds. We frequently
saw pictures of the manger with the Virgin Mary kneeling beside
it, her eyes cast down in the familiar pose. I had no idea at that
time what the word "virgin" meant. Perhaps it was just Mary's
first name. Most of the girls I knew in the South had double
names—Bobbie Sue, Martha Ann, so why not Virgin Mary?

The second story in importance was the narrative of the death
and resurrection of Jesus. Pictures of Jesus on the cross were also
familiar to me, but I never understood why Jesus had to die for
my sins as I was so regularly told that he did. Nonetheless, we
learned the details of the betrayal of Judas, the denial of Peter
and the doubt of Thomas, and we heard the accounts of the
penitent thief, Joseph of Arimathea and the women at the empty
tomb. There were, however, no Easter pageants in which we could
participate or see these stories dramatized, and so these details
were not nearly as vivid as the Christmas ones.

We also learned by memory such things as the Ten Commandments, even though I had no idea what it meant to covet,
and committing adultery brought up no mental images for me
whatsoever! The stories from the Bible were reinforced by hymns
that I learned in church, which seemed to narrate them to music.
I was always moved by the hymn that invited us to "Go to dark
Gethsemane,"[1] where we might observe the Lord's anguish. It was

---

1   The words were written in 1825 by James Montgomery; the music, by Richard
Redhead in 1853. The tune was called Petra. It was Hymn 77 in the 1940 Episcopal
Hymnal. See bibliography for details.

clear that we were supposed to feel guilt as we recalled the final events in Jesus' life.

So deep was the Bible's presence in our cultural life that we actually made fun of it and enjoyed the mischief of singing about some of its stories, especially if they had the power to titillate our imagination. Perhaps this was a way of creating intimacy with the holy—at least I think that was one of our motivations. At church camp one of our favorite songs to sing around the campfire was entitled "The Baptist Sunday School." It was special fun to laugh about the Baptists. This was not an attempt to be religious bigots or to make fun of our Baptist friends; it was just taking cognizance of the fact that the Baptists were in our part of the world numerically larger than any other Christian tradition, so we always defined ourselves against them. We used to say, "The Baptists are outnumbered only by the sparrows." The chorus to that campfire song went like this:

> *Young folks, old folks everybody come*
> *Join the Baptist Sunday school and have a lot*
> *of fun.*
> *Please check your chewing gum and marbles*
> *at the door*[2]
> *And you'll hear some Bible stories that you've*
> *never heard before!*

In the verses of this song we came to the content of particular Bible stories, which followed a four-sentence form that had a limerick-like quality to them. There were numerous verses and, if one knew the Bible well enough, one might actually make up new ones! The ones that were particularly popular with us were just a little "naughty," just a bit off color. I am certain that is why they appealed. The two I remember best illustrate this appeal:

---

2   Some versions said, "Check your guns and razors at the door," but that was too hostile to make it in my community! The original author is unknown.

Pharaoh had a daughter, she had a winsome smile,
She found the baby Moses a-floating in the Nile.
She took him home to Poppa with that same old
        tale
Which is just about as probable as Jonah and the
        Whale!

And:

Salome was a dancer, she danced before the King.
She wiggled and she wobbled and she shook most
        everything.
The King said, "Salome, there'll be no scandal
        here."
Salome said, "To heck with that," and kicked the
        chandelier.

Yes, at our church camp we took liberties, made fun of and with
the Bible and felt rebelliously sinful in doing so.

Later, when I first heard George and Ira Gershwin's classic
American opera *Porgy and Bess,* I would hear that same rebellious note in their song about the Bible, sung by a character
named "Sportin' Life." The song was entitled "It Ain't Necessarily So," which suggested that even the stories one read in the Bible
were themselves not "necessarily so." One verse of those lyrics
again contained the naughty-sexy theme:

Methus'lah lived nine hundred years
Methus'lah lived nine hundred years
But who calls dat livin' when no gal'll give in
To no man what's nine hundred years.

While doubts about the Bible's authority were allowed in fun
or at play, once we went into church, we discovered that the Bible
brooked no challenges. When scripture was read in our church
worship services, the end of that reading would be accompanied

by some version of the phrase: "The Word of the Lord," or "This is the Word of the Lord," or "May God add a blessing to the reading of his [*sic*] Word," to which members of the congregation might respond, as if on cue like well-trained kindergartners, with some version of the refrain: "Thanks be to God." One did not go far in my young world without encountering this assertion that the words of the Bible were identical with the "Word of God." It was and is a bold claim. It is also a claim, I was destined to learn, that depended for its sustenance on a great amount of biblical ignorance. One surely does not want to read much of the Bible if that claim is to remain intact. Perhaps that is why so many people in the Bible Belt pay only lip service to the call to read this book. The fact is that in the Bible Belt the Bible is not read with any regularity. If that had ever been done, then far too many unanswered questions would have been raised about just what kind of God it was who would say and do the things recorded in Holy Scripture.

If the Bible is God's Word, for example, how would we deal with a passage in which the prophet Samuel instructed Saul, the king of the Jews, in God's name, to engage in a war of genocide against the Amalekites, in which he was to kill every man, woman, child, suckling, ox and ass among the Amalekites (I Sam. 15:1–9)? How can this passage be called the "Word of God"? If it is God's Word, why would we want to worship such a God? What kind of God could inspire the psalmist to write in God's "holy Word" that the people of Israel would not be happy until they had dashed the heads of the children of their Babylonian enemies against the rocks (Ps. 137:8–9)? Beyond those rather bizarre episodes, what is one to do with the biblical definitions of women as subhuman, the biblical acceptance of slavery as a legitimate social institution and the biblical admonitions to execute homosexual persons? All of these attitudes are quite clearly present in the Bible. For people to maintain with any real conviction the claim that the Bible is the "Word of God" means that their minds have to be closed to truth that has in our time become universally accepted. Certainly no thinking person can today still view the

Bible as a revelation of God that dropped from heaven, fully written, divided into chapters and verses and bearing the divine imprimatur.

We know now that the Bible is a small library of books composed over a period of about one thousand years between roughly 1000 BCE and 135 CE. Many of these biblical books did not have a single author. Some of them were edited and re-edited over as long a period of time as five hundred years before they reached the form in which they found inclusion in the Bible. Can the "Word of God" actually be edited? Why did God not get it right the first time? What human being would have had the hubris to add to or delete from the "Word of God"? Yet that kind of editing happened, we now know, probably in every book in the Bible. Another fact to embrace is that none of the authors of the books in the Bible wrote thinking that they were writing the "Word of God." That was something decided much later by someone else. Have we ever wondered by whom these decisions were made and on what basis? Among those who still make this claim for the literal sacredness of the entire Bible, we need to know whether they are suggesting that each book of the Bible is equally holy, or that each reflects the "Word of God" with equal fidelity. The mainstream Christian churches do not seem to believe that, for the lectionaries that guide the reading of the scriptures in their worship leave out some books altogether! Can one skip a portion of the "Word of God" as no longer worthy of being heard? Such attitudes reflect uninformed claims for the Bible that are universally dismissed in the circles of biblical scholarship. Why is this scholarship not communicated to the Sunday worshipers of the world?

Let me be specific with certain popular assumptions: Moses did not write the documents we call the "books of Moses," or the Torah (Genesis to Deuteronomy)! Indeed, Moses had been dead some three hundred years before the first word of the Torah was put into written form. David did not write the book of Psalms! Solomon did not write Proverbs! The gospels were not written by eyewitnesses, but by at least the second and, in the case of the

Fourth Gospel (as the book of John is often called), perhaps even the third generation of believers. The book of Revelation does not predict the end of the world or convey any hidden messages about modern-day history! Why do we still allow ourselves to be tyrannized by this kind of uninformed biblical non-sense, regardless of the "authority" claimed for that book by the mouths that still utter these claims?

During the era in which the books of the Bible were written almost everyone believed—indeed, did not even question—the assumed fact that the earth was the center of a three-tiered universe and that God lived just above the sky. How else could God vigilantly watch human behavior and keep the divine record books up to date and ready for Judgment Day? No one in that time had any idea that the sun was part of a galaxy that contained two hundred billion other stars. No one had ever heard of a germ or virus, so in the Bible sickness was interpreted as punishment from the all-seeing God. The bubonic plague in the fourteenth century was viewed as a particularly violent expression of God's anger and was popularly blamed on a scandal in the papacy, which produced a pope in Rome and a pope in Avignon. Weather patterns, from heat waves to hurricanes and tornadoes, which seemed to come out of the same sky that God was thought to inhabit, were regarded as expressions of this same divine wrath. Even today this perspective remains in fundamentalist religious circles. The killing earthquake that rocked Haiti in January 2010, causing the death of some two hundred and thirty thousand people and devastating the whole nation, was explained by one televangelist as God punishing the Haitians for "making a pact with the devil and throwing the French out," events that occurred in the early years of the nineteenth century! In the Bible mental illness and epilepsy were also assumed to be (and were interpreted as the result of) demon possession. Can any modern doctor believe that?

Given these realities, we need to ask just how the claim made by anyone that the Bible in any sense is the "Word of God" can be sustained even for a moment without violating every rational faculty that human beings possess. Yet this claim is still made by religious voices, and it is frequently made without apology. Religious representatives not only say these things, but they also act them out in public with neither embarrassment nor shame. In fact this biblical mentality, frequently worn as a badge of honor, has played a large role in America's national life.

In the history of the United States in the late nineteenth and early twentieth centuries it was the Democratic Party that wore this badge, nominating on three different occasions (1896, 1900 and 1908) a biblical fundamentalist named William Jennings Bryan to be their presidential candidate. Three different Republicans, William McKinley, Theodore Roosevelt and William Howard Taft, defeated him and thus kept this attitude from getting established in the highest political office of this country. In the early years of the twenty-first century, however, this mentality shifted to Republican candidates, and one president, George W. Bush, actually asserted that God had chosen him to be president! President Bush's mentality was not an isolated claim in his party, as those who came to be called "the religious right" found a home in religious Republicanism, packaged as "family values," and they produced a plethora of candidates who opposed evolution, saw the turmoil in the Middle East as the fulfillment of biblical prophecy and sought to impose a narrow religious agenda on this complex nation. An Arkansas Baptist preacher actually became a viable presidential candidate.[3]

How is it possible that such irrational and, at least in scholarly circles, such universally dismissed attitudes toward the Bible can still in the twenty-first century have such power and even appeal? To answer these questions we will have to journey deep into our religious origins.

A worthy starting place would be to seek to understand why we have historically built around the Bible such a firm aura or defense shield to protect it from any serious investigation. That aura is quite distinguishable and that defense shield is far

---

3   Mike Huckabee, former governor of Arkansas and an ordained preacher.

more powerful than most of us can imagine, for it is constantly reinforced.

Look first at how the Bible is treated in church. In the more liturgical churches the choir and the officiants process in at the start of worship, and one of them will normally carry the Bible high as if it is to be worshiped or adored. If this action registers at all on the worshipers it heightens a definition that this book itself somehow participates in the holiness of God, which would of course preclude anyone from being critical of it in any way without facing the charge of being sacrilegious. Next, when the gospel selection for the day is read there is frequently a second procession, this time into the congregation, with the Bible or a book of gospel readings once more elevated. Then the reader, who is normally an ordained person, a practice that seems to say that only officially designated "holy people" can read the "holy gospel," will announce: "The Holy Gospel of our Lord and Savior, Jesus Christ, according to _____," filling in the blank with the name of the evangelist to whom that day's reading is ascribed. The congregation responds with the words: "Glory be to you, O Lord." While this is going on the reader may make the sign of the cross on the gospel and then on his or her head, lips and heart. The reader may even spread the smoke of incense over the gospel book. It is hard to know what these magical gestures mean to the reader or to the congregation, but they do all tend to communicate that the reading about to be heard is of the greatest and gravest significance, thereby enhancing the aura around the Bible. When the gospel reading is complete, the reader then proclaims: "This is the Gospel of the Lord," to which the congregation responds: "Praise be to you, Lord Christ." With that much folderol gathered around the simple reading from the gospels week after week, month after month, year after year, it seems clear that the claim of special sanctity for the Bible would be riveted deep into the people's conscious and subconscious life. Are we not assuming in these activities that this book has a kind of unearthly power that we fail to respect at our peril? When those practices become the tradition of a lifetime, are we not making it all but impossible to study the Bible in a modern and rational way?

Now add to these practices the way the Bible is traditionally published. It is not like other books. It normally has a black, floppy leather cover, frequently with a gold cross embossed upon it. It is traditionally printed on tissue-thin pages that are gilt-edged. The words of Jesus are frequently printed in red ink. They are presumably the "holy of holies" and leap off the page demanding attention. Until fairly recently most Bibles were kept in the Elizabethan English of the past, peppered with words like "thee" and "thou," phrases like "believest thou this" and many other verbs ending in "eth" and "est." It was as if the Bible had a special holy language that we were not supposed to translate. Indeed, until the time of the Reformation it was a crime to put the words of the Bible into the common language of the people, so the text remained in Latin long after Latin ceased to be used in common speech. The leaders of the church did not want the uneducated to know the content of the Bible. John Wycliffe,[4] an English vicar in the fourteenth century, who did translate the Latin Vulgate into English, was rewarded after his death for this heresy: the powers that be had his exhumed body burned at the stake. The hiddenness of the biblical text kept the "myth" of the Bible's sanctity from ever being challenged by anyone outside the church hierarchy.

To keep the Bible shrouded in unapproachable mystery was easy so long as education was considered the privilege of the ruling classes and not the right of the masses. There was no need to prevent people from reading the Bible since most of the people could not read, period. Universal education is a relatively modern accomplishment. So in this pre-literate time people got the content of the Bible, not from reading it, but from seeing works of art that ranged from paintings, to stained glass in houses of worship, to the "Stations of the Cross." People then, not having the biblical text before them, made the assumption that these artistic

---

4   John Wycliffe lived from 1328 to 1384 and completed his translation of the Bible into English in 1382.

pieces reflected accurately the historical occasions that were being depicted. Biblical literalism was thus once again burned deeply into the psyches of Western people. I recall one portrait of Matthew writing his gospel, painted by Caravaggio, which shows an angel guiding Matthew's hand so that he would record only the "Word of God" in the words of the gospel. No one in that world knew, for example, that the virgin birth was a ninth-decade addition to the Christian story or that the ascension of Jesus was a tenth-decade addition. No one understood the fact that the narratives of the crucifixion are quite different in each gospel, that almost all of the details of the Easter story appearing in one gospel are contradicted in another. Even the educated people of this time did not always have the ability to read the gospels side by side. No one knew that there were not "seven last words" spoken from the cross, that one of the thieves did not become penitent until Luke was written about sixty years after the cru-cifixion, or that Judas became more evil and Pontius Pilate more holy with the writing of each gospel and thus with the passing of time. Literalism was not only encouraged, but it was also seen to be the only possibility for understanding the Bible. It thus served to keep biblical knowledge quite limited. We are the inheritors of these traditions.

The final symbol of how this aura or defense shield around the Bible was shaped is seen in the fact that the Bible has tradi-tionally been printed with two columns on each page. This has resulted in the Bible being quite different from all other books except for dictionaries, encyclopedias or other reference and resource books. No one simply reads the dictionary. No one reads the encyclopedia. One goes to these two resources to get answers. Moreover, one does not normally argue with the an-swers of a dictionary or an encyclopedia. By printing the Bible in this format are we not forcing into the subconscious minds of the people the conclusion that the Bible too is a book to which we go for answers, an authority that cannot be and must not be doubted?

Around the Bible for centuries this aura has been encouraged and this defense shield created. This is what accounts for the almost tenacious hold that biblical literalism has had on the people of the Western world. We have in our world today the reality that many people are still clinging quite frantically to the biblical formulations of their past. Some spend enormous energy fighting Darwin, attacking secular humanism as it arises in the society and liberalism, all of which are symptoms of the lack of scholarship available in many churches. That is why in the United States we continue to take seriously the religious vote, the television evangelists, and even a pope who visited Africa with its civil strife, its rampant spread of AIDS and its poverty, and conveyed as his only message a condemnation of the use of condoms! Religious leaders seem to believe that if they allow one crack in their carefully constructed religious or biblical defense system, then the whole thing will collapse in ruins. That is the stance of hysteria, not the stance of either faith or hope, though it masquerades as both.

The primary response to this mentality, and it is a response that is growing rapidly, is to abandon all religion and to take up citizenship in the "secular city." Proponents of this stance no longer see any relevance in religion or the Bible for their lives today. They are not interested in twisting their minds into first-century pretzels, in order to read the Bible or into fourth-century pretzels, in order to say the creeds or into thirteenth-century pretzels, in order to engage in contemporary forms of worship. They find it impossible in their modern frame of reference to conceive of a theistically understood deity, living somewhere external to this world, endowed with supernatural power and ready to invade history to come to our aid, to answer our prayers. They find the concepts of miracle and magic to be outside their worldview. They dismiss readily ideas like that of a "fall" from perfection into "original sin," which is supposed to account for evil and which requires an external rescuer to save us from our sins. These ideas are completely foreign to what they now know about the origins of life and its evolution. They see no alternative to dismissing all religion in general and Christianity in particular, regarding it as something left over from the childhood of our humanity, and they want little to do with it. For such questioners either biblical literalism or the rejection of all religion seem to be their only choices.

One factor that both of these responses have in common is that they share a similar profound ignorance about the Bible. The fundamentalists who quote the Bible as their final authority clearly know little about how the Bible came into being and, thus, why that approach is so totally incompetent. Those who do not find any value in the biblical tradition wind up rejecting the very things that biblical scholars themselves almost totally reject, but these secularists know so little about the Bible that they are not aware of this fact. When I read books written by the new breed of militant atheist writers, who have become both best-selling authors and household names, I find myself perplexed as to how to respond to them. I have no desire to attack them or to rise to God's defense. The religion, the Christianity and the Bible that they reject are the same religion, Christianity and Bible that I reject. My problem with such writers is not located there. It is rather in the apparent fact that they do not seem to know that there is any other way. Why should they, since the church has worked so hard not to allow other possibilities to become visible?

My desire is to work in that very arena and to close that gap in knowledge at least in regard to the Bible. I am not the enemy of the Bible. I am the enemy of the way the Bible has been understood and the way the Bible has been used. I do not think for one moment that the Bible is in any literal sense the "Word of God." It is a tribal story, as this book will reveal—a pre-modern story, an ever-changing and ever-growing story. It came into existence, as every other book does, out of the experience of human beings seeking to make sense out of the life they are living and the things they are experiencing. I want to take my readers into this Bible in a new way. I want to plumb its depths, scale its heights and free its insights from the debilitating power of literalism. I want to make some of its characters come alive—those who probably have vestiges of history attached to them, like Moses, Joshua, Elijah and Elisha, even though that kernel of history is well hidden under layers of myth and fantasy, as well as some who are surely pure literary creations, like the Samaritan woman by the well, Lazarus who was raised from the dead, the "beloved" disciple, and even the figures of Joseph the earthly father of Jesus, Joseph of Arimathea who provided Jesus' tomb, and Judas the betrayer. I want people to see how the God of the Bible changes through its pages from a supernaturalized, warlike tribal chief into a more abstract personification of the realities of love, justice and universalism, a God who calls us beyond our security walls into a new experience of what it means to be fully human and into dimensions of a new consciousness.

I have wrestled with the Bible for more than sixty years. I have broken open my own fundamentalism, walked through valleys of meaninglessness in which I was certain that God had died and then found my way back, not to the security of yesterday's religious certainty, but to an understanding that does not hesitate to go through the Bible in order to transcend it, and thus that provides no security. I want to help people to develop a faith that goes so deeply into the essence of Christianity that they can walk beyond Christianity into that toward which Christianity can only point. I seek to enter and to introduce others to what Paul has called "the glorious liberty of the children of God."

I ask no one to agree with my conclusions, but rather to journey with me toward a new place and to see both the Bible and Christianity from that new context. I want to re-claim[5] the Bible for a non-religious world. In this process I hope people will be open to those understandings of the Bible that are commonplace in academic circles, but still almost unknown in the pews of churches. If we see in religion a way to certainty in our religious convictions, then there will inevitably be great disillusionment with religion. If, however, religion can be seen as the quest to find

5   Deliberately and by choice I am using a hyphen in the word "re-claim." I do so for these reasons. First it matches the usage in the title and second it is used in the title to capture a more action-oriented meaning. The hyphen and the capitalizing of "claim" is designed to catch the attention of the reader. Without the hyphen and capital letter the word "reclaim" sounds like something that would occur at a local lost and found.

integrity in our spiritual pilgrimages, then we can walk together and in this process discover, I am sure, some Bible stories "that you've never heard before," as the old camp song had it, and even be led to the Gershwin conclusion that some things, perhaps even most things, in the Bible "ain't necessarily so," at least not in the literal sense that we have learned them. The stage is thus set for our journey to begin.

It is a journey that will probe the sources out of which the Bible's words originated and the liturgical uses to which the Bible's words were put and by which their meaning was compromised, shaped and expanded. It will be a journey that leads us to make clear distinctions between the human experience of the divine and the human words used to describe and explain that experience. It will be a journey in which we will learn that human words are limited. They can only point to truth; they can never capture it, a fact that is demonstrably true of scripture, creed and doctrine. This journey will force us to embrace insecurity as a virtue and to dismiss security as a vice. Finally, it will be a journey into the depths of human life, serving my conviction that the only road into divinity is through humanity and the only doorway into eternity is through time.

So we raise the curtain, watch the drama unfold, and step boldly into the content of what is clearly the most influential book the world has ever known.

PART II

The Formation
of the Torah

CHAPTER 2

Breaking Open the Books of Moses

The Bible began to be written only a short time ago, relatively speaking. When one considers the fact that the universe is some thirteen billion, seven hundred million years old and the birth of the planet earth can be reliably dated between four and a half and five billion years ago, the beginning of Bible writing near the year 1000 BCE is very recent. Scientists now date the appearance of human life on this planet somewhere between four million and two hundred and fifty thousand years ago, depending on how one defines human life.[1] The beginning of civilization is placed by anthropologists between ten thousand and fifteen thousand years ago. The person we call Abraham, who is regarded in the Bible as the founder of the Jewish nation, is generally dated about the year 1850 BCE. Abraham is, however, a vague memory even in the Bible, since he lived about forty-five generations before the first word of the Old Testament was written. People have, however, unfortunately been trained primarily by the Bible itself, to think

---

1   Hominids have been discovered that are four million years old. If we define the human as a creature that has crossed the boundary from consciousness into self-consciousness, a date as recent as two hundred and fifty thousand years ago can be intellectually defended.

that the biblical story actually begins at the moment of creation. Bishop James Ussher, a seventeenth-century ecclesiastical figure in Ireland, using the Bible's "inerrant words" and its internal dates, including the nine hundred and sixty-nine years that Methuselah was supposed to have lived, asserted that creation actually occurred on October 23 in the year 4004 BCE. One of his later contemporaries, James Lightfoot, added the note that it was at 9:00 A.M. Greenwich Mean Time! If we, however, want to analyze the Bible effectively, the first thing we need to comprehend is the fact that the earliest part of the Bible to be written was recorded only about three thousand years ago, between 950 and 1000 BCE. That fact alone immediately introduces a note of radical relativity into the biblical assertions made by many people.

We now understand that everything that we know about Abraham, which comes to us in that story, has to have been passed on orally for about nine hundred years before it entered a somewhat more settled and static written form. Those data alone force us to embrace the fact that this biblical story cannot ever have been historically accurate as pious but uninformed people have traditionally claimed; this book inevitably has the character of folk tale and myth in which the facts of history are all but lost inside the developing tradition. Abraham, for example, might well not even have been a Jew! His place of origin, we are told, was the city of Ur in the land of the Chaldees. He was later identified with the shrine at Hebron in what is now Palestine. Isaac, who is described as his son and became the second of the Jewish patriarchs, was identified with the shrine at Beersheba, an hour south and west from Jerusalem. The third great patriarch was named Jacob, and in the Bible he was identified with the shrine at Bethel in the northern part of the land that would someday be near the southern edge of the so-called Northern Kingdom. This identification of the three formational ancestors with three shrines in the land opens up the possibility that they may originally have been unrelated Canaanite holy men whose lives were subsequently intertwined and interpreted as the founding fathers of the Jewish people. A motive for doing just that is seen in the

Bible itself, for riding on the backs of these patriarchs in Jewish folklore was the justification for the Jewish invasion of this land that occurred around 1250 BCE. The general purpose of these patriarchal tales in the book of Genesis was to justify the military claim the Jews made that they were conquering this land only because God had promised it to their ancestors hundreds of years earlier. As rational claims go these statements make no sense at all, but as propaganda they constituted then, and still do now, powerful influences in human history.

Other facts about the biblical story are even more threatening to those who treat the Bible as if it had a divine origin, and who pretend that in its words both historical accuracy and literal truth have been captured. Moses, who is an even more pivotal person in Jewish history than Abraham, may well also not have been a Jew, but an Egyptian or a half-Egyptian. His name certainly is quite Egyptian: the traditional name of the pharaohs was Ramases, the "Ra" coming from the name of the Egyptian sun god and "Mases" having the same consonants and thus being etymologically almost identical with the name of Moses. Moses lived in the thirteenth century BCE, but the stories about Moses in the Torah, including the exodus from Egypt, the presumed crossing of the Red Sea and the giving of the law at Mount Sinai were not written until the tenth century BCE, or some three hundred years after his death. This means that everything we know about Moses in the Bible had to have passed through at least fifteen generations of oral tradition before achieving the more permanent status of a written form. How much did these crucial Moses stories grow in that oral period? Did the Red Sea come to replace the Sea of Reeds as the setting for the splitting of the waters story? Did the discovery of the droppings of the tamarisk tree in the wilderness, with its white flaky residue lying on the ground, give rise to the story of God raining down heavenly bread called manna on the hungry Hebrew people? Did an eruption of burning natural gas in that oil- and gas-rich desert give rise to the story of God's call to Moses at a burning bush that was not consumed? What was the process through which the community's code of laws, including the Ten Commandments, went before they settled into the familiar form that we find in Exodus? Is the fact that there are three different versions of the Ten Commandments in the Torah an attempt to explain the biblical story that Moses broke the clay tablets containing the Ten Commandments when he saw that the people of Israel had forsaken the God who had brought them out of Egypt for a Golden Calf, and that he therefore had to return to Sinai to get a second version?[2] How much of the story of the exodus from Egypt is history and how much of that narrative has been bent to conform to the developing liturgy of the Passover, a festival which was designed primarily to let the Jewish people observe liturgically and annually the moment of their national birth? None of these questions could be raised until the idea that the Bible is not an eyewitness account of ancient history was both faced and accepted. No eyewitness wrote any of the materials. One of the most ostentatious book titles I have ever known was *Present at the Creation* by a famous secretary of state, Dean Acheson.[3] He was, however, describing the pressures present at the creation of Harry Truman's presidency and especially his foreign policy. No one was present at the creation of the world to write about it. In fact, writing did not begin among human beings any earlier than twenty thousand years ago at the most! With each new discovery human beings have been driven to temper their claims for the literal accuracy of the Bible. No, this book was not revealed directly by God to anyone, nor was it dictated by God on high to some willing earthly scribe or channel.

In the late 1800s, a group of scholars in Germany led by Professors K. H. Graf and Julius Wellhausen began to study rigorously the details of the first five books of the Bible—Genesis, Exodus, Leviticus, Numbers and Deuteronomy. These books, called the Torah or the books of Moses, constitute for the Jews the most sacred part of the Hebrew scriptures. So important was the Torah to the Jews that traditionally it was required to be

2   The three versions of the Ten Commandments are found in Exodus 20, Exodus 34 and Deuteronomy 5.
3   See bibliography for details.

read in its entirety on the Sabbaths of either an annual cycle[4] or a three-year cycle[5] in the synagogues of the Jewish world. These two scholars, together with their junior staff members, began to apply to these texts the developing insights of literary criticism. To do this, they had to set aside the claims that these works were somehow divinely dictated and even the idea that these books somehow possessed a magical relationship with truth. The results of their work, which is now referred to as the Graf-Wellhausen theory, were salutary, and more than anything else these two men opened the doors to a new academic interest in the Bible itself.

Analyzing primarily the first five books of the Old Testament Professors Graf and Wellhausen discovered that there were many observable differences that could be discerned in the texts of the Torah itself. This discovery, in turn, led them to the conclusion that the Torah consisted of several strands woven together of what had once been independent material. One strand, for example, referred to God by the name Yahweh, or at least by an unpronounceable set of consonants that were written as YHWH. Where Yahweh was used as the name for God the text also called the holy mountain of the Jews Mount Sinai. There was another strand of the Torah that called God by the name of Elohim, and where that name was used for God, the holy mountain of the Jews was referred to as Mount Horeb. A third strand of Torah material reflected life in the Kingdom of Judah in the seventh century BCE, which was well after the split between the Northern Kingdom and Judah and even after the Northern Kingdom had been destroyed by the Assyrians. Still another strand appeared to be dated during the time of the exile in the sixth century BCE after Judah had been defeated by the Babylonians and its

---

4   The annual cycle for the reading of the Torah appears to underlie the synoptic gospels of Mark, Matthew and Luke, as we will see in later chapters. See also my book *Liberating the Gospels: Reading the Bible with Jewish Eyes* for details. The synoptics present the life of Jesus against the background of the one-year cycle.

5   The Fourth Gospel seems to reflect a three-year Jewish liturgical cycle. That is why the Fourth Gospel presents Jesus' public ministry as lasting three years. My work on this theory on the gospel of John itself will appear, Deo volente, in 2014 under the proposed title *The Fourth Gospel: Tales of a Jewish Mystic*.

people relocated to the land of Babylonia. When these scholars began to separate these various strands from one another, other insights became available. The material that called God YHWH appeared to be centered in Jerusalem, for it extolled the institutions identified with Jerusalem, such as the royal line of Davidic kings, the high priest and the Jerusalem Temple. It reflected that period of Jewish history in which the Jewish nation was undivided and all of the Jewish people were ruled from the capital in Jerusalem. The strand that called God Elohim reflected the values of the northern part of the land of the Jews that achieved independence from Jerusalem rule around 920 BCE in a rebellion that occurred following the reign of Solomon. That rebellion was led by a northern military general named Jereboam against Solomon's son and heir, the newly crowned Jerusalem king named Rehoboam. That revolt by the people of the north was successful and it brought into being a new Jewish state called the Northern Kingdom, or Israel. Ultimately, this new nation built a new capital and worship center in the city of Samaria, and it traced its Jewish roots back primarily to Joseph, whom it referred to in the Elohist material as the "favorite son" of the patriarch Jacob. Joseph was said to be the child of Jacob by his favorite wife Rachel, and Jacob was said to have endowed Joseph with, among other things, a distinctive coat of many colors. The patriarch Joseph in this Elohist narrative was always juxtaposed to his older brother Judah, who remained the dominant ancestral figure of the Jewish people whose life centered in Jerusalem. Judah was the son of Jacob by Rachel's older sister Leah. According to the Elohist version of this story Jacob had been tricked into marrying Leah, whom he did not love, rather than Rachel, Leah's younger sister, whom he did love. This chicanery was orchestrated by the father of these two sisters, a man named Laban. Only by marrying Rachel's older sister did Jacob also manage to win Rachel as his second wife. Leah was described in this text, rather cruelly, not only as being unloved, but also as having eyes that popped out of her head like those of a cow.

This Elohist document was designed on many levels to counter the claims made by the tribe of Judah that Judah was destined to rule over these northern tribes. That kingdom was thought to consist of ten tribes in number. In the service of this theme the Elohist writer went so far as to assert that Judah betrayed his younger brother Joseph by selling him into slavery for twenty pieces of silver. In time, however, Joseph was said to have used this act of treachery to save all of his brothers, including Judah, from death by starvation. He accomplished this, so the story goes, by taking them down into Egypt, where they remained, the Bible says, for four hundred years, eventually falling into slavery, from which Moses would ultimately lead them in the exodus to freedom in their "Promised Land."[6]

As these strands came to be isolated from each other, people became aware of the fact that the two narratives reflected quite different times in history. That was when Professors Graf and Wellhausen recognized that they had, in fact, cracked the code of biblical origins. From that day to this the study of the Torah has been radically altered and new conclusions had to be formed. The first five books of the Torah were not written by Moses at all, or indeed by any single author. These books, still regarded as being sacred, were a composite of written materials that had been blended and intertwined into a single story over a period of as much as five hundred years. With that realization, biblical scholarship had taken an enormous leap into modernity. The old claims, held so tenaciously for so long by so many, were shaken to their very foundations. The era of critical biblical scholarship was being born. Since that time the four-source theory of Graf and Wellhausen has been modified and changed in many ways. Some scholars have indicated that they believe there are two distinct strands in the "E" (or Elohist) document. The dating of each strand has been shifted in several directions. The importance of the presumably single Elohist strand has thus

---

6   This story, greatly shortened in my text, can be read in full from Genesis 37–50.

been downgraded. All of these insights are worthy of our time, but they are beyond the scope of this book. They are also not capable of making sense for readers until the insights of Graf and Wellhausen have been fully understood. So I will now, for clarity's sake, proceed to develop the four stands as these two scholars first presented them. Modifications can always come later—and they will.

CHAPTER 3

The Yahwist Document

The Original Narrative

The Torah is the Jewish name for the first five books of the Bible, Genesis through Deuteronomy. In the Torah are stories representing a combination of myths, folk tales and political propaganda, with only the slightest bit, if any, of actual historical memory. The opening biblical stories, from Adam and Eve through the flood, have absolutely no connection with history, despite the fact that some of the world's more foolish people still go on expeditions trying to locate Noah's ark on Mount Ararat. The first shred of anything close to real history in the Bible appears in the Abraham story, and that, as I noted earlier, is indeed only a shred. Even Moses, the greatest hero in the Jewish story, while clearly a person of history, is nonetheless not accurately delineated; most of the details of his life are hidden in the shadows of myth and liturgy. Many scholars today believe that the biblical portrait of Moses might well be a composite of more than one person, for example. There were also probably many exoduses out of Egypt and many journeys through the wilderness that were in time melded together around campfires into a single story. When we get to the Moses stories contained in the book of Deuteronomy, we are dealing with a time some five hundred to six hundred years after the death of Moses; that gap between event and the recording of that event renders history, for all practical purposes, beyond our reach. In other words, most of the accounts in the Torah are not history at all, at least not in any technical sense, but are rather interpretive folklore.

Even after the constant repetition of facts such as these, it is hard to penetrate the religiously uninformed mind-set for which these facts are highly inconvenient. So listen carefully as I trace in more detail the beginning of the writing of the biblical story by isolating the various strands that we can now identify in these books. I begin with what is called the "Yahwist document," which scholars today believe is the oldest part of the Torah and thus the earliest part of the Bible to be written.

The activity of writing history, which is what the Torah purports to be, is an activity that normally starts only when a nation has become established and senses an identity and a security that is strong enough to allow its people to look at their common life with some objectivity. While the Jews were fleeing Egypt, journeying through the wilderness, or invading and conquering the land of the Canaanites, there was little time or interest in transforming the life they were experiencing into a written historical narrative. It is worth repeating that in the ancient world, a person who could actually write was rare. It was a skill possessed in the tenth century BCE in the Middle East by less than one-tenth of one percent of the entire population. Thus the person who wrote this first part of the Torah can be presumed to have been high in either government or ecclesiastical circles. Writing also required considerable wealth, or at least access to wealth, since both parchment and ink were very expensive. We can assume, therefore, that both education and wealth characterized this original author of the first part of the Bible, and that the author reflected the attitudes and the biases of the ruling classes which he represented. I use the word "he" not to be insensitive, but to recognize the fact that in this period of history the privileges of education and status had simply not yet been offered to or anticipated by women.

The Yahwist document got its name from the previously mentioned fact that this narrative referred to God by the name Yahweh (YHWH), the name it claimed had been revealed to Moses at the "burning bush." Those four Hebrew letters were in some way intended to be identified with the verb "to be," and so these letters were translated in the book of Exodus to mean "I am that I am." Since the verb "to be" is the foundational verb of any language, it seemed to be a fitting name for the deity who was regarded as the foundation of the tribe's identity. The name of God as YHWH—"I am"—was also destined to play a major role in later Jewish history when the "I am" claim was made for Jesus by his disciples, as we will discover later.[1]

When this Yahwist strand of material is lifted out of the Torah, in which it is now embedded, and separated from the later strands, its historical setting becomes immediately visible. The context is clear. The Jewish nation has been established. Saul, the first king, a member of the tribe of Benjamin, has been unable to secure his throne. The later biblical narrative describes Saul as a melancholy, depressed man who could not unite the various tribes of Israel into a cohesive national whole.[2] When Saul and almost all of his sons, including his presumed heir, whose name was Jonathan, were killed in a battle against the Philistines at Mount Gilboa, the vacated throne was claimed by Saul's military captain, a man named David. There was one descendant of Saul who seemed to have a legitimate claim to this throne. His name was Mephibosheth (II Sam. 9:1–8), and he was the son of Jonathan and thus the grandson of Saul. He was a crippled lad and David was said to have shown him great kindness even as he kept an eye on him as a figure around whom a rebellion might be organized. David was the clear hero of this Yahwist writer and was portrayed as chosen by God while still a youth and then anointed

---

1   Only the Fourth Gospel states that Jesus used the "I AM" phrase to identify himself. I will discuss that later when we come to the gospel of John.
2   His story is told in I Samuel.

with oil by the prophet Samuel to be the future king of the Jews. Indeed, David, the youngest of the sons of Jesse, was designated "king in waiting" while still a shepherd boy keeping his father Jesse's flocks. As tends to happen to a popular leader, heroic tales had obviously gathered around him in the memory of the people. It was said of the young David that he had killed a lion, a bear and finally the giant Goliath, a Philistine. Most of these stories have the same amount of history in them as the account of George Washington cutting down the cherry tree or Abraham Lincoln living in a log cabin.

When David moved, following the death of Saul and all his sons, to claim the throne for himself, the Yahwist writer suggests that he immediately instituted a series of political maneuvers to solidify that claim and to win popular support. He ordered a national time for mourning the death of King Saul and his sons. He punished anyone who appeared to take pleasure in Saul's demise. He made plans to conquer Jerusalem, the city of the Jebusites, to make it his new capital. If he was to be successful in uniting the disparate tribes of Israel into a single entity, he needed a neutral city to serve as the symbol of that unity. These tactics appear to have worked. With his power at home firmly established, David began to expand his realm with a series of military victories. When he had completed a reign of approximately forty years, he accomplished the passing of his crown on to his son Solomon. Nothing less than that would have served to establish the continuity of his nation. A dynasty, a royal family, was the primary symbol of that continuation. Among his last acts, according to this narrative, was to delegate to his son Solomon the task of making Jerusalem, not just the political center, but the spiritual center of the nation. This meant that one of Solomon's first responsibilities was the building of the Temple in Jerusalem.

With these three institutions now established—the throne and royal line of David, the capital city of Jerusalem and the building of the Temple by Solomon—the time was right for someone to narrate their national story and to set the Jewish nation into the stream of history. That was the setting in which, in all probability, a court historian—perhaps a member of the royal family, perhaps a priest associated with the Temple, or perhaps someone who was both—was commissioned, probably by the king himself, to write the history of this Hebrew nation. This is how the first strand of that material, which would later be called "sacred scripture," came into being.

The date was sometime after the year 950 BCE. King Solomon had been on the throne for at least a decade—enough time for the Temple to have been completed. The Jewish people had become wealthy because tribute money from David's conquests was now flowing into Jerusalem. This part of the Middle East was at peace. The Temple, thought to be God's earthly dwelling place, was functioning, and the life of the nation was widely believed to be resting safely in the arms of its two protectors, God and the king. So the time had come for someone to tell the story of this nation's origins. The one we now call the Yahwist writer thus took up this task.

When the story of the Yahwist writer was complete, the image of Israel as God's "chosen people" was secure, having been buttressed by the claims made in this narrative. These claims were basically three: God had chosen the House of David (and thus the tribe of Judah) to rule over the chosen people; the will of God was expressed through the Temple in which God lived as a protective presence, and the high priest specifically and the Temple priesthood in general, alone, were designated to order the religious life of the nation as the sign of God's continuous presence.

As soon as this Yahwist narrative was complete, it began to be read first as part of the liturgy of the people gathered in the Temple and after the exile in synagogues in which Judaism was practiced. That is the destiny of all writing when it becomes sacred scripture. That is to say that scriptures become scriptures because they are used in liturgy. In that process this narrative, with its power claims, achieved the status of being "God's revealed truth." This elevated status was certainly encouraged by the priesthood, who were well served as an atmosphere of sanc-

tity began to grow around these words. That status also served
the interests of the royal family, since what came to be called
"God's Word" affirmed their divine right to rule. The role of
Jerusalem as the ultimate symbol of this now established Jewish
national life and the people's national unity was celebrated. In
this manner the vested interests of each of Jerusalem's power centers were solidified. The Jewish people, so recently a loosely knit
confederation ruled by local judges and worshiping at shrines
located in Hebron, Beersheba and Bethel, now found unity in a
new federation that was being imposed on them from Jerusalem
by king and high priest as nothing less than an expression of the
will of God.

In a world in which there was no division between church and
state (i.e., religion and politics), this first narrative text in what
was to become the Bible was, in fact, a very political document:

- By tracing the Jewish story from the creation of the world
  to the call of Abraham, this narrative went from the
  universal beginning of human history to the dawn of the
  Jews' national life.

- By relating the stories of Abraham, Isaac, Jacob and
  Joseph, this narrative established, as both legitimate
  and moral, the Jews' claim to land that they had in fact
  conquered.

- By incorporating the ancient shrines of Hebron,
  Beersheba and Bethel into the story of the Jews, thus
  identifying the religious traditions of the past with a
  new center in Jerusalem—which was destined to become
  those lesser shrines' ultimate and grander successor—this
  narrative unified the worship life of these people.

- By telling the story of the noble history of the Jews prior
  to falling into slavery in Egypt, this narrative rebuilt their
  national reputation.

This was political propaganda at its best, a powerful and effective attempt to define what it meant to be a Jew, a member of the chosen people.

What would happen, however, if and when the Jewish nation was ever to be divided in civil war? Such a rebellion would have to be against the scriptures as well as against the Temple and the king. That was destined to occur sometime after the year 920 BCE and with the death of Solomon. That was when the second strand of material that composes the Torah began its journey into being, and so we turn next to that story.

CHAPTER 4

The Elohist Document

The Torah Expands

If one is going to read or study the Bible in any meaningful way, it is necessary to embrace the events of history out of which and against which each individual book of the Bible was written. None of them was created in some kind of a vacuum. This is as true of the gospels as it is of the Old Testament.

Most scholars, for example, are convinced that the Jewish war with Rome, which began in 66 CE in Galilee and ended in 73 CE at Masada, shaped the content of Mark, Matthew and Luke in a dramatic way, perhaps even determining what was remembered about Jesus. In 70 CE, in the midst of that war, the city of Jerusalem fell and the Jewish nation for all practical purposes disappeared from the maps of the world until it was restored in 1948 under the plan that had been set out in the Balfour Declaration of 1917.[1] To read the gospels with no sense of this particular and specific historical context leads to dramatically ill-informed understandings. Not only did the cataclysmic effects of this war

---

1   There was a momentary return between 132–135 CE under the leadership of a charismatic figure named Bar Kokhba, but it did not last and so is generally ignored.

shape the apocalyptic "end of the world" chapters found in the first three gospels (see Mark 13, Matthew 24, Luke 21), but I would argue that the story of Jesus' transfiguration, told first by Mark and then repeated in Matthew and Luke, but omitted in John, makes no sense at all unless the reader is aware that when this story was written the Temple in Jerusalem had recently been destroyed in that war. This is, in fact, one of the ways that we are able to date the gospels so accurately.

In a similar manner no one can read about or understand how the second strand of the Torah, which came to be called the "Elohist document" because it referred to God by the earlier Canaanite name El or Elohim, came to be written without being cognizant of the historical context that produced it.

Somewhere around the year 920 BCE a civil war broke out in this tiny Jewish nation between the Hebrew people of the north and the Hebrew people of the south. This war resulted in a permanent division of these people into two national entities: one was called the Northern Kingdom, or Israel, and the other was called the Southern Kingdom, or Judah.

While the historical division occurred about 920 BCE, the roots of the tension can be located in a far more ancient time. Some historians have found evidence that seems to suggest that the Jewish people did not have a single unified past and were never a single people at all. These data suggest that the escaping slave people from Egypt, about whom the book of Exodus writes so lavishly, were not all of the Hebrew people, but perhaps only those who would later be identified as the Joseph tribes.

Certainly Joseph was the central figure, according to the biblical narrative, in the settlement of the Hebrews in Egypt. At the time of their exodus from Egypt, the biblical narrative tells us that they had become first an underclass and finally slaves in Egypt, because a pharaoh arose in Egypt "who knew not Joseph" (Exod. 1:8). Joseph, according to the Hebrew oral tradition that stretched back some four hundred years, if we can believe the timeline in the book of Genesis, had risen to power in Egypt, achieving a position in the land second only to that of the pharaoh. According to the book of Genesis, he had achieved this prominence through his prescience and foresight, which enabled him to build up the food supply in the time of plenty and then to administer it in the time of famine. This allowed the Egyptian nation to survive hard times. As the nation's leadership changed and the aforementioned pharaoh emerged "who knew not Joseph"—that is, who no longer appreciated the contributions the Hebrews had made to Egypt's national life—that pharaoh began a campaign of oppression against them, which in turn led to rebellion and escape. When the Hebrews made their exit, the book of Exodus informs us that they took with them the bones of Joseph, so he could be buried in the soil of his former home (Exod. 13:19).

According to these scholars of ancient history, however, more Semitic people appear to have been included in the Hebrew nation than just the fleeing slaves of the Joseph tribes. Indeed, the established, pre–civil war Hebrew nation appeared to be a far stronger combination of Semites than a marauding band of former slaves could ever have become. Consider for example that under the leadership of Joshua around 1200 BCE they formed a conquering army that was mighty enough to defeat and overrun the settled Canaanites. Turning to the Torah itself these same scholars find evidence which suggests that during the wilderness years the escaping slaves came together to form common cause with another group of nomadic Semites in an oasis named Kadesh (Num. 20:1–22). It was there that their common ethnic kinship was recognized. Eventually the two groups formed a political alliance and began to think of themselves as a single united people but organized into a loose confederation that recognized their differences.

Even their folklore made it clear that while they appreciated their kinship, there was always a distinct difference between the two groups. This ancient division was explained in the biblical story, to which I have previously alluded, in which it was said that their ancestral father Jacob, whose name had been changed to Israel, actually had two primary wives. Leah, the first one, was the mother of Judah, whose descendants formed the tribe that settled the southern part of Canaan. Rachel, the second wife, was the mother of Joseph, whose descendants settled the northern part. There were of course other tribes—indeed twelve, it was said—but they tended to be satellites of the two major tribes. Much later, after the civil war, the Northern Kingdom of Joseph's descendants would be called the "ten tribes," while the powerful southern tribe of Judah stood almost alone. The twelfth tribe, Benjamin, named in Genesis as Joseph's younger brother, became in effect a satellite tribe of Judah and lost its identity.[2] The whole Jewish nation was, thus, more an alliance or a confederation than it ever was a unified people. The biblical book of Judges described this locally organized phase of tribal history. Survival as a recognizable people in that day, however, required these various loosely related groups to become a strong and unified nation. The only way they knew that might allow them to achieve that goal was to be governed by a strong single leader. That is why the Hebrew people began to exert pressure to have a king. There was a long struggle between local leaders and those who argued for a federal state, and that struggle is reflected in the book of Samuel (I Sam. 8:5–22).

The first king of this newly unified nation, according to biblical history, was a Benjaminite named Saul. Perhaps it was a political asset to Saul that he was not a member of the two major, competing groups. Saul, however, was not able to bring about the needed unity, which was best symbolized by his inability to pass the throne on to his son. The second king was David, who came to power as Saul's military captain. He was a member of the dominant tribe of Judah. Among the political realities of having a member of this particular tribe become king was that it raised the anxiety of those in the northern part of the nation, the home of the Joseph tribes. The northerners believed that any semblance

2   Levi, who is in the Bible one of the sons of Jacob by Leah, became not a geographical unit, but a religious unit, the Levites. Joseph's tribe was split and named for Joseph's two sons Ephraim and Manassas. Together they dominated the Northern Kingdom.

of their own local control and power was jeopardized by allowing a king from the tribe of Judah to rule over them. David, however, with both military and political skill, managed to quell these doubts and unify the country. He moved the government to the neutral city of Jerusalem, heretofore the city of the Jebusites, and he reigned for approximately forty years before passing on the throne to his son Solomon, who in turn reigned for another forty years. We noted in the previous chapter that it was during the reign of Solomon that the Yahwist strand of the Bible was probably created, and that is why it affirmed the institutions that undergirded Judah's power and control. That document also assumed that any rebellion against the king, his capital city of Jerusalem, or the Temple with its high priest was nothing less than rebellion against God. One would hardly have written this negativity toward any idea of secession so deeply into the story of a people's national history had not rebellion and revolution been a constant threat.

The tensions between Joseph and Judah, north and south, had obviously never been dormant, then. Those tensions appear to have been greatly exacerbated during the reign of Solomon as the people of the north felt that they were overtaxed to provide wealth and grandeur for the people of Jerusalem. When Solomon died around the year 920 BCE the throne passed in an orderly fashion to his oldest son, a man named Rehoboam. The people of the north, however, were not ready to pledge their allegiance to Rehoboam without some changes in the way the king related to the people of their region. They demanded an audience in which to present their grievances and to negotiate changes before they were willing to accept Rehoboam as the ruler. The spokesperson for these claims of the people of the north was a military general named Jereboam. The negotiations were not successful, and when they collapsed the new, and perhaps rash, young King Rehoboam, King David's grandson, decided that he must put this rebellion down with brute force. The people of the north then organized themselves under Jereboam for resistance, and in the ensuing civil war they won their independence. There were now two Hebrew states.

There was, however, another serious problem that had to be addressed. This successful revolution had removed the people of the north from the House of David, the city of Jerusalem and the Temple with its official priesthood. In the process of doing that it had also rendered the only existing sacred story of the Jews inadequate to guide worship in the breakaway realm. These rebellious northern tribes could hardly continue to call sacred the Yahwist document, which on almost every page judged them with its own words, by suggesting that they were rebels against God, against God's anointed king, against God's holy city and against God's dwelling place in the Temple! In time this newly independent country had not only to build its own separate institutions, but also to write its own sacred story. Leaders of the new Northern Kingdom quickly set about the task of establishing their own monarchy, but on a very different and far more democratic basis. They demanded that their king be chosen by the people and thus also that he be subject to removal by the people. They requisitioned a hill and in time they built on it the city of Samaria to be their capital. They set up the ancient shrines outside Jerusalem to be worship places to rival the Temple in Jerusalem. Eventually these seceding tribes would also find it both compelling and necessary to take the crucial step of writing a new version of their sacred history that might be more compatible with their values and their unique history.

To the degree that we can isolate the two strands in the Jewish sacred story, we can see the differences. For the writer of the second strand, the Elohist document, it was Joseph, not David, who was the ultimate hero. We see that idea developing in the story about Joseph, where he was portrayed not only as the child of Jacob's favorite wife, Rachel, but as Jacob's favored son. This document also reflected contemporaneous tensions, describing a conflict between Judah and Joseph in their early years as brothers. This writer deemphasized Jerusalem, relativized the importance of the Temple and resanctified the ancient shrines in the north. Finally the divine right of kings, so important to the political security of the Southern Kingdom, was dismissed by this narrative, which claimed that the king must always be subject to the will of the people. If the king violated his trust, the people were deemed to be competent to remove him. This claim obviously solidified the legitimacy of the northerners' rebellion against King Rehoboam, but it also made it difficult for a hereditary kingship ever to develop in the Northern Kingdom.

While these differences were sharp, many of the stories in the two histories were nonetheless quite similar. Exactly when the Elohist narrative first achieved written form is hard to say, but my best guess would be before 800 BCE, though editing and additions continued well after that. Later study has shown that the Elohist narrative as we now have it represents more than a single original document. At this moment in biblical history, however—the moment when the Elohist narrative was recorded—there were two Hebrew nations, two kings, separate worship centers and two versions of the sacred scripture. These two competing nations fought each other in numerous indecisive wars. They tended to form opposing and competing alliances with foreign powers. When Assyria became the major Middle Eastern power, the Northern Kingdom joined Syria in armed resistance, while the Kingdom of Judah formed an alliance with Assyria and accepted vassal status in exchange for Assyrian protection.

In 721 BCE the Assyrians conquered the Northern Kingdom and exiled most of its people to foreign lands under their control. Then they imported other conquered peoples to repopulate the land that had once been the nation called Israel. In time these foreigners intermarried with the remaining Hebrews, and their descendants became known as the half-breed Samaritans. After the destruction of the Northern Kingdom, we assume that some unknown person managed to escape to the south and to take with him or her a copy of whatever then constituted the Elohist document. Over the years in Jerusalem the two sacred stories from these competing halves of the Hebrew people were woven together, not seamlessly, but actually. The dominant Yahwist version was given priority, but the Elohist story, even with its divergent view, was preserved as part of the sacred story of the Jews.

By the turn of the century, certainly before 690 BCE, the sacred story of the descendants of Jacob, whose name was said to have been changed by God to "Israel," had now become the Yahwist-Elohist version, and the second stage in the formation of the Torah was complete.

CHAPTER 5

The Deuteronomic Writers

The Third Strand of the Torah

The book of Deuteronomy is not the final part of the Torah historically, but it is the final book of the Torah as the Bible was compiled. It was also a primary part of the third strand in the Torah's development. The book of Deuteronomy was both an addition to the Yahwist-Elohist combined tradition and a new editing of the entire story. The name Deuteronomy comes to us from the combination of two Greek words: *deutero,* which means "second," and *nomas,* which means "law." This name thus means the second giving of the law, and in that title the story of the book's origin is probably exhibited. Listen to its story as the Bible reveals it.

In 621 BCE in the Southern Kingdom, now called Judah and thus its people were called "Jews," a period of growing fervor for religious reform was apparent. This fervor was encouraged and shaped by a group of prophets, among whom Jeremiah might well have been one voice, though that is a guess more than a conclusion. These prophets focused their hopes on their young king, Josiah, who had succeeded to the throne at the age of eight when his father, King Amon, was murdered by his own servants. Josiah was a king who, in the eyes of these prophets, "did what was right in the sight of the Lord and walked in the way of his father David; he did not turn aside to the right or the left" (II Kings 22:1–2). Perhaps that was because King Josiah was attentive to and a supporter of the worship of the Temple, thus ingratiating himself to this school of the prophets. When the king reached the age of twenty-six, he ordered major renovations to be done on the Temple, which presumably had fallen into some disrepair and neglect under the reigns of previous kings, including his father, all of whom were in the royal line of King David. It appears, however, that many pagan practices had been allowed to take root in the Temple. Josiah proposed in his call for renovations not only a physical restoration of the Temple, but also the purging from its life of these alien practices. He was thus hugely popular with the religious authorities and especially with the prophets.

During this restoration, however, unexpected events occurred that were destined to shape the worship life of the entire country. The context of the story is strange, but the details are important. First, the second book of Kings tells us that this renovation was to be done with money that had been collected from the people over the years (and presumably not spent by previous kings), so the project would not require new taxes. That was, needless to say, quite popular. Second and still mysterious, it was ordered that no accounting of the expenditures on this renovation by the authorities would be required, for it was said of the people who would be in charge that "they deal honestly" (II Kings 22:7). Next came an electrifying discovery. During the actual work of the renovation the workers found, perhaps hidden behind some of the plaster that was being torn away, a book that purported to be "a book of the law." The book even claimed to have been written by Moses, who by this time had been dead for some six hundred years. The book, discovered by Hilkiah the high priest, was sent to the king by a man named Shaphan, who was described as "the secretary in the house of the Lord" (II Kings 22:12), who in turn read this book in its entirety to the king.

When King Josiah heard the words of this newly discovered manuscript, the biblical writer tells us, he tore his clothes in an act of public penitence because it was obvious that the "Word of the Lord" found in this book had not been obeyed by previous kings and by bygone generations of God's people. Complicating matters, a female prophetess named Huldah was produced and she declared—in her most solemn voice, I'm sure—that unless the commands of this book were obeyed, God would bring "disaster on this place and its inhabitants." Huldah went on to say that because good King Josiah had responded with penitence and had "humbled himself before the Lord," by tearing his clothes and weeping publicly, so long as he was the king these terrible punishments would not occur (II Kings 22:14ff). When this message was delivered to the king, skillful political planning to manage the process of change was carefully developed.

Josiah, empowered by the "Word of God" that he had "found" in this newly discovered book, clearly now had the authority to proceed. This book after all bore the name of Moses and it was said by the prophetess Huldah that obedience to the commands of this book had the ability to hold back the wrath of God so long as this faithful king was alive. The words of this new book were then ordered to be read to the whole people and a new covenant, reflecting the values of this "discovered" document, was adopted. After being publicly agreed to, the covenant established that this book would from that day forward govern the common life of the people of Judah. A great reformation of the worship practices in the Jewish Temple and throughout the land of Judah was then carried out. The reformers removed from the Temple all the vessels made for deities other than Yahweh (II Kings 23). All idolatrous priests were deposed. All houses of male Temple prostitutes, associated with the fertility rites of the deity known as Baal, were closed and torn down. Religious shrines suspected of encouraging pagan worship were destroyed. All mediums, soothsayers and fortune-tellers were put out of business. Josiah, in the kind of bold act that frequently marks religious zealots, even went into what had once been the Northern

Kingdom and destroyed the rival shrines in Samaria and Bethel. This Deuteronomic reform also required that the Passover be celebrated only in Jerusalem, where its liturgical purity could be guaranteed. The prophets of Yahweh said of King Josiah that there had been "no king like him, who turned to the Lord with all his heart, with all his soul and with all his might, according to the Law of Moses; nor did anyone like him arise after him" (II Kings 23:25).

One major purpose of worship, usually hidden under pious words, has always been the human attempt to please the deity, even to manipulate the deity in order to win divine favor, blessing and protection. That was certainly the intention and the hope of those who engineered this enthusiastic reformation. In all probability they were, not to be cynical but to draw the obvious conclusion, also the ones who wrote, planted and "discovered" this new book of Moses. They then orchestrated and engineered the political campaign that led to its adoption. They believed that if they obeyed the rules outlined in this book, God would extend divine protection over their land.

We do not know the names of the people who constituted this group of reformers. They are simply called the "Deuteronomic writers." By the power of their leadership in this reformation, however, they took the previous sacred story, at that point including only the strands known as the Yahwist-Elohist document, and incorporated into it the book of Deuteronomy, "the second giving of the law." Then they set about to edit the entire sacred story into a consistent narrative until it became identified as the Yahwist-Elohist-Deuteronomic version of the scriptures. The third strand of material that would someday be called the Torah was now in place.

The great hoped-for protection of God, which the reformers believed would come to them if they followed these new directives and worshiped God properly, did not, however, materialize. The distress and hard times that had fallen on the land of Judah not only continued, but actually seemed to intensify. The book of II Kings (specifically II Kings 23:26) recorded the fact that, despite these wide-ranging reforms, "still the Lord did not turn from the fierceness of his great wrath, which his anger had kindled against Judah." The Lord was heard to warn that just as Israel (the Northern Kingdom) had been removed from the face of the earth, so Judah (the Southern Kingdom) would also be removed if its people did what was unpleasing to God. The only caveat of hope lay in the assertion that this destruction would not occur so long as King Josiah lived.

A few short years later, Josiah was killed on the battlefield of Megiddo by Pharaoh Necho of Egypt, who was fighting against Josiah's ally, the Assyrians. His death was so devastating to the Jews that Megiddo came to be thought of as the site where the ultimate battle that would precede the end of the world would occur. Armageddon is nothing but the modern spelling of Megiddo. The deluge that had been promised by the prophets to come only after the death of King Josiah now began to fall on the Jewish nation. It came in the form of defeat, devastation and the removal of the Jewish people from the land of Judah into Babylonia in an exile that was destined to last some two to three generations. It was in that desperate period of Jewish history that the final strand of material that was to constitute the Torah was written. We turn next to that story.

CHAPTER 6

The Priestly Document

The Fourth Strand of the Torah

The Holy Scriptures all have human authors who lived in a specific time and place. Only those readers who ascribe an external, revelatory, supernatural source for these ancient texts will find this insight disturbing. There is, however, no rational argument in the world that would support a divine or revealed source for the sacred writing of any religious tradition. This truth becomes quite obvious as we begin to look at the final major strand that made up the Torah.

As the previous chapter noted, the defeat of the Southern Kingdom by the Egyptians, an ally of the Babylonians, at Megiddo presaged greater defeat to come. By the early years of the sixth century BCE, Nebuchadnezzar, the king of the Babylonians, had subdued the Assyrians (who had themselves been the conquerors of the Northern Kingdom) and had consolidated his power in his own land sufficiently to enable him to begin a war of conquest. Signing a pact of alliance with the Egyptians to neutralize them, he looked for further fields to conquer. Sweeping out of the north he defeated every nation in his path until he arrived at the walls of Jerusalem, where he began a siege around the year 598 BCE.

Jerusalem was eminently defendable, located as it was high on a fortress-like hill and possessing an internal water supply. This city had not been conquered by a foreign army in the last four hundred years. The Jewish strategy before marauding armies was always to retreat inside the walls of "Fortress Jerusalem," where sufficient food supplies were kept to wait out almost any siege. Normally, the enemy would grow weary in the dullness of waiting and a negotiated settlement would be reached, leaving Judah free but poor. Jerusalem had thus, at least in the minds of its citizens, developed a sense of invincibility, causing the people to assert that, since it was clearly the earthly dwelling place of God, God would not allow this holy city to be either conquered or destroyed. The Babylonians, however, proved to be more persistent than any previous enemy and their siege lasted for two full years, by which time both the food supply and the weapons of war were exhausted. Rocks and spears hurled in conflict, while reusable in theory, were not retrievable. Finally, the Babylonians breached the walls of this city and their army poured in, destroying everything before them. Even God's house, the Temple, was leveled.

The Babylonians rounded up the captive people and pre-pared them for deportation to Babylon. Only the elderly and the physically impaired would remain. The period of Jewish his-tory known as the Babylonian captivity, the Babylonian exile, or simply the exile was about to begin (II Kings 24–25). A puppet ruler named Zedekiah, of the House of David, but loyal to Judah's new master, was placed on the throne. All others were forced to march into resettlement in Babylonia. This experience would remain the darkest moment in Jewish history until it was superseded by the Holocaust in the twentieth century.

While the first wave of Jews entered the Babylonian exile around the year 596 BCE, a second wave came in 586 after an abortive and unwise rebellion led by Zedekiah was put down by the Babylonians and all of the identifiable descendants of King David were executed. Both those exiled in 596 and those who made up the second exile carried with them their sacred story, which at that time consisted of the consolidated and edited version made up of the Yahwist, Elohist and Deuteronomic strands.

When these Jewish exiles left their homeland of Judah, they left everything that they had ever known. They would never again see their sacred soil. They were removed from the land over which their Temple had once been dominant and separated from the traditional fasts, which once gave their lives a sense of order and purpose. The exiles, however, felt that once they had been removed from the land over which they were certain God had ruled, they had in fact been removed from God. According to Psalm 137, the conquered Jews were taunted by their captors. The words of this psalm are plaintive:

> *By the waters of Babylon we sat down and wept, when we remembered thee, O Zion. As for our harps we hanged them upon the trees that are therein. For they that led us away captive required of us then a song and melody in our heaviness: Sing us one of the songs of Zion. How shall we sing the Lord's song in a strange land?*

These conquered and exiled Jews were destined to live as slaves or as a perpetual underclass in a land where the name of their God was never to be spoken in public. They did not believe that God could even hear their prayers in this foreign place.

Their spiritual crisis was even deeper than this. In this primitive time the defeat of a nation was also understood to be a defeat for their God. This meant that the God of the Jews had been demonstrated to be impotent in the face of the Babylonian deities. This crisis was experienced by the Jews as if their God had been destroyed. If they were to continue to be believers, they had to become, to use a phrase I would coin some twenty-six hundred years later, "believers in exile."[1] They were now separated from everything that undergirded their understanding of God. It was a crisis of dire proportions in which their God would either perish or change dramatically. There were no other alternatives.

---

1   The subtitle of one of my books, *Why Christianity Must Change or Die*, was *A Bishop Speaks to Believers in Exile*.

Most ancient peoples did not survive such an ordeal intact. This norm had in fact been the fate of the people of the Northern Kingdom. In only two or three generations they had completely lost their identity and were soon absorbed into the general population, becoming what we now call "the ten lost tribes." The only hope a conquered people had for survival lay in their ability to remain separate and distinct from their neighbors, thus making it impossible for amalgamation to occur. These southern Jews, now exiled in the city of Babylon, had as their driving passion the ultimate hope that someday, in some unknown future, either they or their descendants, if still cohesive and recognized as Jews, might have a new opportunity to return to their homeland and rebuild their nation and their holy city of Jerusalem. This hope became their dream and the dominating value which motivated them while in captivity.

Included among those who were taken into exile was in all probability the man we know today as Ezekiel, along with a number of other priests. Almost inevitably these priests became the new leaders of the exiled people, moving at once to instill into the consciousness of these conquered people the virtues of remaining separate from the Babylonians as the means necessary to guarantee their dream of a return someday to reestablish their nation and to fulfill what they believed was its God-given purpose—namely, to be a blessing to the nations of the world.

In the service of this hope these priestly leaders identified three essential marks of Judaism, which they set out to stamp so deeply on the psyches of their people that these marks would serve to keep them separate from the others in Babylonia:

- First, they reintroduced the Sabbath, making it the sign of Jewish national identity. The Jews became known in Babylonia as those strange people who refused to work on the seventh day. This custom disrupted work crews to which they had been assigned as laborers, causing frustration and anger to grow among the Babylonians. At the same time, however, this practice served to identify the Jews in the minds of the Babylonians as "different," perhaps even weird, which in turn aided the Jewish desire to remain separate.

- Second, these priestly leaders urged upon their people the adoption of kosher dietary laws, mandating that the food that the captive people ate had to be not only kosher, but also prepared in kosher kitchens. This meant, effectively, that all social discourse with those who were not Jews was cut off. Since Jews could not eat with non-Jews, there was little chance that close relationships with Babylonians could ever grow, since it is a fact that most human relationships develop through the act of eating together.

- Third, these priestly leaders revived the practice of circumcision as the distinguishing mark of a Jewish male, literally cutting that mark into their bodies at the time of puberty. This made it impossible for a Jewish male to hide his Judaism from the world, and thus it served to make intermarriage difficult.

The plan worked. The Jews became a people separate from all others. All of these practices were imposed on the people as religious mandates, which meant that to violate them was tantamount to violating God. These priestly leaders then decided that the sacred story of the Jewish people had to be revised to demonstrate that these traditions had been part of Jewish life and practice from the very beginning of their nation's history. This included the idea that these practices must, therefore, have been mandated by God. To accomplish this task these priestly writers undertook a new and major editorial revision of the then-existing Yahwist-Elohist-Deuteronomic story. This fourth strand of material would come to be called the "priestly document," or the "P" document, as a way of seeking to identify its primary architects.

When the Jews left their Babylonian captivity, which they did in waves from fifty to two hundred years later, their sacred text had been substantially rewritten and greatly expanded by these priestly writers. Now this Jewish sacred story reflected two major themes. First, it made mandatory the Jewish struggle for survival, which was to be accomplished by making isolation from their captors a primary religious requirement; and second, it delineated a new understanding of their ultimate mission in this world, which was to return someday to their sacred soil and re-build their capital city of Jerusalem, in which their ordered life of worship could once again be centered in the Temple. These goals alone, they came to believe, would fulfill what they understood to be their national calling and their national destiny. The stated mission of the priestly writers was to create such a deep sense of what it meant to be a Jew that their identity would never again be compromised individually or corporately. This could be done, they believed, only by asserting that their sacred scriptures were in fact the absolute law of God. Since these scriptures expressed the will of God, the Jews' obedience to the Torah had to be total and complete. Reflecting that belief, priestly editorial changes in-dicated that the mandates of Sabbath observance, kosher dietary laws and the requirement of circumcision for all the males of the tribe were now said to have been original parts of their covenant with God. Then into the Torah they wrote rules designed to govern every aspect of their common life. This was a monumen-tal revision, but when it was complete the nature of Judaism had been set, not in stone, but in literal scriptures.

The opening chapter of the Torah was thus rewritten to reflect God's command at the beginning of the world that all Jews must obey the Sabbath. This was the meaning of the new seven-day creation story, which now introduced the older creation story that featured Adam and Eve. This new Jewish account of their origins was actually modeled on a Babylonian story of God cre-ating the world in a specific number of days. The priestly writers suggested that creation was accomplished in six days so that God could obey the Sabbath by resting from the divine labors on that day. All Jews were then required to follow the divine example. This creation narrative moved in beautiful stages from the idea of the Spirit of God brooding over the chaos of darkness in order to bring forth life, to the story of how light was separated from darkness on the first day. On the second day, the narrative reported, a firmament, which was to be called heaven, was made to separate the waters above the earth from whence the rains came, from the waters below, which at that time presumably covered the entire planet. On the third day the waters of the planet were gathered into one place and called the seas, and thus separated from the dry land, which came to be called the earth. This dry land was enabled to bring forth grass, herbs, fruit trees and vegetables to be used for food as soon as living creatures arrived. On the fourth day God created the sun to illumine the day and the moon to light the night, thus dividing day from night, and in the process creating both seasons and years. God was also said to have made the stars on that day. On the fifth day the fish of the waters and the birds of the air were created and ordered to fill the sea and the sky. On the sixth day God made the beasts of the fields—that is, "everything that creeps on the earth." Finally, on that same day and as the last divine creative act, God made the man and the woman, together, instantaneously, both in the image of God. These first human creatures were then ordered to be fruitful, to multiply and to fill the earth. The work of creation was now finished, and God pronounced the divine task to be both complete and good. So on the seventh day God inaugurated the Sabbath of rest, blessed it and hallowed it, enjoining its observance upon the subsequent generations of the Jewish people as their sacred duty. This whole creation story was the product of the priestly school of writers who made survival the highest goal of the Jewish people during the Babylonian exile. This creation story was designed, not to inform people about what happened at the dawn of creation, but to make the Jewish observance of the Sabbath the original rule and defining mark of Judaism (Gen. 1:1–2:3). This opening salvo from the priestly writers implicitly announced that the sacred story of the Jews had been reshaped to aid their goal of tribal survival as a distinct group of people called by God to live faithfully in and through a critical experience.

Once that purpose is noted and understood, then the other priestly editorial changes can be seen and observed. In the story about God providing manna to the hungry Jews in the wilderness on their original trek from slavery in Egypt to what they believed was their Promised Land, the priestly writers inserted new details to reinforce the Sabbath. The manna from heaven was said now to have fallen only on six days of the week so that neither God in sending, nor the people in gathering up this heavenly gift, had to violate the Sabbath by working on that day of rest (Exod. 16:4ff).

When the priestly writers came to the story of the Ten Commandments, which were said to have been given by God at Mount Sinai, they added their creation story motif to the Sabbath Day commandment as a necessary commentary (Exod. 20:8–11). The earlier reason for the Sabbath (see Deut. 5) was that the Jews were called to remember from the days of their slavery in Egypt that even slaves were entitled to a day of rest. Now, however, the order of creation itself was the reason the commandments gave for a strict observance of the Sabbath.

The priestly writers then sought to locate each of the marks of Judaism needed for their survival as a nation inside the earlier narratives in order to give them the authority of having come from Moses. That was when the kosher dietary laws were written into the book of Leviticus as among the commands of God given through Moses (Exod. 34:24, Lev. 11:1–23). That was when circumcision was written back into the stories of both Abraham (Gen. 21:4) and Moses (Exod. 4:25) as something mandated by God from the beginning to these ancient figures. The elaborate rites of Jewish worship that mark the book of Leviticus were spelled out in detail and adapted to the Jews' exile status, so that they could be observed even in captivity. This was also when synagogues were created to replace the Temple and in these local teaching centers, the reading and the teaching of the Torah was carried out Sabbath by Sabbath. Even the story of Noah was adapted so that Noah would have on board sufficient animals (seven pairs) to carry out all of the required ritual sacrifices without jeopardizing the future of any species of which there was supposedly only a single pair that made it into the ark (Gen. 7:1–5).

The revisioning process orchestrated by the priestly writers went on for many years. It was thus not the product of a single author or even a single generation, but it accomplished its stated purpose. It stamped an identity on the Jewish people that was destined to become indelible. As we have seen, the priestly revisioning was designed to mark the Jewish people as different and thus to keep them isolated and racially pure. Only then would they carry the hope of the world expressed in their messianic dreams. With these priestly changes the Torah was now formally established as the Yahwist-Elohist-Deuteronomic-Priestly version. This biblical text had by now more than doubled in size. Great chunks of new material had been added, mostly to govern worship and behavior. In addition to the Genesis account discussed above, priestly additions included most of the book of Exodus after the story of Mount Sinai (Exod. 20), all of the book of Leviticus and significant parts of Numbers, as well as editorial revisions of the entire text. It may not have come into its finished form until as late as the fourth century BCE. There is a narrative in the book of Nehemiah (chapter 8) in which a group of Jewish people, having returned from the exile and having rebuilt the Temple in Jerusalem, were gathered "before the Water Gate." There, upon orders from the governor, Nehemiah, Ezra the priest had delivered to him "the book of the law of Moses," which he then proceeded to read to the people in its entirety. This reading occurred, we are told, on the first day of the seventh month of the Jewish year. That was the day on which the New Year, or Rosh Hashanah, was to be celebrated and the people covenanted to be bound by this law. What Ezra read on that day was in all probability pretty much the substance of the now-complete Torah, the first five books of the Bible.

Two of the qualities that have marked Jewish life through history were now in place. First, the passion to keep themselves separate from Gentile infiltration in order to survive as a recognized people during the exile got interpreted, when the Jews returned to their homeland, to be a passion for ethnic purity. Genealogies were kept so that people could demonstrate their blood lines and prove their unpolluted Jewish heritage. This led to purges of those husbands, wives and children who were not demonstrably full-blooded Jews, as well as to the judgment, found in New Testament times, that Gentiles were by definition unclean and thus to be avoided. It also led to a violent prejudice against those who came to be called Samaritans. Not only had the Jewishness of the Samaritans been compromised, but their religion had been corrupted by foreign and thus pagan elements that the Samaritans had welcomed. Jewish prejudices against those thought of as half-breeds and heretics went deep and they were validated and legitimatized by appeals to the "Word of God" found in the law said to have been dictated by God to Moses. In time this prejudice against both the unclean Gentiles and the heretical Samaritans would usher in some less than admirable parts of Jewish history, which would in turn create their own Jewish protest. We will look at that development later.

The other quality was the elevation of the Torah into the status of "holy of Holies" in the Jewish scriptures. The essence of Judaism would in time be said to contain both the "law and the prophets." The Torah was the law.

With the Torah now formed, we will follow the biblical story until the prophets begin to emerge.

PART III

The Rise of
the Prophets

The Transitional Books

Joshua, Judges and Samuel

The first of the so-called books of Moses carries the Jewish tradition from creation to the birth of their tribe in the story of Abraham, then on through the patriarchs of Isaac, Jacob and Joseph, through whom they wound up as sojourners in Egypt. The Jews then sank into an underclass of slave laborers. That is the story line in the book of Genesis.

Then the great moment of the exodus finally arrived as slavery was escaped and the Jews' journey in the wilderness toward the Promised Land became part of the national history. During that journey they had a series of related adventures, from the splitting of the Red Sea, to being fed miraculously with heavenly bread called manna, to the giving of the law on Mount Sinai. Moses was the hero of this saga, which fills the books of Exodus, Leviticus, Numbers and Deuteronomy. Fittingly, we are told of the death of Moses in the last chapter of Deuteronomy and a new leader named Joshua is introduced.

Now, moving beyond the books of Moses, we see that Joshua leads the military invasion by the Jews of the land of the Canaanites until they are presumably conquered. Next we learn about how the land is divided up and how the tribes of Israel, named for Jacob's twelve sons, settle in various parts of this land and a loose confederation of people that will someday evolve into a unified nation comes into being. As we proceed through this period, we will see the rise of what came to be called the prophetic movement and we will examine how it was ultimately the law, identified primarily with Moses, and the prophets, identified primarily with Elijah, which defined Judaism. We now turn, therefore, to examine the Jewish story between the giving of the law at Mount Sinai to the emergence of the prophets to produce the "twin towers" of the Jewish religion. It is a fascinating story.

I think it is fair to say that behind the books of Joshua and Judges there are some echoes of history, but they are faint indeed. There were constant invasions of the settled lands of Canaan by marauding nomadic bands of people, and one of them, led by Joshua perhaps, may have been more dramatic than others. Beyond that, however, we cannot treat the books of Joshua and Judges as history. They are too deeply overlaid with myths, folk tales, hero stories and nationalistic propaganda to be understood as literal history. Nonetheless, they do provide insights into the character of the Jewish people: We can see in these books some of the identifying marks of Judaism in their most embryonic forms. Besides that, the stories are wonderful and memorable.

We begin with the book of Joshua. Is the portrait drawn in that book one of a real-life person who was remembered as Moses' successor, or do we meet in these pages a composite of many leaders who lived after Moses? I do not believe we will ever be able to answer that question with any sense of confidence.

What we are told in the book of Joshua is that Joshua was the successor to Moses. He was of the tribe of Ephraim, which made him a member of one of the two Joseph tribes. In the Joshua cycle of stories we discover that Moses' acts appear to have been repeated and wrapped around Joshua, in order to endow him with the political power that accrued to Moses. Certainly the splitting of the Jordan River so that the people of Israel could walk across it on dry land on their way to conquer Jericho is a version of the story of Moses splitting the Red Sea, simply retold about Joshua.

The conquest of Canaan by Joshua is portrayed in the Bible as being both quick and total, but later history shows Jews and Canaanites living side by side, even intermarrying, long after the time of Joshua, which would seem to indicate that Joshua enjoyed something less than a total victory. The present book of Joshua relates only three major military campaigns carried out by this new commander. They are the battle of Jericho, which is told in great detail as a supernatural story of walls miraculously falling at the sound of Joshua's trumpets, the battle against the kings of the south and finally the battle against the kings of the north. In neither of the final two accounts are we given anything but very scant details. The overall story is quite misleading to the modern reader. Joshua is described as being in only those epic battles, with each battle being described in terms of a world conflagration. The so-called kings he battled, however, were more like mayors of various villages than they were heads of state. After these three victorious campaigns the Bible suggests that the Jewish people settled down into a series of closely related regions under the leadership of local judges.

The most remembered story in the book of Joshua, and one that was quoted in a seventeenth-century dispute when the Christian faith was challenged by the new learning about the size of the universe, is the account of Joshua stopping the sun in the sky (Josh. 10). The context of the narrative was a battle between the Israelites and the Amorites. The battle was going well for Joshua; the army of the Amorites was not just defeated but routed. The sun, however, began to go down in the western sky and the defeated Amorites soon would have the cover of darkness under which they could escape. Joshua, we are told, took this concern to God, presumably in prayer. God appeared to answer Joshua by stopping the sun in the sky to allow him more time to slaughter his enemies. It was not a very noble purpose for creating the first instance of daylight saving time! In this passage God is portrayed as interfering with the laws of nature, manipulating such things as the law of gravity and the orbit of heavenly bodies in the sky—and all for the sole purpose of allowing Joshua more daylight for killing. God was surely pro-Jewish in this tribal story, but God also appears to have been less than noble and even less than moral. We recognize again the human origins of this book.

The reason that this text is destined to live in history is that it was cited by the Vatican in its condemnation of Galileo for the "heresy" of suggesting that the earth was not the center of a three-tiered universe. In that generally accepted seventeenth-century view, the earth was the static center of all things and the sun rotated around the earth. The Bible assumed the accuracy of this cosmology. That worldview is what Galileo challenged so deeply. In the conflict between the church and Galileo, this text in Joshua, assumed to be the "Word of God," was used to seal Galileo's fate. In that period of history, if something contradicted the revealed and inerrant truth of the Bible, that contradiction was to be dismissed—and so it was in this case too. So the church leaders proclaimed that the Bible's overt statement that God had stopped the sun on its journey around the earth was clear proof that the sun rotated around the earth, making the earth the center of the universe. Galileo was therefore incorrect and guilty of heresy as charged. He was then condemned to be burned at the stake. The sentence was later modified in deference to Galileo's age, his poor health and probably because he had friends in high places in the Vatican. His case was probably not hurt by the fact that he had a daughter who was a nun. His sentence was reduced in the end to the requirement that he recant his "heresy" publically, house arrest for the balance of his life and his agreement never again to publish his thoughts.

That moment, which constituted one of the most embarrassing episodes in Christian history, inaugurated the science-religion battle that would rage over the next four centuries. That battle was not eased by the Vatican's decision in 1991 to issue a public document announcing that the Catholic Church now believed

Galileo had been right! This document was issued a few years after space travel had begun, which would have been quite impossible if Galileo had not been correct. Both of these events—the church's denouncement of Galileo and its subsequent belated endorsement—constituted dark moments in which fundamentalism, this time in a Catholic manifestation, was used to retard the advance of human knowledge and thus served to elevate this text in Joshua to the status of the best known, even topping the fact that "Joshua fought the battle of Jericho and the walls came tumbling down." Beyond these two narratives, people have very little sense of this transitional book in the Hebrew scriptures.

One further note. The name Joshua is the anglicized pronunciation of the Jewish name Yeshua. "Jesus" is the attempt to render that name understandable first in Greek and later in English. So Joshua and Jesus are simply two spellings of the same name, identical at their origin. That fact will play a large role in the story of Jesus when the New Testament comes to be written.

After the book of Joshua comes the period of "the judges" in Jewish history. This is a time that produced a series of folk tales, narratives that are quite distinct even in the Bible. People tend not to be familiar with these stories, except for the narrative about the strong man, Samson, and his dramatic undoing at the hands of his lover, Delilah (Judg. 13–16). As delightful as the story of Samson is, it is only one of many that we find in the book of Judges. There is also the account of a woman named Jael, who finds the number-one enemy of her people, a Canaanite general named Sisera, delivered miraculously into her hands. After giving him a glass of milk laced with sufficient drugs to render him unconscious, she proceeds to nail his head to the floor with a mallet and a tent peg. It is a rather gory story! At the climax of this story the literal text of the Bible says: "He sank, he fell, he lay still at her feet, he fell; there he sank, there he fell dead" (Judg. 5:27). It is a convoluted sentence, but it indicates fairly clearly that Sisera was in fact dead. A spike through the temple pinning the victim's head to the floor is a pretty effective murder weapon.

There is also the story of Jephthah and his rash vow to sacrifice anyone who comes out to greet him on his return from a
military victory. The innocent one who gets trapped in this vow
turns out to be his own daughter. She is given time to "mourn her
virginity" and then she is put to death (Judg. 11).

Then there is the story of Ehud, the judge who, because he
was left-handed, was deceptive enough to drive his sword so
deeply into the stomach of Eglon, the hugely fat king of Moab,
that his hand actually disappeared in the king's flabby flesh. Some
of the later prejudice toward left-handed people was born in this
narrative (Judg. 3).

Perhaps the most repellent story in the entire Bible is the narrative in the book of Judges about a man who traveled with his
concubine to Jerusalem where, to save himself from abuse, he
offered his concubine to the men of the city for the purpose of
gang rape. When they had done their worst to her, they threw her
unconscious body on the porch of the home where this man was
staying. He then proceeded to carve her battered and unconscious
body into twelve pieces, sending part of her to each of the twelve
tribes of Israel to call them to arms (Judg. 19). Many of the
themes of this story are repeated in the Genesis story of Sodom
and Gomorrah. One could hardly read this passage in church
on Sunday morning without revulsion. This narrative is a lot of
things, but the "Word of God" is not one of them. The stories
found in the book of Judges are not necessarily stories that inspire, teach or can be used to enhance life.

This period in Jewish history is not unlike what's going on
in the modern-day nation of Afghanistan, where real leadership
resides in the tribal chiefs, who rule various parts of the nation
with an iron hand. These local Jewish judges were in fact the
political rulers at that time. It is also analogous to that period of
American history when the people of this nation lived under the
Articles of Confederation as a loose union of states with little
or no national power. Having just endured the life of submissive colonists ruled by a foreign power, these early Americans
were not eager to cede local authority to anyone, including a

national government. The Israelites at this time likewise had searing memories of their oppression at the hands of the Egyptians.
Having found freedom, they were now not eager to be submissive
to a distant authority again. That is a natural reaction, but it is
hardly ever a permanent solution. The American colonies could
not have maintained their independent life had they not become
a unified nation. The tribes of Israel could not have maintained
their independent life had they not become a nation. The new
union in both of these nations was, we recall, quite fragile, and
both the Jews and the citizens of the United States were tested by
secession. It came to the Jews some eighty years after the kingship of David had been established. It came to the United States
some seventy-three years after the United States established its
central government under the presidency of George Washington.
The process of nation building always seems to go through certain inevitable stages.

The period of the judges came to an end under the leadership
of the final judge, whose name was Samuel. He is clearly the pivotal figure in this period of Israel's history, as that nation transi-
tioned from being a disorganized nomadic people in the wilderness
to becoming an established nation with a central government.

As seems to be the case with every pivotal figure in Jewish history, Samuel became a significant figure whose memory would
later shape Jewish messianic thinking. Certainly the Jesus story
shows the influence of Samuel at a number of places. Samuel had
something of a miraculous birth. His mother, Hannah, had been
unable to have children until, as the story says, "God intervened
to answer her prayers." When Samuel was born Hannah was said
to have sung a song that is quite similar to the Song of Mary that
we call the Magnificat (compare I Sam. 2:1–10 with Luke 1:47–
55). When Luke tells the story of Jesus going up to the Temple at
the age of twelve, there are many similarities with Hannah taking
Samuel to the shrine where Eli the priest lived (compare I Sam.
1:21–28 with Luke 2:41–52).

Samuel was also the pivotal figure in the establishment of the
Jewish monarchy. At first he was said to have resisted the pressure

from the people to have a king, warning them that kings can be tyrants (I Sam. 8), and yet finally he anointed Saul to be the first king of the unified Jewish nation (I Sam. 10). When Saul proved to be a poor choice, Samuel sought out and anointed a shepherd boy named David, the son of Jesse, to be the second king, and it was David who established the lasting monarchy (I Sam. 16). It was also during the reign of King David that a lone man, armed with nothing except a sense of his belief in the immutable moral law of God, challenged King David publicly for what he believed was the king's immoral behavior (II Sam. 12). By that act this man established the so-called prophetic principle, which was rare indeed among the ancient nations. That prophetic principle proclaimed that even the king must live under and be judged by the law of God. Ultimately this principle would make Israel a very different nation from all the other nations of the world. To this man's story and its role in the rise of the prophetic movement we turn next.

CHAPTER 8

The Story of Nathan

All Are Subject to the Law

The prophets of the Hebrew scriptures are not religious versions of Drew Pearson or Jeane Dixon.[1] They do not predict future events. Instead, prophets are those who are in touch with values, truth and God. They thus see the issues of life more deeply than other people see them. By standing on the shoulders of others, they can perceive future trends and speak to them before others even see them developing.

There have been artists to whom prescience has been attributed. A well-known Spanish painter, for example, painted a scene prior to the Spanish Civil War that portrayed his country torn apart in a violent struggle.[2] The Bible might well have called him prophetic. He saw what there was to be seen as inevitable, but not everyone was able to see it.

The power of the prophets was derived not from the established structures of the social order, but from each prophet's own

---

1   Drew Pearson was a political columnist in the middle of the twentieth century who liked to predict future events. Jeane Dixon was a psychic who patterned herself as one who could divine the future.
2   *Guernica* by Pablo Picasso.

unique vision. Prophets almost always stand outside the boundaries of either political or ecclesiastical authority. The established
authority of religious institutions has almost always resented the
prophets, for they were neither ordained nor trained. They are
free spirits who somehow spoke with an authority that established figures wished they possessed. The ability to speak to those
in power in a way that demands their attention is the signal mark
of the prophetic spirit.

None of this, however, answers the question of just why it was
that the role of the prophet was able first to appear and then to
rise in Israel to such heights that the religion of Israel was said to
rest with equal weight on those aforementioned "twin towers"—
the law (the Torah) and the prophets. It all began, I believe, in a
charismatic confrontation between Israel's most powerful king
and a man armed only with a sense of God's righteousness. That
story, told in II Samuel (chapter 12), remains instructive today.
We listen to its incredible words, told accurately, but not literally;
hence I place this story in italics.

*King David lived in the biggest and tallest house in the city
of Jerusalem, which meant that when he was out on his rooftop he could look down on the rooftops of all of Jerusalem's
citizens. One afternoon, when he was doing just that, he spied
a beautiful woman taking a bath in what she assumed was the
privacy of her own rooftop. The king was smitten with her
charms and at once sent a messenger to her with an invitation to
visit the palace to have a tryst with her king. The woman came.
Perhaps in the power equations of that world she had no choice,
perhaps she wanted to come—the text doesn't tell us and so we
will never know. The two of them, nonetheless, became lovers
at least for this brief time. When the lovemaking was over the
woman, whose name was Bathsheba, returned to her home.
This was likely neither the first nor the last such affair that King
David had, and he probably did not think much about it once
the rendezvous had ended. So it was that weeks passed and
memories faded until they were newly awakened by a message
arriving at the palace directed to the king's eyes alone. The mes-*

*sage read: "King David, I need you to know that I am expecting
your child." It was signed Bathsheba.*

When David read the message, he responded in a typically
male, evasive way. "You are a married woman," he said, "why
do you assume I am the father of the baby?" That is the first time
that we learn from the biblical source that this tryst the king had
had was an adulterous relationship with a married woman. To
this fairly natural question Bathsheba responded immediately,
"I am indeed a married woman, but my husband, Uriah, is a
soldier in the king's army. He has been fighting the king's wars
under Joab, the king's military leader, and thus he has not been
home for months. There is no doubt, O king, that you are this
baby's father."

Still unwilling to accept responsibility, the king decided on an
alternate course of action. It was plan B. He would grant Uriah a
furlough so that Uriah could come home, enjoy the privilege of his
wife's bed and then, in this pre–DNA testing world, they could say
this baby came early. It would not be the first time that tactic had
been employed. So permission for leave was conveyed by a royal
messenger to the captain in the field and a very surprised Uriah
found himself being granted an unasked for and unprecedented
furlough. What King David did not anticipate, however, was that
Uriah had the makeup of the "original Boy Scout." He was a soldier first and foremost and as such he was drunk with the cama-
raderie of warfare. "It would not be fair or appropriate for me,"
he said, "to enjoy the comforts of my home and my wife while my
buddies are bleeding and dying on the battlefield from which I
have somehow been removed. Therefore, in solidarity with them,"
he concluded, "I will not enter my home on this leave." So in a
quite ostentatious way Uriah set up a pup tent on the walk beside
his home and spent his entire leave there. On viewing this, David,
feeling trapped, began to develop plan C.

Once again a sealed royal order was conveyed to Joab, the
commanding officer, this time by the hand of Uriah himself. In
this letter David commanded Joab to organize his army into a
V-shaped wedge and to hurl that wedge at the gates of his en-

emy's capital city. Uriah was to be placed at the front tip of this wedge, where his death was all but inevitable. It was done. Uriah was struck down and killed. Joab then notified the king that his problem was now solved. King David, in response, sent for Bathsheba and she became a member of his harem. Finally King David felt that this situation was under control.

This outrageous kingly behavior did not, however, escape the notice of a highly respected holy man whose name was Nathan. He decided that he must confront the king about the king's action. The reputation of Nathan was such that the king, unsuspecting of what was to come, granted him the audience that he requested. It must have been a strange confrontation. Here was King David in his chambers, surrounded by all the wealth and opulence of royalty. Standing before him was Nathan, armed only with a sense of righteousness derived from what he believed was the moral law of God that permeated the universe. When the two of them were alone, Nathan said to the king that an episode of gross injustice had occurred in the king's realm and he felt compelled to bring it to the king's attention. The king, who was the ultimate judge of his people, encouraged Nathan to speak on. Nathan did so in terms of a parable.

"A certain poor man," Nathan told the king, "had a single ewe lamb that was treated as a pet in his family. This lamb was fed from the family's table, slept in the family's home and shared in the family's love. Another man who lived nearby," Nathan continued, "was very wealthy and owned great flocks of sheep. One day this rich man had a distinguished visitor that he was required, according to the mores of his culture, to honor at a banquet. Instead of taking a lamb from his own extensive herds, however, he went to the house of his poor neighbor, took his only ewe lamb, the family pet, and slaughtered, dressed and roasted it to set before his guest. The rich man and his guest dined sumptuously while the poor man and his family were grief-stricken." Nathan let the pathos hang quite poignantly as he finished his story. David, upon hearing this tale, was filled with anger and declared: "The man who has done this thing must surely die."

Then in one of the Bible's most dramatic moments, Nathan fixed his eyes on the king and said: "King David, thou art the man!"

The king, thought (by himself and others) to be all-powerful, had been called by the prophet Nathan to answer for his deeds. No one is above the law of God, he learned. That was a lesson rare in the ancient world—indeed, it was a message unique to the people of Israel. David might have been divinely chosen to be king, as the biblical story suggests and as the royal family always claimed, but the king of Israel still lived under the authority of the law of God and must answer for his behavior.

David, to his great credit, did not banish Nathan from his presence. Rather, apparently hearing the voice of God through the words of Nathan, he publicly repented. He performed open acts of penance designed to win restitution. When the child of this adulterous liaison died shortly after his birth, David, together with the biblical writers who recorded this story, interpreted this death as divine punishment. Perhaps in a further act of trying to make things right, David lifted Bathsheba out of the anonymity of the harem and installed her in the public role as his queen. Their second child was born a while later. His name was Solomon, and he was to be the successor to David's throne and the one who would solidify the royal line of the House of David that was destined to last, at least in the Southern Kingdom, for over four hundred years.

When Nathan's act of courage was included in the sacred story of the Jewish people, it entered the annals of Jewish memory. By becoming part of the Jewish scriptures, this story was destined to be read in worship settings over the centuries and in time to become identified as containing an essential mark of Judaism. In retrospect Nathan was called a prophet, and because of that designation the prophet's role in Jewish life was established as essential and formidable. It was the duty of the prophets to speak for God in the citadels of power, to claim for God's law a place of absolute influence and to assert that there is no one in the land who is not subject to the law of God. Monarchy was not absolute in Israel from that moment on. This was destined to become the single most important factor that made the Jewish nation different from all the other nations of the ancient world. One never knows the ultimate power of a single courageous prophetic word.

CHAPTER 9

I and II Kings, Elijah and Elisha

Step Two in the Prophetic Tradition

The man Samuel was more of a judge than he was a prophet. He was also a power broker, choosing and anointing the first two kings of the Jewish nation. When Samuel passed from the scene it was Nathan who really established the role of the prophet, as we have just read. Someone else, however, had to pick up that role and solidify it before it could become an identifiable part of the life of the Jewish people. That is exactly what two remarkable and colorful figures did, and their story dominates the biblical drama in that period of Jewish history between Nathan's confrontation with King David and the rise of the so-called writing prophets in the eighth century BCE. Their names were Elijah and Elisha.

Their stories are found in the Bible between I Kings 17, where Elijah suddenly arises in the text, and II Kings 13, where Elisha makes his final appearance and his death is recorded. Between those two points are some of the most dramatic narratives in the entire Bible. While these two figures were on the stage, they dominated the biblical account. Their adventures were fanciful and sometimes even farcical, but they were always entertaining. Both of these figures were destined to play an important role in the Christian story in two primary ways. First, the name of Elijah was identified later in Jewish history with the mythical figure who would herald the coming of the messiah. The story of John the Baptist, who was assigned that anticipatory role by early Christian interpreters, was remembered and written about through the lens of Elijah. In the first biblical portrait of John the Baptist, which is found in Mark, we note that John the Baptist was clad in Elijah's clothing, fed on Elijah's diet and placed in Elijah's wilderness. Second, in some other parts of the tradition, the messiah was himself said to be a new and greater Elijah, and so it was that Elijah, and to a lesser degree Elisha, also shaped the content of the Jesus story. When we come to our consideration of the gospels themselves, I will amplify these hints very substantially. For the moment, however, let me now lift both of these personalities into the spotlight so that we might examine them closely.

Elijah was called the Tishbite because he hailed from Tishbe in Gilead, an area east of the Jordan River in the Northern Kingdom. His emergence into the Jewish story was very dramatic. There was a drought, which affected the whole nation and for which Elijah was somehow given full credit. Elijah, it seems, had predicted this drought to King Ahab and his wife, Queen Jezebel, of the Northern Kingdom, and he claimed that it was divine punishment for their sins; thus he was held responsible for it. Fearing for his life at the hands of this enraged royal couple, Elijah fled first to the Brook Cherith, which was located in the desert. He was clearly a larger-than-life figure already, for it was said of him that God provided for his needs by having the ravens bring him bread to keep him alive during the famine that he presumably had caused. When the drought continued so long that the waters of this brook began to dry up, Elijah fled further to the east, to the region known as Zarephath.

In Zarephath he had a dramatic encounter with a widow, who was the mother of a solitary son. Elijah first asked her for water and a meal cake, but she replied that she was down to her last bit of flour and oil and she planned to use those to make a final meal for herself and her son before they both died of starvation in this relentless famine. Elijah, however, assured her that if she did as he requested, her supply of both flour and oil would never run out. Here we have what we should begin to recognize as a familiar biblical theme—namely, that in a time of hunger God will supply adequate food by some miraculous act. It was the story of Moses and manna in the wilderness; it will reappear in the Elisha cycle of stories; and, in its most familiar form, it is the meaning of Jesus feeding the multitudes with five loaves and two fish. I identify this theme here so that we can be on the lookout for it later in this journey through the Bible. This widow soon reappeared in the Elijah cycle of stories when her son died and Elijah raised him back to life in the first biblical episode that suggests that the power of raising one from the dead was possible for a human being.

In the tradition of Nathan, who dared to witness to his understanding of truth in the citadels of power in the Jewish nation, Elijah is portrayed as confronting King Ahab time after time, winning for himself from Ahab the title of "the troubler of Israel." The next issue between the prophet and the king was over whether or not Baal and Asherah, who were the deities worshiped by the fertility cults of the Canaanites and supported by Queen Jezebel, would be allowed to stand in the nation of the "chosen people" beside Yahweh, the God worshiped by the prophet Elijah. It is clear in this story that Baal worship was still vibrant throughout the land. In Elijah's mind the land was not big enough for both deities. Elijah, therefore, challenged the priests of Baal and Asherah to a duel on Mount Carmel. Four hundred priests of Baal and four hundred and fifty priests of Asherah accepted this challenge, lining themselves up against the solitary and quite heroic figure of Elijah. The contest was to determine which God, Baal or Yahweh, would respond to the prayers of that deity's priests or prophet by sending fire from heaven to burn up the sacrificed bull that had been laid on the altar. The priests of

Baal went first, dancing, chanting and even cutting themselves with knives in pleas to Baal and his female partner, Asherah, for heavenly fire. Their pleas, however, were to no avail. The fire from heaven never came. Elijah, who must have been a hair shirt of a personality, taunted them from the sidelines with suggestions that perhaps their God was sleepy, until finally it became his turn.

In a dramatic display of confidence, Elijah poured barrels of water over his altar and the sacrificed animal until the water filled the trenches around the altar, a detail which surely was designed to heighten the power of the miracle. One wag, trying to account for the supernatural elements of this story, suggested that while it looked like water, it was really liquefied natural gas. That would indeed have made a difference! Then Elijah called down the fire of God and it came, devouring the sacrifice with flames and licking up all the water in the trenches. Elijah, clearly the winner in this contest, was not gracious in victory. He proceeded to cut off the heads of all the "false" priests with his sword. Then he moved quickly to use his newly recognized power to purify the worship of Israel, removing all vestiges of Baalism. Elijah's ability to call down fire from heaven appears to have become his special gift: The biblical story will record two more occasions on which this prophet employed this power.

Elijah is also the first person in the Bible of whom an unambiguous narrative about ascending into heaven is told. The details are dramatic, involving a fiery chariot drawn by magical fiery horses and propelled by a whirlwind. That story will reappear in the New Testament, most prominently in the book of Acts, and be retold about Jesus, as we shall see when we come to that part of the biblical story.

Following this ascension story Elijah's handpicked successor, Elisha, comes to the Bible's center stage and we watch as familiar Jewish themes are repeated in the cycle of Elisha stories. Miracle stories in the Bible are frequently told over and over again, but about different people. Moses, Joshua, Elijah and Elisha, for example, all seem able to split a body of water so that each can navigate through a heretofore watery obstacle on dry land. Elisha, like Elijah before him, also has some less than desirable qualities. In a fit of anger about being called bald-headed he causes two she-bears to come out of the woods to devour some little children. He appears able to cause a borrowed iron axe head to float on the top of a river so that it can be found. He too can raise the dead and he can cure foreigners of leprosy by having them wash in the Jordan River. Like Moses and Elijah before him, he has power over the weather and uses it to punish the Jews for their sinfulness, especially the unfaithfulness of the king. Elisha also appears to be able to cause a barren woman to conceive. This power too has appeared before in the biblical story in the narratives about the births of Samson and Samuel. I suspect this is the seed out of which will ultimately come the story of Jesus' miraculous birth to a virgin. The story of Jesus' birth had to manifest a more dramatically heightened form, one fit for a messiah, than did the stories of the births of the more ordinary John the Baptist, Samson or Samuel.

The narratives that floated around these two ancient and not always positively portrayed figures, Elijah and Elisha, were filled with miracles, magic, fantasy and folklore, all built once again, as we have noted before, on what was probably a mere germ of history. They, however, greatly solidify and clearly establish the role in Israel that a prophet can and must speak with authority as a voice for God, to whom even the mighty are subject, and thus they demonstrate that no one can escape the moral law of God.

Elijah and Elisha tend to blend together in the Bible so that it is hard to keep them separate. Even their names are so similar that they are frequently confused. Sometimes things commanded for Elijah to do are completed either in the life of Elisha or even later in Jewish history. It seems obvious that Queen Jezebel's vow to remove Elijah's head as he had done to her priests of Baal at Mount Carmel finally gets its fulfillment when another queen, one named Herodias, the wife of King Herod, has John the Baptist's head removed—another attempt to tie Elijah and John the Baptist together. As we shall see quite clearly when we get to the

Jesus story, many Elijah themes are developed, magnified and reused to interpret the life and meaning of Jesus.

These two figures, Elijah and Elisha, are deeply emblazoned in Jewish history, and they form a bridge to the writing prophets of the eighth century BCE and beyond, who in turn help to transform the God that the Jews worshiped from a rather vindictive and bloodthirsty tribal deity into a universal presence, incorporating into the divine identity a new sense of oneness, a transforming love and a searing understanding of divine justice. Ultimately the prophets create a deity who turns away from the requirements of worship and sacrifices and who demands that the people give this God honor primarily by living out what "God" means in relation to one's fellow human beings. God is taken out of liturgy and plunged into life. That is quite an accomplishment!

PART IV

Introducing the
Writing Prophets

The Prophetic Principle

Ancient and Modern

I f one takes the book of Daniel out of the Old Testament, a
much clearer view of the writing prophets of Israel becomes
visible. Daniel, written during the time of the Maccabees
and not during the earlier Persian period, as it pretends to
be, really does not fit the prophetic tradition. The fact is that the
book of Daniel should be in the Apocrypha (a collection of later
Jewish writings that we will consider briefly at the end of chapter
26), not in the Old Testament, but that would upset those people
who like to predict the end of the world by quoting from Daniel,
so it is not likely to be removed.

Excising Daniel for a moment, the remaining prophetic works
are those of Isaiah, Jeremiah, Ezekiel and those called minor
prophets. That latter designation includes those books from
Hosea to Malachi—a collection that was originally called the
"Book of the Twelve." These writing prophets, called this because
unlike their predecessors they tell their own story, can be looked
at through a number of lenses. Our first observation is that, if we
treat the Book of the Twelve as a single volume, which is the way
the Jews regarded it, all four texts—Isaiah, Jeremiah and Ezekiel

and the Book of the Twelve—are about the same length. The reason for this has nothing to do with the profundity of the content, but rather with the length of the scroll on which the words were written. That also helps us to understand why new writings, once they were judged worthy of inclusion in the sacred texts, were simply added to space on an available scroll. Jeremiah and Ezekiel, while having extraneous additions, nonetheless appear to represent a single author, but Isaiah and obviously the Book of the Twelve are not. Isaiah has been identified as the work of at least three writers who are separated in time by as much as three hundred years. The book of Zechariah, one of the Twelve, is today viewed as the work of at least two writers (chapters 1–8 and then 9–14), separated in time by a minimum of at least a century. There is even widespread speculation that the final book of the Twelve, Malachi, is really a third portion of Zechariah (which would make it chapters 15–18) and that this is why this book, which tradition calls Malachi, actually has no name, Malachi being a Hebrew word that simply means "my messenger." Malachi was a nameless voice crying in the wilderness. I go into these preliminary explanations to set the stage for our consideration of the content of these various prophetic texts by the writing prophets, whose work was incorporated into the sacred scriptures of the Jewish people over a number of centuries.

We began this section by looking at how the prophetic principle first got established in the life of Nathan. We then traced that principle through the lives of Elijah and Elisha. We now begin to look at those prophets whose work forms sixteen books of the Old Testament. In the journey through the writing prophets we will note how time and time again the role of a prophet is defined and redefined.

There is no such thing as a self-proclaimed prophet, a fact that is widely misunderstood by religious folks. To be a "prophet in residence" is not a role for which one can apply, nor can anyone study for a prophetic career. The designation of prophet is bestowed by history alone, and normally well after the end of the potential prophet's life and career. Prophets are recognized in retrospect and thus usually posthumously.

Are there any modern-day prophets that might help us to understand the role of the biblical prophet more adequately? I think of three people immediately: Martin Luther King, Jr., Nelson Mandela and a less well known person named Aleksandr Solzhenitsyn. All saw and affirmed the humanity beneath dehumanizing systems. King and Mandela spoke to the humanity of people of color, Solzhenitsyn to the humanity of those oppressed by an economic system. Each of them spoke from outside the normal power positions of authority. King was a neophyte in the field of religion, a local pastor. Mandela was a resistance leader whose power actually grew while in prison. Solzhenitsyn was a literary man, an author. Let me bring them briefly into our awareness.

Martin Luther King, Jr. became the voice of America's oppressed black population, which had been both systematically and legally separated from the mainstream of society and wrapped inside a cocoon of prejudice and fear. King stood before the political world as one who was unwilling to accept for himself or his people the status of outcasts, which first slavery and then segregation had imposed on them. He confronted the leaders of the insensitive ecclesiastical establishment in his famous letter from a Birmingham jail. He was regularly arrested by local police, vilified by local politicians and newspapers, and spied on with telephone taps by none less than J. Edgar Hoover, Federal Bureau of Investigation head, who we now know was a deeply closeted and self-denigrating homosexual. Ultimately Dr. King was murdered when he sought to lead the garbage workers in their strike for decent wages in Memphis, Tennessee. Above all else Dr. King gave hope and dignity to his people. He called this nation into both repentance for the past and dreams for a society based on racial justice in the future. In that society, he said, the proper value assigned to people was that they be judged by the "content of their character" rather than by the "color of their skin." Well after his death in 1968, a grateful nation created a national holiday to honor his memory. Forty years after his death, his legacy was further seen in the fact that an African American named Barack Obama achieved the highest pinnacle of political power in the United States, an unthinkable idea in pre–Martin Luther King days. In campaigning for the Democratic nomination in 2008, Senator Obama quoted Dr. King every time people suggested he was too young and therefore too inexperienced for the high office he was seeking. Dr. King had once referred, noted Obama, to the "fierce urgency of now." When forces of change coalesce around a candidate and lift that candidate to center stage, that is the signal that the time is now. "This is our time, our moment," Senator Obama declared, and the people responded. The history of this nation was changed by Dr. King. It was fitting that after his death, this nation designated him a prophet.

Nelson Mandela helped to organize the African National Congress, a political paramilitary resistance group, which was declared illegal by the apartheid government of South Africa. He was arrested on more than one occasion, was vilified as a communist and was confined on Robben Island for as long as eighteen of his twenty-seven years of imprisonment. Yet by the sheer power of his unarmed person he maintained the leadership of his people and their course and ultimately outlived his enemies with the quality of his life and his determination. When apartheid crumbled, the white establishment turned to Mandela as the only person who could unite his nation. Mandela responded by seeking to bring about the reconciliation of his nation by the power of forgiveness. He appointed his close friend Archbishop Desmond Tutu to head up the Truth and Reconciliation Commission. Tell the truth, discover forgiveness and be reconciled. Those who were willing to do that would not be charged with a crime nor would they be incarcerated.

Mandela went on to become the founding father of a new South Africa and a grateful nation, both white and black, acclaimed him a prophet who had brought human beings to a new sense of wholeness.

Aleksandr Solzhenitsyn's story is a little different, but his life was no less effective. Solzhenitsyn spoke through his literary talents to the centers of communist power in the old Soviet Union. When that country's leadership got to the place where they were unable to bear the weight of his words, he suffered the prophet's fate. The Soviet leaders had him expelled from the writers' union, imprisoned in the gulags of his day and finally banished from his homeland. They were unwilling to execute this nemesis to the established order because the intellectuals of the world publicly came to his support. People as diverse as Jean-Paul Sartre in France, W. H. Auden in England, and Arthur Miller, Truman Capote and John Updike in America made the Soviet treatment of Solzhenitsyn a matter of international concern. While Solzhenitsyn lived in exile in Vermont, his books were read everywhere. *One Day in the Life of Ivan Denisovich* and *The Gulag Archipelago,* among others, made the case against the demeaning of humanity by his government a worldwide concern. People in the West thought of him as their champion, not understanding that the prophet is not the servant of any one person or institution, but only of the truth. This became obvious when Solzhenitsyn was invited to be the commencement speaker at Harvard University in Cambridge, Massachusetts, in 1978. People across the United States and the Western world expected to hear words of commendation from one anti-communist to this anti-communist nation. They listened for him to validate their positions and indeed even their prejudices. This expectation was a clear example of the old adage that "the enemy of my enemy is my friend." A prophet like Solzhenitsyn, however, served a different master, and—as prophets tend to do—he marched to the beat of his own drummer. In that address he called America "spiritually weak, mired in materialism." He chastised our government for its ineptitude in the defeat in Vietnam, suggesting that our leaders had been too hasty in retreating before the evils of communism just to satisfy local political pressures. He went on to criticize the press for violating the standards of decency and to condemn any government that believed it could defend freedom by using the tactics of dictators, like tapping telephones, invading privacy and launching wars of aggression.

Under Russian President Vladimir Putin, Solzhenitsyn was finally allowed in his old age to return to Russia, where he died. His death was a front-page story in America with long biographical sketches detailing his role in history. In Russia, his death was merely noted with no attendant fanfare, fulfilling the observation made by Jesus that a prophet is not without honor "save in his own community or among his own people" (Mark 6:4).

Tributes, however, do not make a prophet. Prophets rise after their death when people begin to realize that someone of great vision has lived among them. In two generations Solzhenitsyn came to be hailed as a prophet, honored in his homeland and ranked with other Russian literary giants, like Tolstoy and Chekhov, as one who has made a difference.

That is also the way it was with the biblical prophets. Each of them was dead long before any of their writings were lifted into the body of sacred scripture by their descendants. Only when the Jewish powers-that-be decided that such figures as Isaiah, Amos, Micah and Zechariah were prophets, people whose words demanded to be heard by every generation, were their writings elevated from the words of an angry troublemaker into words in which and through which the voice of God had been heard.

Do all of the biblical prophets speak with equal weight and authority? Of course not! I do not believe the world would be significantly poorer if the words of Haggai, Nahum or Zephaniah had not been preserved. The fact is that most people who say they value the Bible today have no idea what the message of these particular books was or is. Yet people are still moved by Hosea's understanding of God as love; by Amos' portrait of God as justice; by Micah's clear distinction between liturgy and life; by Jonah's understanding of the boundaries of prejudice; by the universal vision of Malachi; by the magnificent portraits of the "Servant," or "Suffering Servant" found in II Isaiah, and by the image of the "Shepherd King" found in II Zechariah. It was also largely through the words of the prophets that first-century Jewish people processed their experience with Jesus of Nazareth.

We turn now to look at these writing prophets. I invite you, my readers, to break out of your stained-glass prisons in which the power of the prophets has been lost and to enter with me into the study of these voices that the Jews came to revere, and begin to understand how they shaped our history and our lives.

CHAPTER 11

The Isaiahs I, II and III

The book called Isaiah is not a cohesive whole. Indeed it reflects writing that occurs over about three hundred years of history, obviously far beyond the life span of a single writer. Scholars have identified in its pages the work of at least three authors, one of whom wrote in the eighth century near the time of the fall of the Northern Kingdom; one of whom wrote in the late sixth century at the time of the return of the people of the Southern Kingdom from the Exile in Babylonia, and the final one who wrote in the late fifth century, a generation or so after the Exile. All that these three authors have in common is that, through an accident of history, each shared space on a scroll that was first named Isaiah.

I Isaiah

Bernard Baruch, a Jewish American from Camden, South Carolina, was well known in the first half of the twentieth century as the unofficial advisor to presidents. He played key roles in the think tanks of Presidents Woodrow Wilson, Franklin Roosevelt and Harry Truman. As the son of a surgeon who served on the staff of Confederate General Robert E. Lee, dealing with power seemed to come naturally to him. David Gergen, a native of

Durham, North Carolina, also played a key role in American history, in his case in the last half of the twentieth century, serving as an advisor to Presidents Nixon, Ford, Reagan, George H. W. Bush and Clinton. Baruch and Gergen were representatives of that rare ability to ride a long political tide and to provide objective analysis in the midst of partisan conflict and thus to guide the ship of state through choppy waters.

The biblical figure we call I Isaiah might be seen as the Bernard Baruch or the David Gergen of the ancient world. His writings are found in the book of Isaiah, chapters 1–39. His life spanned the reigns of four monarchs who ruled in Jerusalem: Kings Uzziah, Jotham, Ahaz and Hezekiah. According to the dating system of Old Testament scholar William F. Albright, these four kings ruled between 783 and 687 BCE, a total of ninety-six years.[1] I Isaiah was center stage, according to our best efforts at reconstruction, for more than fifty of those years, a tribute to his longevity. This man tells us himself when he emerged into public view—it was "in the year that King Uzziah died" (Isa. 6:1)—and he lived through one of the most difficult periods of biblical history.

The great power abroad in the world during those days was Assyria. This warlike nation had succeeded in conquering or reducing to vassal status most of the nations in the Middle East. As we have seen, in 721 BCE the Assyrians destroyed the Northern Kingdom called Israel and deported its people from their land into foreign countries for resettlement, from whence they never returned. Despite the legendary attempts to explain their fate, the fact is that these Hebrews simply disappeared into the DNA pool of the Middle East. Theirs was the same fate that had earlier befallen the Canaanites, the Philistines, the Amorites, the Amalekites, the Edomites and many other once previously identifiable tribes of people.

The prophet Isaiah may himself have been a member of the royal family, all of whom were descendants of King David. He certainly shared their lifestyle, educational background, values

---

1   From Albright's book *The Biblical Period from Abraham to Ezra*. See bibliography for details.

and perspectives. Perhaps it was this "blood relative" connection that provided the doorway through which he walked into his prophetic and perhaps even his priestly career in the upper echelons of political power in Jerusalem.

I introduce I Isaiah by isolating a few passages from his writings that have entered the consciousness of the Western world sufficiently to be familiar to many people. First among these passages is his oracle about whether or not God was moved by ritualistic activity and sacrifices. In 1:11–15, Isaiah writes:

> *What to me is the multitude of your sacrifices?*
> *I have had enough of the burnt offering of rams. . . .*
> *I do not delight in the blood of goats. . . .*
> *Incense is an abomination to me. . . .*
> *When you spread forth your hands,*
> *I will lift my eyes from you.*
> *Even though you make many prayers,*
> *I will not listen.*

It was a powerful denunciation of an understanding of worship that is designed to manipulate the deity. The proper purpose of religion, Isaiah has God propose, is an alternative to sacrifices. It is that the people "remove the evil of your doings from before my eyes; cease to do evil; learn to do good, seek justice, correct oppression, defend the fatherless and plead for the widow" (1:16–17). This tension between the activities of worship and the quality of the lives of the worshipers, noted so powerfully in the words of I Isaiah, has always been present in both Jewish and Christian religious life.

Also in I Isaiah are the words that Lyndon Johnson, president of the United States from 1963 to 1969, quoted regularly during his political life, first as Senate majority leader and then later in the White House: "Come let us reason together, saith the Lord" (1:18). Unfortunately, Johnson's idea of reasoning together was for his opponents to line up, drop their pants and have the LBJ brand burned into what the Bible called their "hindquarters."

Probably the most influential passage of Isaiah in religious history occurs in chapter 7, where the prophet writes in verse 14 the words that were later translated to read: "Behold a virgin will conceive and bring forth a son and you shall call his name Immanuel." That text was the inspiration that caused Matthew, the writer of the second gospel, to create the narrative that we now know as the virgin birth. That narrative, a ninth-decade addition to the Christian story, was destined to shape both the Christian creeds and later doctrinal development, despite the fact that the proper translation of that verse states not that "a virgin will conceive," but that "a woman is with child." The word "virgin" is simply not present in Isaiah's work. We shall return to this text when we come to the gospel of Matthew.

The final part of I Isaiah that has been influential in religious history is that prophet's description of what the coming of the Kingdom of God would mean, which is found in his apocalyptic chapters 34 and 35. Here the prophet begged the nations of the world to listen. He informed them that the Lord was angry and would avenge the nations of the world for their evil, bringing about the Kingdom of God on earth. It would be, said Isaiah, a day of vengeance against the enemies of God's people. Clearly tribal religion was in full force! I Isaiah, however, did not stop there. He continued by saying that the coming of "the day of the Lord" would be marked by the presence of fulfillment and wholeness. Listen to his words:

> *The wilderness and the dry land shall be glad,*
> *The desert shall rejoice and bloom,*
> *Like the crocus, it shall bloom abundantly*
> *And rejoice with joy and singing. . . .*
> *Then the eyes of the blind shall be opened,*
> *And the ears of the deaf unstopped;*
> *Then shall the lame man leap like a hart,*
> *And the tongue of the mute sing for joy.*
> *The waters shall break forth in the wilderness*
> *And streams in the desert;*

The burning sand shall become a pool,
And the thirsty ground, springs of water. . . .
And a highway shall be there,
And it shall be called the holy way. . . .
And the ransomed of the Lord shall return,
And come to Zion with singing. (35:1–10)

This passage in Isaiah shaped the gospel story of Jesus dramatically and probably accounts for the fact that healing miracles beginning in the eighth decade of the Christian era came to surround the memory of Jesus as a way of proclaiming him to be the messiah who would inaugurate the Kingdom of God.

These are just a few of the major contributions that the prophet we call I Isaiah made to the development of Judaism and later of Christianity in chapters 1–39 of this book, which scholars have determined were written in the latter years of the eighth century BCE. When most people think about the prophet Isaiah it is not from these chapters that their image is normally drawn, but from what we now call II Isaiah. Keep in mind, however, that in the time of Jesus and for the first nineteen hundred years of Christian history, the entire book of Isaiah was viewed as a single whole.

II Isaiah

If I were to ask an ordinary group of people, even church people, to tell me about the message of the prophet we call II Isaiah, most of them would turn glassy-eyed and retreat into silence. Yet if I were to ask the same group if they had ever heard or even sung in a production of Handel's oratorio entitled *Messiah*, almost every hand would go up. One sad fact about our educational system, both secular and ecclesiastical, is that few people seem to know that Handel's *Messiah* is in large measure a musical rendition of II Isaiah and that the "expected" one about whom II Isaiah writes in this work is not Jesus, but a mythical figure that we know simply as the "Servant," sometimes called the "Suffering Servant." It is about this "Servant," not Jesus, that Handel sets to music II Isaiah's words to form a magnificent contralto solo: "He was despised, rejected, a man of sorrows and acquainted with grief." The confusion of the "Servant" with Jesus should not be surprising, since the earliest gospel, Mark, drew heavily upon II Isaiah to compose the narrative of the crucifixion, a fact that we will examine in detail when we get to the gospels. II Isaiah also figures deeply in both Luke and the Fourth Gospel's portrayal of Jesus. It was the "Servant" who was punished in place of the guilty one. It was about the "Servant" that II Isaiah wrote: "Surely he has borne our griefs, yet we did esteem him stricken, smitten by God and afflicted; but he was wounded for our transgressions, he was bruised for our iniquities, the chastisement of our peace was upon him and with his stripes we are healed" (53:4–5, KJV).[2]

The words of II Isaiah have shaped Christianity so deeply that we have, by a process of religious osmosis, absorbed much of it into our conscious and unconscious minds. When II Isaiah's words then got literalized in Christian history in the form of doctrine and dogma, the significant distortions that mark the Christian faith today—distortions focusing on blood, sacrifice, guilt and atonement—began to take shape. That was, however, not the original meaning of II Isaiah's words. What then was that original meaning and who is the "Servant"? To answer this question we must undertake an historical analysis of II Isaiah. It is clear to me that this writer had the greatest influence on human history of all the Jewish prophets.

Turning to chapters 40–55, which constitute II Isaiah, we note first that these chapters were written by an unknown Jewish person who lived during the time that the Babylonian exile was coming to an end, roughly between 550 and 500 BCE, or close to two hundred years after chapters 1–39 had been written. What brought the exile to an end was the rise to power of the Persian

---

2   Because of the familiarity of the text from Handel's *Messiah*, I will use the King James Version of the scriptures in this segment.

Empire (roughly modern-day Iran), which challenged the hegemony of the Babylonians (roughly modern-day Iraq). Cyrus, the
king who led the Persian onslaught, awakened such hope among
the captive Jews that II Isaiah described him with these words:
"How beautiful upon the mountain are the feet of him that
bringeth good tidings, that publisheth peace, that bringeth tidings of good that publisheth salvation, that saith unto Zion, thy
God reigneth" (52:7, KJV). Cyrus was well known for his policy
of allowing conquered, exiled peoples to return to their homeland, and in this reputation the Jews vested their hopes as Persian
power grew. The captive Jewish people, who were destined to be
the beneficiaries of Cyrus' policy, were by now the grandchildren
and even the great-grandchildren of those who had originally
been taken from their homes by the conquering Babylonian army
a half-century or so earlier. Thus they saw Cyrus as God's instrument, who would allow God's will to be accomplished by permit-
ting them to return to their home.

The beauty of Jerusalem, the glory and grandeur of the land
of the Jews, had been passed on by word of mouth through their
parents and grandparents to the second and third generation of
exiles. These magnificent word pictures of their homeland now
fed their desire to return to that idealized but promised place.
As time passed, their fantasies grew, as fantasies always do, in
the absence of reality. They were, therefore, thrilled at the pros-
pect of going back to the land they believed God had promised
to their ancestors. It was to accomplish this purpose alone—
their reason for living, as it were—that they attempted to keep
themselves intact as an identifiable people. If they were going
to reclaim what they believed was their national destiny, to be
a blessing to the nations of the world, they were convinced that
they must return to their homeland and reestablish their nation's
glory. That destiny, they believed, could come only from a revived
nation, with the city of Jerusalem reestablished in the place many
still believed stood at the center of the world. The claim was even
made by the Jews in exile that it was in Jerusalem that heaven and
earth actually touched. Those were the motivating thoughts that

fed their yearning to return to their ancestral homeland. When the defeated Babylonians no longer had the power to keep them in bondage, the migration back to their homeland began.

These exiles, however, were not prepared for the sight that greeted them when they reached the land of which they had for so long only dreamed. They discovered a Judah that was a waste-land and a Jerusalem that was no more than a pile of rubble. It took only one glimpse at this devastation to put an end to their restoration dreams, their fantasies and their hopes. There was no way a nation so defeated and so downtrodden as this one could ever aspire to become "a light to enlighten the Gentiles" (42:6). They saw no way to rise from this powerless present, no way forward that would enable them ever again to dream of fulfilling their vision of their destiny as "God's chosen people."

It was at this point that a nameless writer—we call him II Isaiah only because his words were placed on the partially filled scroll of Isaiah—took in this vision of despair. I imagine him sinking into a period of intense depression and hopelessness him-self. He walked through his own "dark night of the soul." When he finally emerged, however, he took his quill in hand and began to sketch out a new role and a new vocation for the Jewish people based on the newly established fact that never again would they be powerful, never again could they dream about being rulers and never again would they be listed among the respected peoples of the world. In his dramatic words he personified this downtrod-den and defeated Jewish nation under a literary symbol that he simply called the "Servant." That is the context in which this mythical figure emerged in the writings of this unknown prophet in Jewish history.

It would be the role of the "Servant," wrote II Isaiah, to bear affliction, to endure the pain of being among the world's outcasts. The "Servant," however, must never respond to hatred with hatred or to hostility with hostility. The "Servant" must, rather, absorb these attacks upon his dignity and return them as kindness. The "Servant" would thus drain the world of its anger and, in the process, transform that anger into love, thus creating wholeness. The "Servant" would pay the price of the dis-ease of others by allowing that dis-ease to become his own without ever seeking to get even. In so doing the "Servant" would bring life to the world: "By his stripes we are healed" (53:5).

This proposed new vocation for the "chosen people" of God was not popular. No one is drawn to the masochistic possibility of perpetual suffering. The human desire is always to get even, to act in self-protective and thus survival-oriented ways, to become winners through the use of power. So over the years of post-exilic history II Isaiah's vicarious image of the "Servant" who suffered for others languished. Yet the words of this unknown visionary Jew of the exile were written into the blank space at the end of the work of the prophet Isaiah. This meant that over the years his incredible words would be read periodically in the synagogues and would become endowed with not just the authority of the name Isaiah, but with the authority of God. In this way the words of II Isaiah, along with his portrait of a radically different role for the Jews in human history, became, almost inadvertently, part of the scriptures of the Jewish people.

In the first century CE the disciples of a Jewish man named Jesus found in II Isaiah's portrait of the "Servant" a way that enabled them to understand and to interpret the meaning of their experience with the one who had taught them that love must embrace even their enemies and who himself was crucified for his efforts. They saw Jesus as the embodiment of the "Servant" role—that is, as one who would absorb the world's anger and hatred, transform it and give it back to them as love. So they leaped on this image and used it to tell the Jesus story.

Quite apart from this later Christian interpretation of II Isaiah, what we have in this remarkable book is the picture of a new breakthrough in human consciousness. Here in the words of this unknown sixth-century BCE person, we see a portrait of human life that has finally transcended the survival mentality of our evolutionary past. If the "survival of the fittest," so natural to all living things in the jungle, is allowed in self-conscious human beings to become the purpose of living, then human life will finally grind down to a single survivor, upon whose death the grand experiment with self-conscious life will disappear from the face of the earth. We human beings have arrived atop the world's food chain, but if we cannot evolve into a consciousness that is not consumed with our own survival, then genocide is our human destiny. Only a new consciousness can break this cycle. In II Isaiah a portrait of a human life that has transcended the survival mentality emerges, suggesting that life is a gift that is meant to be given in love for another. How amazing it is that an unknown Jew some twenty-six hundred years ago grasped this idea and portrayed it so eloquently, creating in the process the holiest part of Jewish religious history, carrying in his words a profound hope for a human future. II Isaiah's inclusion in the Bible is one of the reasons we call that book the Holy Scriptures. We need to note, however, that II Isaiah carries us only through chapter 55 of the book we call Isaiah. There are still eleven more chapters on this scroll, which constitute the work of yet another unknown prophet. We turn next to consider III Isaiah.

III Isaiah

Most scripture scholars today believe that they have definitely identified a third author in the book of Isaiah, who deserves at least a brief treatment to make sure that our biblical study is complete. Chapters 56–66 are attributed to this third author. Both the content and the context of these final eleven chapters indicate that they were written at least a generation after chapters 40–55.

The setting of III Isaiah appears to be some years after the return from Babylonia chronicled in II Isaiah. The despair that had led that unknown voice to create the dramatic portrait of the "Suffering Servant" seems to have faded away. Perhaps by this time the suffering role had been deemed as not a desirable vocation and so the Jews had jettisoned it. Yet something compelled them to seek and to find another way to fulfill both their

Jewish and their national destiny. By the time III Isaiah writes, the people are caught up in the mundane issues of the human struggle to survive. Against great odds they are now busy trying to reestablish their nation, to rebuild their Temple and to restore their customs in order to place the imprint of Judaism once more on their homeland. They still believed that this land had been given to them by their God and that God would not bless this land until it was filled with an ordered life reflecting the customs and practices of Judaism.

These people were struggling with their circumstances, wrestling with their fate in the past and trying to find a way to look to their future. The land had been ravished, not just by invading armies, but recently by drought. Crop failure was common, leading to rampant hunger. Their ability to defend themselves against wandering marauders was scant. Far from seeing in this despair a new call from God, as had been proposed by the genius of II Isaiah, they had now returned to the activity of playing theistic games in order to help make sense of their plight. So they wondered why it was in these hard times that God seemed intent on sending divine wrath to punish them and apparently wanted to make their suffering ever more difficult.

The answer they came up with in this final part of Isaiah's scroll is quite similar to the answer we will soon find in other, less than inspiring books like Haggai and Nahum. The people in III Isaiah judged that the reason for their hardship was their failure thus far to erect and restore God's dwelling, the Temple, in Jerusalem. They listed their other misdeeds in a litany of confession, "talking oppression and revolt, conceiving lying words and uttering them from the heart" (59:13). These misdeeds, they argued, have displeased God so there was no justice (59:15). This theme is frequently heard in the pages of scripture, yet it also reveals a point of view against which the book of Job will soon contend. It represents the ancient problem of defining God as an external being with supernatural powers. If God has the power to intervene and does not do it, one of two things becomes obvious: Either God is impotent and not able to intervene, a point of view which destroys theism completely, or God is angry at something or someone and is determined to punish the offenders. The former would force us either to rethink what we mean by God or to abandon the concept as worthless. The latter is the constant attempt on the part of human beings to preserve the illusion of God's justice. Perhaps the people of III Isaiah's day feared that their life experience might lead them to conclude that God is nothing more than a human projection and thus a human delusion.

It was the facing of the possible truth of this last alternative during a later time of suffering and pain that drove many Jews out of both belief and religion during and after the Holocaust. One has only to read Elie Wiesel's chronicle, entitled *Night,* of his years in a German concentration camp to see this conclusion begin to form.[3] The biblical story in Exodus had asserted that God had the ability to intervene in history with miraculous supernatural power to free the Jews from bondage and to end their slavery in Egypt. Why then, they wondered, did not God intervene in the twentieth century to save the Jews from an even greater peril found in the death camps in Nazi-controlled Europe? These victims accordingly, having no other understanding of God to consider, discovered that their belief in this external supernatural deity declined after the Holocaust. It was not persecution and suffering, however, but rather the knowledge revolution of the last five hundred years, which challenged all of the underpinnings and presuppositions of supernatural religion. That brought the same issues front and center for Christian people. In both traditions we find the same inner struggle to find meaning in religion today that occupied the mind of III Isaiah well over two thousand years ago.

The time that III Isaiah describes appears to be the last years of the sixth century, somewhere around 515–510 BCE. An intense battle for survival often brings out the worst qualities of human beings. "Every person for himself or herself" is the rule of the day. There was thus bitter enmity between rival groups in Judah at this time. Those who had migrated back to what they thought

---

3   See bibliography for details.

of as the holy land a generation earlier resented the latecomers, who made the lives of all the resettlers even more difficult. Corruption was ever-present and a low level of community cooperation existed. People were self-interested and vindictive. They saw no future. Feeling the sense of impending doom and even their own potential destruction, they saw little need to work together. The contrast with the situation described in the writings of II Isaiah some twenty-five to thirty years earlier was enormous.

Even in these final eleven chapters there is the further question as to whether they were the work of one single author, our III Isaiah. The style of writing in these chapters is not homogenous, but to postulate a fourth or fifth Isaiah is beyond the scope of this volume. I simply file this hint to signify the lack of unanimity on the issue. III Isaiah ends with this depressing thought: "They shall go out and look at the dead bodies of the people who have rebelled against me. Their worms shall not die. Their fire shall not be quenched. They shall be an abhorrence to all flesh" (66:24). It is not a hopeful conclusion!

Yet there are gems still in these final chapters on the Isaiah scroll and the theme of rebuilding a destroyed land is a noble and laudable one wherever it appears. Isaiah 58:12, for example, reads: "And your ancient ruins shall be rebuilt; you shall raise up the foundations of many generations; you shall be called the repairer of the breach, the restorer of streets to dwell in." That particular text is burned deep into my psyche, because it played a crucial role in my life and ministry during the 1970s, when I was serving as rector of St. Paul's Church in downtown Richmond, Virginia. My predecessor, Joseph Heistand (later the Episcopal Bishop of Arizona), had led this urban church through a major rebuilding activity, which included the completion of a three-tiered parking garage that could accommodate some two hundred cars underneath the parish house. This garage was a commercial venture Monday through Friday and the church's private parking on the weekends and evenings. Income from that garage serviced the debt on the new building until that debt was paid off. Then this congregation decided to designate fifty percent of the continuing garage income to be used to invest in improving the quality of life for the citizens of urban Richmond. We called this initiative the "Isaiah 58:12 program," which sent people scurrying to their Bibles to see what that verse said. We were in this program in obedience to the mandate of this text, calling us to rebuild our ancient ruins and our broken people, and to become the repairer of the breach and the restorer of the streets of Richmond as safe places in which to live. It is out of this experience that III Isaiah was then and remains for me now an important witness in the biblical story in which and through which I continue to hear the voice of God speaking.

CHAPTER 12

Jeremiah

Prophet of Doom

The book of Jeremiah, the second of the works by so-called major prophets in the Bible after Isaiah, is not only a large and complicated piece of writing, but it exhibits no narrative line that can easily be followed or recalled. Most people, including most clergy, could not cite a single passage from this book if you asked them to do so. The book of Jeremiah does not lend itself to memorable prose. I know of no major scholarly work that has been done specifically on this book, nor does anyone come to mind who might be called a "Jeremiah scholar." Yet this book has shaped many aspects of our religious history and quite specifically has helped to form the Christian story. It is worthy, therefore, of our examination.

Many of the familiar images that were incorporated into the birth narratives in the gospels of Matthew and Luke were originally found in Jeremiah. In chapters 26 and 27 of the prophet's work Israel is referred to as a virgin who is to bring forth God's firstborn son, who will keep Israel as a shepherd keeps his flock. It is another image out of Jeremiah, the portrait of Rachel as "weeping for her children who were not" (31:15), which Matthew quotes (2:18) as the biblical basis for his story of King Herod killing the innocent boy babies in Bethlehem in his effort to remove God's promised deliverer.

The following words in Jeremiah, "I will raise up for David a righteous branch and he shall reign as king and deal wisely and shall execute justice and righteousness in the land" (23:5), may have led to the popular theme that Jesus was the heir to the throne of David. It also may be the text that Matthew alluded to when he quoted a prophetic word that Jesus would be called a Nazarene. The Hebrew word for "branch" in the above-quoted text is *nazar,* which may have led to Nazarene. Even the story of Mary and Joseph finding no room in the inn, told only by Luke, may have been based on a passage from Jeremiah, who refers to "the hope of Israel being treated as a stranger in the land by being turned aside," not able to stay "for even a night" (14:8). Besides these, there are other biblical themes found in Jeremiah that deserve at least a brief mention.

Jeremiah along with Ezekiel, his younger colleague, are the biblical voices suggesting that individualism is beginning to appear in the land of Israel about the sixth century BCE. "Every one shall die of his own sins" (31:30), writes Jeremiah. Individualism will shape substantially the Jewish idea of life after death that later emerges in around 200 BCE in a collection of Jewish sacred writings called the Apocrypha (more on those writings later).

There is in Jeremiah a hint of universalism that challenges the ancient tribal mentality. This prophet has God refer to Nebuchadnezzar twice as "my servant" (25:39, 27:6). He also sees the threat that the Babylonians represent as God's instrument for punishing the waywardness of God's people.

A theme finding expression in Matthew's parable of the judgment, identifying God with justice, appears in Jeremiah, who writes: "He judged the cause of the poor and needy; then it was well. Is not this to know me? says the Lord" (22:16).

The identification of Israel with a fig tree not bearing fruit and on which even the leaves have withered (8:13) may be the origin of the story told in Mark that Jesus laid a curse on a fig tree for not bearing fruit, even though, as Mark notes: it was not "the season for figs." This episode occurred just before the cleansing of the Temple (Mark 11:12–26). That fig tree also withered to its roots.

The words of the Negro spiritual "There is a balm in Gilead" come from a text in Jeremiah (8:22). That hymn has made it into hymnbooks across a wide span of denominations, familiarizing generations of churchgoers with the words of Jeremiah, though they rarely know the source.

Jeremiah, like the author of the book of Job, wrestled with the problem of evil: "Why do the ways of the wicked prosper?" (12:1), he asked.

The early Christians called themselves "the followers of the way." That name may have come from Jeremiah, who portrays God as setting before the Jews a choice between the way of life and the way of death and demanding that they choose (21:8).

Other texts from Jeremiah have been used to illumine current events. One thinks of the condition of the American economy in 2009, with the government of the United States having to bail out of bankruptcy financial institutions in trouble because of greed, when one reads in Jeremiah that "everyone is greedy for unjust gain. . . . [T]hey do not even know how to blush" (6:15).

My favorite personal recollection involving a text from Jeremiah came at the start of the first Iraq war in 1991. President George H. W. Bush, trying to perfume his military efforts to push back Saddam Hussein, had Billy Graham come to pray with him at the White House as the bombs began to fall. Outside the White House that same night were anti-war protestors and picketers led by Presiding Bishop Edmond Browning of the Episcopal Church. One of the signs carried in that silent procession quoted words from Jeremiah: "My heart is beating wildly. I cannot keep silent for I hear the sound of the trumpet and the alarm of war" (4:19).

Jeremiah wrote out of a sense of destiny, maybe even a sense of being preordained or predestined for a particular role in life.

As such he has been the inspiration for many who have found themselves in the right place at the right time, who thus have been able to change history. That was what it meant, in Jeremiah's words, to assume the mantle of the prophet. God is reported to have said to Jeremiah in this book, "Before I formed you in the womb I knew you, and before you were born I consecrated you to be a prophet to the nations" (1:5).

Jeremiah's time was similar to that described when we looked at the book of Deuteronomy. It was a particularly difficult and turbulent period of Jewish history. Everything in the book of Jeremiah reflects that fact. Jeremiah watched the power struggle between Assyria and its conquered lands and the rising power of the Babylonians, as that struggle ebbed and flowed in the period between the fall of the Northern Kingdom to the Assyrians in 721 BCE and the fall of Judah to the Babylonians in 596 and again in 586 BCE. His sympathies were clearly with the Assyrians, and so he was destined not to be a winner. A false hope grew among the Jews when Assyria and Babylonia were so consumed by the threat of each other that they would not menace the smaller nations. As soon as the Babylonians had defeated the Assyrians, however, the "Indian summer" of Judah's life came quickly to an end. When the popular young King Josiah, whom we met in our study of Deuteronomy, went out to battle Pharaoh Necho of Egypt as part of his duty to the Assyrians with whom he was in alliance, and was defeated and killed, the hope of the Jews died with him. Jeremiah reflected that hopelessness.

History unraveled for the Jews from that point on. With Josiah's death Judah's sense of security died too. Their Assyrian protector was no longer able to come to their aid. The powerful Babylonians were exercising hegemony. Judah had backed the wrong horse in this political and military conflict and found itself consequently on the wrong side of history. In less than ten years the Babylonians would besiege Jerusalem. When Jerusalem finally fell, the Babylonian exile began.

Jeremiah saw this impending calamity and warned his Jewish nation of its coming with regularity. No one heeded him. His message was so relentless and so hopeless that the Jews actually wanted to kill him. People did not believe that Jerusalem could be conquered. Jeremiah likened what was about to befall Judah to the time when the Jews had been slaves in Egypt. No image could have been more fear-inspiring. When his message came true and his nation was prostrate, Jeremiah was carted off to Egypt, where he died in poverty and of a broken spirit. One image of Jeremiah is that of a weeping prophet, another a madman. Both are accurate. Time, however, is usually a prophet's greatest friend. At some time after his death the words of Jeremiah were added to the sacred story of the Jews and thus were preserved as scripture. So we have access to his words, painful though some of them are, and his truth was validated.

The job of the prophet is to illumine the pain, not to eliminate it, to help people walk through it and to transcend it. It is not helpful to deny the pain and pretend that there is another reality in which the pain is not present. Jeremiah was in this tradition.

CHAPTER 13

Ezekiel

Prophet of the Exile

W hen Americans are asked to name the great presidents of this nation, four names appear more often than any others: George Washington, Abraham Lincoln, Woodrow Wilson and Franklin Roosevelt. What these presidents have in common is that each of them presided over a time of trauma, transition and change in our nation's history: Washington at the birth of our nation, Lincoln during the dissolution of the Union, Wilson over World War I and Roosevelt during both the Great Depression and World War II. This list thus begs the question: Does a nation in crisis call forth great leaders or do leaders become great because they have to deal with a crisis? I suggest that it is the latter, but historians will debate the issue forever.

When we study the biblical prophets, the same question arises. Does a crisis in the life of the Jewish people serve to call great people into leadership, or do these leaders become great because they had to deal with a crisis? Once again I suspect it is the latter, but biblical scholars will likewise debate this forever. There have been two great crises in Jewish history in which the extinction of the whole nation was a real possibility. One was in the twentieth century when six million Jews were exterminated by the Nazi government in Germany. The other was the time of the conquest of the Jews at the hands of the Babylonians and their subsequent exile in the land of Babylonia.

The crisis in the twentieth century called David Ben-Gurion into leadership. The earlier biblical crisis, occurring in the first half of the 6th century BCE, called the prophet Ezekiel into leadership. We now turn to a consideration of this great figure upon whom the continuation of the Jewish nation literally hung.

The book of Ezekiel is the third of what we call the major prophets. Ezekiel is probably not as well known as the first two, Isaiah and Jeremiah, but perhaps he should be. His star burns brightly in the Jewish diadem as a critical life in Jewish history.

It is hard to re-create the person Ezekiel from the text of the book that bears his name, since we now know that the text was edited a number of times, corrupted badly and added to, with chapters 40 to 48 generally regarded as a later addition by another author. Yet there is a real figure who stands in the shadows behind the words of this book, one who lived in history and who changed the character of the Jewish people. Since his life overlapped with that of Jeremiah, they shared some common background. So keep in mind the context of history we described at the end of our study of Jeremiah and also recall our analysis of how the final strand of the Torah, called the priestly document, reflected this same time in history. I shall review it only briefly.

After Babylonia defeated Assyria in the last years of the seventh century BCE its army swept down on and destroyed Judah and Jerusalem in 596 BCE. This was the first time the city of Jerusalem had been conquered in four hundred years. For the "holy city," believed by the Jews to be the dwelling place of God, to fall was devastating. Leading Jewish citizens were then rounded up and marched off to Babylonia to be resettled as an underclass in the service of their conquerors. They appeared destined to disappear as the Jews of the Northern Kingdom had done about one hundred and twenty-five years earlier. Among those exiles, however, was a young prophet-priest named Ezekiel, who was apparently a member of a well-respected priestly family. In that crisis this young man rose to become a determinative figure in their story.

Ezekiel, as we noted earlier, saw his role as that of keeping his people separate and identifiable. This was for him the necessary prerequisite for the Jews' ever returning home and resuscitating their nation. He was also a psychiatrist's delight. He had vivid dreams, perhaps he even dreamed in Technicolor, and he used his dreams to galvanize his people. Two of his dreams made such indelible impressions on future generations that they were turned into Negro spirituals and used to illumine the black experience of being, first, exiled from their native Africa and, second, enslaved by their white oppressors. The first of these spirituals, based on the first chapter of Ezekiel, proclaimed that "Ezekiel saw the wheel, way up in the middle of the air," words that expressed a yearning for deliverance to come from on high (Ezek. 1:15ff). The second, based on Ezekiel 37, was entitled "Dem bones gonna rise again." In a dream recounted in that chapter, Ezekiel saw the Jewish nation under the analogy of a valley filled with dead, dry, fleshless bones. There was no hope of restoration or resurrection. God spoke to Ezekiel in this dream, addressing him by his favorite title, "Son of Man," to ask: "Can these bones live again?" To which Ezekiel replied, "Lord, you alone know" (37:1–3). Hope for a future life for the Jewish nation was at that time beyond Ezekiel's imagination. Behind both of these dreams was the biblical idea that God was the source of life. It is a recurring biblical theme.

In the Jewish myth of creation it was the breath of God that was breathed into Adam, transforming him from an inert body of clay into a God-infused living soul. God's breath had also been identified in the Jewish tradition with the wind that animated the forest. Now Ezekiel's dream proclaimed the breath or wind of God as also having the ability to re-create the lifeless Jewish nation. In this dream the breath of God blew over that valley and caused those dead bones to be reassembled. As the spiritual tells it, "The toe bone got connected to the foot bone, the foot bone got connected to the ankle bone, the ankle bone to the leg bone," and on and on it went until these bones were reassembled and the people were all standing up again. The Jewish nation was destined to be revived with the life force, the breath of God.

That dream now became Ezekiel's task to fulfill. Of course it was a task that no one person could accomplish on his or her own. It would indeed be the task of several generations. One person, however, had to have the dream, see the vision, stamp it on the minds of his people, burn it into their psyches and turn it into a reality. That person was Ezekiel.

Ezekiel's influence succeeded in making "separation" his people's highest priority. They became known as Sabbath day observers and as kosher dietary people, whose male members practiced circumcision. To ground these practices in the sacred scriptures as the revealed will of God became the task of the editors of the Torah. Ezekiel surely inspired this process.

It worked. These Jews were the only defeated and exiled people in human history to return intact to their homeland generations later and to reestablish their nation. That vocation was burned so deeply into the Jewish psyche that it would forever remain a characteristic of these people. They would draw on this image once again in the first century of the Common Era when in 70 CE Jerusalem was destroyed again, this time by the Romans. The Jewish nation was wiped from the map of the world and the Jewish people were once again aliens, scattered across the face of the earth. The Jewish state was not reestablished until 1948. During those years between 70 and 1948 the homeless Jews endured many horrors, much persecution and even the Holocaust, but the lessons of Ezekiel were too deep to be ignored and so the Jews survived once more intact as a recognizable people, able finally to return to the land of their fathers and mothers and to reestablish their national identity.

I do not mean to minimize the pain and dislocation that the return of the Jews to Israel and to the land of Palestine caused in 1948 and since. I do mean to suggest that people who can maintain their national identity for almost nineteen hundred years as a homeless people have performed a remarkable accomplishment. Standing in the shadows of their history is the prophet Ezekiel, who, in my opinion, more than any other Jewish figure, created among the Jewish people a bond with their ancestral lands that no passage of time seems capable of erasing. That is Ezekiel's singular achievement.

CHAPTER 14

Daniel

Misplaced but Potent

History is not well served by the way the Bible is organized. For example, the Torah (Genesis to Deuteronomy), which seems to tell a continuous story, was actually written over a period of about five hundred years and describes events that occurred over as long a time frame as fourteen hundred years. Yet it is always read in worship as if it were a single story, which makes some of its described events little more than historical nonsense. Similarly, we have noticed that a book like Isaiah was written in three parts by three different authors over more than two hundred years. Yet for most of both Jewish and Christian history this book has been read as a single cohesive work, making a proper interpretation of its pages all but impossible.

The same distortion of history is found in the lineup of the prophets. The four so-called major prophets, Isaiah, Jeremiah, Ezekiel and Daniel, are placed in that order in the Bible. Yet Isaiah was written time-wise on both sides of Jeremiah and Ezekiel, and Daniel is in fact a work of the second century BCE that, just to confuse things, purports to be written at the time of the Babylonian exile in the sixth century BCE. Someone who seeks literal truth or literal history in these pages of the Bible will be quite frustrated.

The timing problem becomes most apparent when we reach the book of Daniel, which is a piece of mythological, allegorical writing designed to strengthen Jewish resistance to the Seleucid king Antiochus Epiphanes IV during the period of the Maccabean revolution in the 160s BCE. This means that the book of Daniel is outside the timeline of the traditional Old Testament itself and belongs to the inter-testament years. It is also true that several stories that were originally additions to the book of Daniel—among them Bel and the Dragon, the Prayer of Azarias, the Song of the Three Young Men, and Susanna—were in fact taken out of Daniel and placed into the Apocrypha by later biblical editors, but the book of Daniel itself was kept in the canon of the Old Testament. This act of inclusion means that the stories left in Daniel have become far better known in the Christian world than those relegated to the Apocrypha. We are generally familiar with the narrative of Daniel in the lion's den and with Shadrach, Meshach and Abednego in the fiery furnace. Familiar phrases from the book of Daniel have also enriched our language, like calling God "the Ancient of Days," referring to some impending doom as "the handwriting on the wall," a fatal weakness as "feet of clay," or the facing up to strong opponents as "entering the lion's den." It is also a fact that Daniel in the Old Testament and the book of Revelation in the New Testament are the two biblical works that are quoted most frequently by those who like to predict the end of the world. We have happily passed through many such projected dates in Western history, yet predictions still come from the loony fringe of religion. I do not think they are worth much consideration.

My favorite end-of-the-world story came when I received a warning letter from a priest serving in the diocese of which I was the bishop, saying that the world was about to come to an end. He had a specific date and time on which he seemed to be sure that this would happen. He quoted a number of biblical sources, including Daniel, to prove his point. I must say that I did not begin to make preparations. A few days later I received an invitation from the wife of this priest inviting me to his fiftieth birthday celebration. The party was scheduled for about ten days after the anticipated end of the world. What a relief! Not even his wife believed his theory.

When we turn to the content of the book of Daniel, we discover that it is divided into two primary sections. The first section, chapters 1–6, is a series of stories about Daniel. The second, chapters 7–12, is a series of visions that have played a role in the development of Christian history. The first vision has a character in it known as the "Son of Man." It was Ezekiel who first introduced this phrase to our religious vocabulary in the sixth century BCE. When Ezekiel used it, however, it was just a title by which God called Ezekiel, simply Ezekiel's name. It designated him only as a human being. It had no divine connotations. When this name was attributed to Jesus many years later, however, its meaning was dramatically different. It had become, in fact, a claim of divinity. That title had to have made quite a journey for its meaning to have been transformed that significantly in the time from Ezekiel to Jesus. It did, and it was in one of the visions of Daniel that much of this transformation took place.

The "Son of Man" in Daniel was the name of a supernatural divine figure who would usher in the Kingdom of God and put an end to the persecution of the faithful. Daniel's "Son of Man" also traveled on the clouds of heaven and was given by God dominion, glory and kingship. All the nations of the world would serve him. His throne would be everlasting and of his kingdom there would be no end. We become aware when we read the New Testament that many of these images were attached to Matthew's Jesus story, first in his parable of the judgment, when the Son of Man, acting on God's behalf as the judge, would separate the sheep from the goats (Matt. 25), and second in his account of Jesus appearing as the resurrected one to the disciples out of the sky on a mountaintop in Galilee (Matt. 28:16–20). In that narrative he came on the clouds clothed with the authority of heaven and earth to send the disciples out on a mission "to all the world."

Daniel was also a pivotal book in the Jewish development of ideas about life after death. In the last chapter of Daniel the author refers to the time at the end of the world when the great deliverance would come. "Many of those who sleep in the dust of the earth," says Daniel, "shall awake, some to everlasting life and some to everlasting shame and contempt" (12:2). Reward and punishment from this time on became a major feature of life after death in Jewish and later in Christian circles.

Prior to the second century BCE, the Jewish people spoke little about life after death. The only concept generally abroad was that of Sheol, a place located in the "middle of the earth." It was not a place of reward or punishment; it was simply the abode of the dead. No one looked forward to it. No one was comforted by it. Everyone who died went to it. If it was described at all, it was described as shadowy, filled with shades of life, ghostlike with no sense of joy.

When Daniel was written, religious persecution against the Jews had reached horrendous proportions. The Jews were forced by their enemies to eat food they regarded as unclean. The Temple was itself polluted with the installation of the head of a swine in the Holy of Holies, an unclean animal in the very dwelling place of God. The Jews called it "the abomination of desolation." Those Jews who refused to violate their religious practices were summarily executed. The Apocryphal book we call II Maccabees, written at the same time as the book of Daniel, tells the story of seven brothers who, along with their mother, were arrested and were compelled to eat the flesh of a swine (7:1ff). The oldest brother refused and his tongue was cut out. Then he was scalped and his hands and feet were chopped off. Finally, he was taken, still breathing, to a fire and burned up. With this vision still vivid, the next brother was told he should eat the flesh of the swine or suffer the same fate. He refused and he too was tortured and executed. This procedure continued until all seven brothers had been murdered. Then the mother died. It is a dreadful story.

That story, however, became a powerful instrument in giving birth to a new concept and a new passion among the Jews for life after death. That is what finds expression in the twelfth and final chapter of Daniel. The driving theme was that without life after death for these faithful martyrs, the very justice of God was at stake. If faithfulness to God was not to be rewarded beyond this life, then God could not be just. If that is so, then evil does in fact triumph over God. So heaven and hell became the categories of divine justice and the afterlife was employed to make fair this unfair world. The book of Daniel was pivotal in this transformation and, as such, exercised an enormous influence on the development of Christianity, as the afterlife became crucial to the human sense of justice in both the crucifixion of Jesus and the later persecution of the Christians for loyalty to their Christ. The book of Daniel is not a profound book, but one wonders what Christianity might have looked like if it had not been written. Yet, for me, to think of the afterlife as a place of reward or punishment distorts the concept of life after death completely. That, however, is another story that I told in another place.[1]

---

1   See *Eternal Life: A New Vision—Beyond Religion, Beyond Theism, Beyond Heaven and Hell* in bibliography.

PART V

The Minor Prophets: The Book of the Twelve

CHAPTER 15

Hosea

The Prophet Who Changed God's Name to Love

I n the ancient world important and holy words were written on a scroll. So expensive was both the substance that
formed the scroll and the dye or ink used to inscribe the
words on the scroll that no one would think of wasting the
space, their time or their wealth to record words that were not
deemed to be of significant, perhaps eternal worth. So it was that
a number of prophetic writings were placed onto a single scroll,
just as II Isaiah and III Isaiah were added to the scroll of Isaiah.
This was what occurred when twelve separate works of various
prophetic voices were at some point all transcribed onto a single
scroll—voices that today we call the "minor prophets." They
are not minor in their message, however, so much as they are
minor in their size. These books are today placed by Christians
at the end of the Old Testament and they constitute the books
from Hosea to Malachi. I will treat some of them as substantially as I have treated the so-called major prophets, for these I
have deemed to be worthy of such treatment. A few of them I do
not regard as terribly insightful, so I will treat them in a more
cursory manner. It is, of course, a judgment call, but history has

also revealed that these twelve books are not of equal value and some of them tend to be relegated to complete obscurity by both the Jewish and Christian traditions, although both continue to regard them all as part of their sacred story. I hope I have been fair in the way I have assessed these twelve books. You, my readers, and time itself will be the final judges of this.

Hosea is probably my favorite of all the prophets in the Hebrew scriptures. His story is so real and so compelling, and his expansion of the meaning of God was so closely tied to his personal domestic situation, as to make his witness unforgettable. The story line is not always clear in the text, but the facts, as we piece them together from this book, are that Hosea and his wife, Gomer, had three sons, to whom they gave strange names: Jezreel, Not Pitied, and Not My People. There is some suggestion that Hosea had actually married a prostitute, but I think the data are much more substantial that his wife later became a prostitute and ultimately a slave. We know that Hosea eventually purchased her at a slave market for fifteen pieces of silver and restored her to a place of honor in their home as his wife. It was out of this experience that Hosea came to a new understanding of the unbounded love of God. I have let my imagination amplify these few details, which are about all that we can glean from the text, to come up with the following story, through which I hope to communicate the powerful message of this book. The blanks have been filled in in the manner of all storytellers, but the message is faithful to the text and clear:

Tongues must have wagged in Jewish social circles when the staid and respected holy man Hosea married Gomer, the party-loving, youngest daughter of the old merchant Diblaim. Gomer was known for her dark and flashing eyes and her dancing feet. The tongue-wagging was also driven by the fact that Hosea was an older and settled man while Gomer was much younger, loved the pace of the social scene and was thought of as overtly flirtatious. People wondered if such a union would last. Hosea, however, was obviously proud of his beautiful young bride and he vowed to do all he could to make her happy.

At first, things went well. Hosea seemed to find a whole new lease on life as he accompanied his wife to countless events where he basked in her popularity. The social pace did not slacken after a year or so, however, and Hosea began to yearn for the somewhat quieter life he had known before his marriage. Almost inevitably these realities brought tension into the relationship. From time to time Hosea wanted to leave a party sooner than Gomer, so a compromise was arranged by which he departed earlier and she was escorted home later by their friends. That tactic, though dangerous in that overtly patriarchal society, seemed to work well. When Hosea finally got to the place where he did not want to go out as often, they came to a much more dangerous compromise. On these occasions Gomer would go to a party either with her friends or finally alone. Over the years these solo trips increased until they became the rule, not the exception. An unescorted woman was almost unknown in Jewish society in those days, for it left her vulnerable and unprotected. This was especially so when that woman was by nature a sensuous and fun-loving person like Gomer.

Almost inevitably, those fears and suspicions were fulfilled and the night finally came when Gomer did not return home at all. Alarmed, Hosea immediately began to search for her, but to no avail. She had vanished without a trace or clue.

While Hosea's concern and his search for his wife continued for months, Gomer, now unburdened by her more sedate husband, became the favorite plaything of the Jewish jet set. She rode this track until it stretched into years. Hosea, his love for her still undiminished, refused to give up the search, while Gomer continued her risky ways. Life in the fast lane, however, fades for everyone sooner or later. As the years passed, Gomer was no exception. Yesterday's favorite charmer can always be replaced with tomorrow's younger models. Youthful beauty also does not last forever. Even Gomer had begun to notice that crow's-feet that no cosmetic could disguise were appearing around her eyes. Next she recognized that she was sagging in places she had never sagged before. Inevitably, she had begun *that fateful and inevitable descent of the femme fatale. Once the favorite plaything of the social pacesetters, she now had to adjust to being the plaything of anyone who wanted a plaything. When even that activity had run its course, she became a common prostitute, selling what remained of her charms for enough money to survive. Even prostitution is a competitive profession and the day came when those seeking her services were no longer attracted to her at all. Gomer then descended to the bottom rung on the social ladder, becoming a slave and offering her labor to the family that bought her in exchange for sustenance.*

Through all these downward-spiraling years, Hosea kept up his search for the woman he had married and whom he still loved. With the passing of years, Hosea's search became less frantic, but it was always on his mind. Hosea knew the ways of his world, so, after a significant amount of time had passed, he limited his search to the slave markets, which seemed to him to be Gomer's likely final destination. His was a lonely life. He did not know whether his wife was dead or alive.

Then one day it happened. Hosea wandered into a particular slave market, where the usual riffraff of society offered loud commentary on the human cargo placed on the block. He moved into this crowd just about the time a woman was brought on stage for public inspection. Her hair was matted, her eyes were bloodshot and her face was lined, revealing the toll that the years had taken. The crowd was loud and raucous in its derision, suggesting by their shouts that no one would be so foolish as to pay anything for "that old bag." The slave master tried to ignore them as he sought in vain to secure a purchaser. Their guffaws, however, were not silenced until Hosea, recognizing this woman as his wife, stepped forward and with a clear and audible voice bid fifteen pieces of silver for her.

A momentary silence of the stunned greeted this bid; then the crowd turned to see who had made such an incredibly stupid offer. Fifteen pieces of silver was the top price that young, strong male servants would bring. Only someone significantly naive or totally uninformed would have offered so absurd a price for this battered piece of merchandise. The crowd's abusive shouts now shifted from this pathetic woman, who probably could only hope to be a throw-in on another sale, to the strange man who had made the outrageous offer. This bidder had been duped, they believed, and so they hurled their insults at him, profoundly unaware of the drama being acted out before their eyes.

Taking no notice of their catcalls, Hosea walked forward, paid the offered price, took the woman by the hand and led her past the mocking bystanders until their words faded in the distance. When he reached his home with her, Hosea informed his household that Gomer was not a slave, but his wife, and he installed her back in the place of honor she had once occupied as the mistress of his household and the center of his affection.

Following this experience Hosea began to reflect on his life and on what it meant to serve God. His relationship with Gomer led him to examine what he perceived to be God's relationship to the people of Israel. His thoughts about God began to intertwine with his thoughts about his wife. Just as he loved Gomer regardless of her actions, so, he began to understand, did God love God's people. God's love was not conditional, nor was it tempered by Israel's actions. This definition of God began to grow in Hosea. The love of God was not a commodity to be earned; it was a reality to be entered, something to be lived. His meditation, born in his own pain, paved the way for him to arrive at a new understanding of what divine love really was. God's love cannot be merited and God's love cannot be destroyed, no matter what people do. This was the message of Hosea.

Later in Jewish history, this message of Hosea was seen in Jesus of Nazareth. When the gospels were written, that understanding of love permeated every verse. Jesus was portrayed as praying for his tormentors and giving his life and love away even as people acted as if they were taking those things from him. The message of Jesus that the gospels sought to convey was very clear: There is nothing you or I can ever do, nothing you or I can ever be, that will ultimately separate us from the love of God. As

I read this small book, I discover that Hosea reaches out to love and even to rescue his wife from the consequences of her own decisions, though by the standards of that day she would have been judged unworthy of such a response. That God related in a similar fashion to God's people was the essence of the message of Jesus some eight hundred years later.

Now, let me quickly say that even in this reconstruction of Hosea, we do not know the whole story. A marital relationship is never one-sided. In the biblical text, we do not have access to Gomer's side of the relationship. Hosea may have been an impossibly righteous man. We do know, however, that selfless love is always a doorway into a transforming forgiveness, an expanded life and perhaps even a larger consciousness. We also know that the idea of God being defined as selfless love in the writing of Hosea brought a whole new dimension to the meaning of the worship of this God for the Jewish tradition.

After Hosea lived through this experience and found reconciliation, he still had to write his story and someone somewhere had to make the later decision to incorporate that writing into the sacred scriptures of the Jewish people. That is what enabled Hosea's message to reverberate through the ages. Later generations of people listening to the words of Hosea would then begin to say that in the words of Hosea we hear the "Word of God."

I treasure Hosea for many reasons. His message is real and it counters the anti-Semitic Christian rhetoric of the ages, which suggests that the Old Testament portrays a God of judgment while the New Testament portrays a God of love. Yet judgment is nowhere as severe in the Bible as it is in the New Testament's book of Revelation, where constant fire and flaming pits are promised as the eternal fate that God has designed for sinners; and love is nowhere portrayed more profoundly than in the Old Testament book of Hosea, who turned his personal pain into a new understanding of the limitless love of God.

God does not change over the course of time, but the human perception of God is ever changing, and in the book of Hosea a new breakthrough into the meaning of God was achieved.

CHAPTER 16

Amos

The Prophet Who Changed God's Name to Justice

Not every character in the Bible starts out to be a hero. Indeed, one of the great themes of biblical literature is that it is the meek and the lowly who become the channels through which God is known in new ways. Mary, the mother of Jesus, is portrayed as expressing this theme in a song attributed to her that we call the Magnificat when she is made to utter these words: "For he has regarded the low estate of his handmaiden," but later generations "will call me blessed" (Luke 1:48). The Old Testament prophet who makes this truth powerfully real for me is named Amos. We turn to his story.

Amos was a citizen of the Southern Kingdom of Judah in the eighth century BCE. He lived in the village of Tekoa, near Bethlehem, where he was a herdsman and a keeper of sycamore trees, neither role in life demanding high academic achievement or the credentials that produce great expectations. In those days Uzziah was king of Judah and Jeroboam II was on the throne of the Northern Kingdom. The major powers of the world were preoccupied with their own problems and with each other,

which allowed these two small Jewish states to enjoy a moment
of prosperity, peace and even some wealth. The distribution of
that wealth was, however, hardly balanced. The worship places
of the Jewish world were crowded on holy days and religion was
popular among the greedy ones who dominated the social order.
There thus appeared to be little relationship between the words
of the ideal religion and the practices of people's lives in the
public arena. In many ways that is not dissimilar from periods
in the history of Western capitalism, where with more frequency
than we like to admit, the few have achieved massive fortunes by
the manipulation of the markets, creating a situation in which the
wealthy inevitably become wealthier and, as a direct corollary,
the poor become increasingly poor. This familiar dichotomy, so
frequently ignored in the body politic of the nation, proceeded to
burn itself into the consciousness of this simple herdsman named
Amos. That enhanced consciousness, in turn, transformed Amos
into the proverbial "Hound of Heaven,"[1] allowing him no rest
until he had addressed this issue overtly and publicly. So, in the
power of this compelling idea, he packed his suitcase and journeyed from Tekoa in the land of Judah to the king's special shrine
at Bethel in the Northern Kingdom to make his witness.

When he arrived Amos entered the courtyard of this holy
place, where all of his suspicions were confirmed. He saw the
crowds dressed in their finery busily attending to holy things,
while the poor outside the city gates were largely ignored. Amos
was a picture of the unsophisticated country person who was so
frequently looked down upon by the more sophisticated urban
dwellers. I picture him in bibbed overalls, a wide-brimmed hat on
his head and perhaps a bit of hay between his teeth. His accent
bore a country twang. So he wandered about, speculating on
just how he might manage to gain a hearing. Amos was a clever
man, however, and knew how to appeal to the base instincts of
the people. So it was that he found a corner in the courtyard, set
up a soap box and then, using one of the oldest tricks in human

---

1   The title to a famous poem by Francis Thompson. See bibliography for
details.

history, began to solicit first the curiosity and later the full attention of the crowd. Let me use the techniques of a storyteller, once again, in order to re-create the adventures of Amos.

"Come closer," Amos shouted from his makeshift pulpit. "Let me tell you about the sins of the people of the city of Damascus." Amos knew that everyone likes to hear gossip about the moral weaknesses of their neighbors, and so as he excoriated the Damascans the crowds grew. Next he turned his judgment first on the people of Gaza and then on Tyre, condemning the sinful practices found in both places. The crowd, loving it, grew even larger as Amos continued to appeal to their prejudices about and suspicions of their neighbors. This strange-looking rube from the south said the things they wanted to hear.

Then Amos moved to larger targets, with his oratory rising to new heights as he focused on the nation-states surrounding the Northern Kingdom. First it was the Edomites, and about their sins Amos got more specific. The Edomites had pursued "their brothers with a sword, showing them no pity," and they had allowed anger to "tear perpetually" at the fabric of their society. The ecstatic crowd began to shout, "You tell 'em, preacher." With every loud voice of encouragement, the people congregated around Amos in ever-greater numbers. Next it was the Amorites' turn. According to Amos, they had attacked Gilead and "ripped up the women with child in order to enlarge their borders." As Amos pronounced his message of doom on these nations, the people gathered around him roaring their approval. When he turned to the very unpopular Moabites the frenzy of the crowd exploded.

Next Amos, with the crowd in the palm of his hand and fully attentive, spoke in a bare whisper: "Now let me tell you about the sins of the southern Jews," he said. These Southern Kingdom Jews were the people with whom the citizens of the Northern Kingdom were the most competitive and with whom they had the deepest rivalry. The relationship between Judah in the south and Israel in the north was like that of New Zealand and Australia today. Signs in shops in New Zealand announce that "New Zea-

landers have two favorite teams, the All Blacks [the name of New Zealand's national rugby team] and anyone who is playing Australia." So to hear their Jewish rivals in the south condemned was music to the ears of the Northern Kingdom people. The crowd pressed closer to this strange messenger, and the number of people listening to him continued to increase dramatically. Those southern Jews, Amos said, despise the Torah; they do not keep God's commandments. Their lies cause them to err constantly, but God's justice is sure, he promised, and so Jerusalem will be "devoured by the fire of God." The crowd was ecstatic with enthusiasm, clapping and cheering. No one budged as this crowd-pleasing evangelist reached his climax. Now, with every ear straining to hear, this herdsman arrived at the conclusion for which he had journeyed from Tekoa to the king's chapel in Bethel.

"Now," he said, "let me tell you about the worst people in the world." The crowd could hardly wait to hear who that would be. They were not prepared, however, for what was to come. "You people of the Northern Kingdom," he said, "are the ultimate culprits in God's world. You are the ones who worship ostentatiously in the sacred shrines, but even as you worship, you sell the righteous for silver and the poor for a pair of shoes. You trample the weak in the dust of the earth. You violate one another sexually. You worship at every altar in garments stolen from the labor of the poor. You profane holy places with heavy drinking of wine purchased with fines levied against the meek. You corrupt holy people, encouraging them to violate their sacred vows. You even silence the prophets." The crowd was suddenly silent and the smiles disappeared from their faces. Then Amos spoke of the punishment that God would send. "This judgment is inevitable," he screamed. It was a devastating message. The stunned crowd took a while to recover from shock, so Amos continued to drive home his key insights. Worship isolated from life is of no value. If worship and justice are ever separated, idolatry is the inevitable result. It was a stirring message, but suddenly it was not a popular one.

When the members of the crowd recovered sufficiently to respond, they sent for a priest named Amaziah from the shrine at Bethel and asked him to come to their defense, for they said, "Amos has conspired against you and the land and we are not able to bear his words." Amaziah was the voice of the established religion. He would brook no more of this interference with worship at the king's shrine and so to Amos he said: "O Seer, go home, flee away to your land in Judah. Prophesy there if you must, but you are never to come again to Bethel, for this is the king's sanctuary. This is the Temple of our nation. Your words are not welcome here."

Amos responded to Amaziah, "I am no prophet, nor even a prophet's son. I am a herdsman, a dresser of sycamore trees, yet the Lord took me from my flocks and called me to prophesy to the people of Israel." Once again, he repeated his charges: "The songs of your holy places have become nothing but wailing to the Lord. You cannot worship while you trample the poor. You cannot wring money from the poor to line your pockets with greed. God will turn your sacred feasts into mourning and your pious songs into lamentations." The preaching of Amos was now more than the people were willing to tolerate and so Amos was physically driven from the shrine.

Rejected and defeated Amos returned to his humble life in Tekoa. In this newly imposed exile he wrote out his prophetic message, and that message became known as the words of Amos the prophet. In time people heard transcendent truth in his words and finally these words were added to the sacred text of the Jewish people and were thus read in worship settings in the Temple, synagogues and holy places. That was when people began to recognize that in the words of Amos, they were beginning to hear the "Word of the Lord." That is how the message of Amos came to echo through the centuries. In that process, God was inevitably redefined as justice. It was largely through the contribution of Amos that from henceforth in Judaism worship and justice would never again be separated. Worship, rather, came to be viewed as human justice being offered to God, while justice began to be seen simply as divine worship being acted out. In this context justice became another name for God.

It was through the work of the prophets primarily that God was redefined in Jewish history. The prophets really do matter, not because they were the predictors of the future as so many of us were once taught, but because they were able to see more deeply into the meaning of God and into the nature of our humanity. It was the prophets, more than anyone else, who made it possible some eight hundred years later for people to see and to hear the presence of God in the life of a crucified one named Jesus of Nazareth. That resulted in a new understanding of consciousness in which divinity and humanity seem to flow together as one.

The biblical story was never static, nor is the human understanding of God. It is idolatry and an act of faithlessness when anyone thinks that all truth has finally been revealed and that someone or some institution actually possesses it.

CHAPTER 17

Micah

The Prophet Who Turned Liturgy into Life

I n my career as a bishop I have known churches that spent great time and effort on liturgy and worship. It was clearly the focus, the reason for being, of those congregations, and their budgets reflected this priority. Altar hangings, clergy vestments and the garb of the supporting cast of liturgical characters were always coordinated. Sacristies, where the vestments and sanctuary coverings were stored, were orderly and reflected great care and devotion. These churches also tended to invest heavily in music. A grand organ was generally an essential and, of course, one had to have a grand organist to make the grand organ functional. Then there had to be a professional choir, since an all-volunteer choir might dissipate the beauty of both the organ and organist. Next, for the people for whom the liturgy was designed, there had to be a printed bulletin to guide them successfully through the Sunday liturgical process.

I do not mean to be critical of this. Liturgy that is well done does invite the congregation into the symbols of transcendence. It transforms worship from being the town meeting that it has become in many congregations. Town meeting liturgy is im-

mediately recognized, for it is dominated by announcements
of coming events and a public listing of the sick, the recently
deceased, the soon-to-be married, as well as those celebrating
birthdays and anniversaries. Sometimes these announcements
are overt, while at other times they are camouflaged under the
guise of prayer. These public displays serve to remind people that
they are not forgotten and to massage delicate egos. I wonder,
however, if either the liturgies of grand proportions or those
of a town meeting really understand worship, which means the
act of investing infinite worth in God as well as the calling of
those who are gathered to act out their worship in service to
others. Liturgy is not an end in itself, but a means toward an
end. There was one prophetic figure in the biblical tradition who
understood this better than anyone else. His name was Micah
and he lived in the Southern Kingdom of Judah. To his story
we now turn.

If people have any conscious awareness of the content of the
book of Micah, it is probably a vague recollection of his suggestion that the messiah must be born in Bethlehem, the city of
David's birth. That verse clearly became part of the developing Jewish expectation that the messiah had to be from the line
of David and thus the heir to the throne of the Jewish nation.
This verse from Micah found its way into the birth stories of
Jesus in both Matthew and Luke and thus it gained familiarity
by being repeated in our annual Christmas pageants. Matthew,
the scripture-quoter par excellence, refers directly to this text in
Micah when King Herod asks his scribes to search the scriptures
to locate the place where the messiah is to be born so that he
can redirect the magi's quest to find him. Luke uses this Micah
text indirectly to demonstrate the relationship of lineal descent
between David and Jesus, when he states that it was by order of
Emperor Caesar Augustus that all the descendants of King David
had to return to their ancestral home to be enrolled. While this
is probably the best-known quote from Micah, the power of this
book is not found here, but is located rather in the drama he describes later in the sixth chapter of his small work.

Micah thought of himself as an expert in the law, the Torah. One gets the sense that he yearned to demonstrate his legal skill before the Supreme Court in Jerusalem, but that opportunity had never come to him. In chapter 6, however, he fantasizes about a trial that was designed to be even more dramatic than one that might have occurred in Jerusalem. It had to do with the proper role of liturgy. Under the skill of Micah's pen he envisioned this trial as being conducted before the throne of God, who played the role of the ultimate judge. For Micah the mountains and the hills were drafted to serve as the jury for this trial. Israel was called to stand before this judge and jury as the accused. Micah cast himself in the role of the prosecuting attorney. The trial opens as Micah says to the people of Israel: "Arise, plead your case before the mountains and let the hills hear your voice, for the Lord has a controversy with God's people and God will now contend with Israel" (6:2). Court is open and Micah's grand trial of the chosen people has begun.

The charges are then read out. God demands to be answered by the accused, asking, "What have I done to you? In what have I wearied you?" (6:3). Why, God is demanding to know, do you not understand how to serve me? Then God recites the things that God has done for Israel throughout history: God delivered them from bondage; God raised up leaders for them like Moses, Aaron and Miriam; God gave them the Torah, the law; and, finally, God protected these chosen ones from their enemies. This significant list of divine benevolences has, however, clearly not gained for God the hearts of the people.

Israel, the accused, hearing these charges, feels the pangs of guilt and seeks to make amends. The response of the people, however, is to recite their faithfulness in religious observances and in proper liturgies. Trapped inside this misunderstanding of what it is that God seeks, Israel says, "With what shall I come before the Lord and bow myself before God on high? Shall I come before God with burnt offerings and with calves a year old?" (6:6). Better sacrifices, they suggest, can address this problem.

From God, however, in response to this pitiable plea, comes only silence. The people have responded to God's charges as if

God were interested primarily in religion or in worship. They only wonder whether their religious observances have been deemed by God to be inadequate. With that understanding, these people now vow to enhance their sacrifices. If God is not pleased with the oil that burns the sacrifices or with the year-old calf that is their burnt offering, then maybe God would be pleased if they expanded their worship to new levels of magnanimity: "Will the Lord be pleased with thousands of rams or with ten thousands of rivers of oil?" (6:7). Surely such heightened acts of worship—acts that they presume God desires—would win for Israel the divine favor. God, however, is still silent, and once again the people of Israel interpret this silence to mean that their worship and their offerings are still inadequate and once again they seek to make their sacrificial liturgies more worthy of their disappointed God.

God, do you want us to offer our children, our most precious possessions? Would the reintroduction of child sacrifice satisfy you? That is the meaning of the words that Micah now places on the lips of the people: "Shall I give my first born for my trans-gression, the fruit of my body for the sin of my soul?" (6:7). This dramatic scene reaches a crescendo before God finally responds, and this response forms in my opinion the most powerful words recorded in this prophetic book. Micah sets the stage for God's response: "God has shown you, people of Israel, what is good! And what does the Lord require of you?" (6:8). It is not beauti-ful liturgical words, burnt offerings, animal sacrifices or even ten thousand rivers of oil. It is not even the sacrifice of your most cherished children. The only requirement God lays on God's people, says Micah, is "to do justice, to love mercy and to walk humbly with your God" (6:8).

The trial is over. The verdict has been rendered. One does not please God with acts of worship. The only sacrifice that God values is the offering of lives lived in justice, mercy and humility. The people of Israel must understand anew what the meaning of worship really is.

Micah, like his prophetic predecessors and successors, then wrote down his words for the people, who treasured them at first simply as the inspired words of their prophet. In time, however, someone decided that Micah's words were more than just Micah's words, so his writings were ultimately added to the sacred scriptures of the Jewish people and in that capacity began to transcend their original setting, to be read in worship across the centuries and to be pored over by the rabbis.

The human understanding of God was always growing, evolving and changing in the Jewish scriptures. In the writings of Micah, the people learned that worship is not about form and ceremony. It is not about wearing vestments in a particular style, about chanting the liturgy in effective ways. It is not about a sacred prayer book or a grand organ. It is not about where the altar is located, the style of the liturgy or the nature of one's prayers. Worship is always and foremost about living faithfully and ascribing ultimate worth to a God who is manifested in the fullness of human life.

Throughout the national history of the Jews, it was the prophets, who stood outside the sacred traditions, and not the priests, who stood within these traditions, who again and again caused the understanding of God to grow. It was the prophets who slowly, but surely, transformed the tribal God of the Jews into a set of universal principles. It was the prophets who made Jesus of Nazareth possible. Jesus was clearly in the prophetic tradition of Judaism. In episode after episode in the gospel narratives Jesus set aside religious rules so that the ultimate principle of justice, based on the conviction that no life falls outside this love of God, could become operative. In Christ, said Paul, there is neither Jew nor Greek, male nor female, gay nor straight, baptized nor unbaptized, bond nor free, Catholic nor Protestant, Jew nor Muslim, Hindu nor Buddhist. To assert this reality as the ultimate meaning of God is the essence of worship. So worship is, therefore, not about liturgy, but about life. Worship leads us not to build ecclesiastical institutions, but to humanize our world. This is the "Word of God" heard in Micah by which all liturgy must be judged.

CHAPTER 18

Jonah

Definer of Prejudice

It was a profound shock to the people of Judah when the city of Jerusalem fell to the army of the Babylonians in the early years of the sixth century BCE. This city had not been conquered by an invading power since 1000 BCE. They had come to believe it was indestructible. When Solomon erected the Temple in Jerusalem, the people began to think that this holy city now lived under the protection of its indwelling deity. Both of these ideas were shattered with the city's fall in 596 BCE. The subsequent relocation of the Jewish people into a Babylonian exile only continued the shock and increased the despair.

The depth and pain of these reactions was located in the firm belief that somehow the Jews were God's chosen and favored people. Yet the destruction of Jerusalem and the exile of the people seemed a strange way for the "chosen people" to be treated by their God. Life has to be endured as it comes, however, and so the Jews lived apart from their holy city and their sacred soil for several generations. Finally, when the Persians defeated the Babylonians the Jews were allowed to return and resettle their native land. These Jewish pilgrims, the descendants of those who had been exiled, then journeyed to their ancestral home. They came in smaller and larger groups over the next two centuries.

The Jews dealt with this trauma in their history by trying to explain why God had allowed the defeat and exile of the chosen people. All of their understanding of God compelled them to find some rationality in this experience. This was especially true when a sufficient number had returned in the latter years of the fifth century and even into the early years of the fourth century to allow them finally to begin to rebuild their country. They wanted to make sure that God's wrath would not descend on them again. To accomplish this they needed to know how they had offended God so that this behavior would never be repeated and thus result in yet another defeat and exile.

Their first explanation suggested that their forefathers had not been faithful to the covenant and so God had punished them. This suggestion was, however, emotionally unsatisfying since it placed blame for their misfortunes on their own ancestors and thus dishonored their parents in direct violation of the Ten Commandments. Then they hit on what seemed a better idea. Alien influences were to blame, they said. Some of our weaker ancestors had married foreign partners. These Gentiles present in our common life then brought corruption to our nation, first by polluting the true faith and second by compromising the racial purity of God's people. With that explanation of the cause of both defeat and exile, the way to avoid a future disaster seemed clear. They must purge the nation of its non-Jewish elements by banishing them from the land. The half-breed children of these unholy unions must also go. The new land of the Jews must be for Jews only. So the law was decreed and vigilante squads were loosed on the populace with instructions to check blood lines back to the tenth generation in order to guarantee the racial purity of the newly established Jewish state. The true worship of a racially pure Jewish people was the only way to secure God's blessing. The Jewish state thus entered a period of internal violence. One can read about this history in a number of books contained in the Old Testament. We have met it before; we will meet it again.

It was because of the atmosphere produced by this mentality that an unknown Jewish person, presumably a man since women were not taught to write at this time, went to his home to devise a means of challenging these prevailing attitudes. He could not attack them openly in a public, political way, for that would be interpreted as inviting a new defeat and a new exile. He had to confront these attitudes obliquely, until their destructiveness was made clear. He had to find a way to hold up a mirror and to force the ruling authorities to look directly into it. Taking his quill in hand he decided to write a fanciful story filled with the exaggeration of a world of make-believe, but so enchanting that everyone would want to hear it. In the privacy of his home, he did just that. When he had finished, a text of this story appeared suddenly and anonymously in Jerusalem at the height of the ethnic cleansing. The town crier gathered some people around him in a public square, and this is the story he read:

Once upon a time there was a prophet in Israel whose name was Jonah. God called to Jonah and told him that he must go to preach to the people of Nineveh. "Nineveh!" proclaimed Jonah. "You must be kidding. That is an unclean Gentile city. Why would you want me to do something that weird?" God was adamant, however, and God's message was clear, so Jonah had to respond. He did so in the classic way that people do when they are told by an authority figure to do something they really do not want to do. Jonah said yes but he meant no, since he had no intention of obeying. Jonah, however, went through all the motions of leaving. He went to his home, packed a suitcase, went down to the port and booked passage on a boat, but his ticket was to Tarshish and not to Nineveh. One does not go by sea to Nineveh. He reasoned, however, that if caught, he could claim that he had misunderstood and by that time, God would surely have had second thoughts anyway.

All went well as Jonah boarded the ship, unpacked his suitcase in his stateroom, put on his Bermuda shorts, got a good book and positioned himself topside in a deck chair as the ship pulled out into the Mediterranean Sea. The trip was unevent-

ful until a dark cloud in the sky seemed to be shadowing the boat. Aware of this dark presence, the captain tried to escape it by turning the boat first to the right and then to the left, but the cloud turned in concert with the boat. While the rest of the sky was clear and blue, this cloud got darker and darker and from within it came flashes of lightning, the roar of thunder and finally rain. So strange was this phenomenon that the captain drew the obvious conclusion: *Someone up there does not like someone down here.* In what he regarded as a scientific fashion, he sought to identify the culprit. He drew straws and the lot fell on Jonah. "What is this that you have done, Jonah?" the captain asked. "Well, God did tell me to go preach to the Ninevites, but I knew that God could not possibly care for the Ninevites, so I booked passage on this boat instead." The captain, who did not care for Ninevites either, understood and thought he could ride out the storm, until a bolt of lightning struck nearby and a wave from the sea swept over the boat, hurling Jonah's deck chair from one end of the ship to the other. That was when the captain weighed his own security against Jonah's decision and decided that Jonah had to go. So, with the help of three deck hands, Jonah was seized by his limbs and on the count of three the men heaved him overboard.

Jonah never hit the water. God had created a great fish (the word "whale" never occurs in this story), which had been swimming in tandem with this boat, waiting for its moment in the drama. Jonah fell into its open jaws, which closed over him, and Jonah found himself living in the belly of this great fish. Jonah had amazing adaptive qualities, so he settled down to make his new home comfortable, rearranging the furniture and hanging the curtains. For three days and nights, Jonah lived in this new, but somewhat confining, Mediterranean condominium, until even the great fish could not tolerate Jonah any longer (perhaps he smoked!). So it was that with a great primeval belch, the fish threw up Jonah, who tumbled head over heels onto a conveniently located sandbar in the midst of the sea. As Jonah was clearing his head and taking in his new situation, he heard a voice saying, "Jonah how would you like to preach to the people of Nineveh?" With the stench of the fish's belly still clinging to him, Jonah didn't have to think long. "Okay, God," he said, "you win. I'll go."

Once Jonah was in Nineveh, but still convinced that God was making a mistake, he opted for a new form of resistance. In Frank Sinatra fashion, he concluded, I'll do it, God, but I'll do it my way! I'll preach to the Ninevites, but I'll preach by muttering under my breath and I'll do that only on the back streets and alleyways of the city. So around the city Jonah went, muttering: "God says to repent. Repent and turn to God," hoping no one would hear. To his amazement everyone heard. Crowds poured into the streets from every house and condominium of the city, confessing their sins, tearing their clothes in repentance and begging for God's mercy. Jonah was apparently the most successful evangelist in the history of the world! Modern televangelists would eat their hearts out for this kind of response.

Jonah, however, was angry. Storming out of the city, he said: "I knew this would happen, God. That is why I did not want to come. These wretched people deserve punishment. I know you, God! I know you will forgive! Why, God, does your love not stop at the boundaries of my ability to love?"

Jonah found a spot outside the city where he sat and sulked. The sounds of the revival could be heard as "Sweet Hour of Prayer" was being sung by the penitents. God was strangely silent, however, and night fell. When Jonah awoke, a giant plant had grown up near his head. During the day Jonah found protection from the desert sun in its foliage and sanctuary from the biting desert wind in its trunk, but God was still silent and night fell once more. That night God created a worm that ate the giant tree, leaving only a small pile of sawdust. When Jonah awoke, he was distraught at the loss of his beloved tree. He wept, mourned and felt the depth of bereavement. Finally, God broke the divine silence and said, "Jonah, how is it that you can have such passionate feelings and empathy for this tree and yet you appear to have no compassion at all for the

one hundred and twenty thousand people who live in Nineveh,
to say nothing of their cattle?"

The book of Jonah ends there. Imagine that story being read
on the streets of Jerusalem while ethnic cleansing was taking
place in the city. As the reading unfolded, the people listening to
this story roared at the depth of Jonah's bigotry until they real-
ized that Jonah was a fictional portrayal of themselves.

The book of Jonah remains in the Bible to this day to counter
human attempts to say that the love of God is bounded by the
limits of any human being's love or by any religion's inability to
be inclusive. There are no boundaries on the love of God. That is
the message of Jonah. In God there are no human distinctions of
tribe, sex, race or sexual orientation. God's invitation is "Come
unto me, all ye . . . ," not "some of ye." We are to come "just as
I can, without one plea," as the old evangelical hymn proclaims.
How dare popes or archbishops of Canterbury or religious institutions anywhere define anyone as beyond the limits of God's embracing love! When any ecclesiastical leader or religious tradition
excludes or diminishes any child of God for the sake of "unity"
or by defining God's love as limited, the book of Jonah stands as
biblical judgment on that leader and those attitudes.

CHAPTER 19

I and II Zechariah

Shapers of the Jesus Story

If you were to search the scriptures for a book called II Zechariah, you would not find it. There is only a single fourteen-chapter book called Zechariah, buried in the Bible between Haggai and Malachi. This book is, however, not a single work by a single author, although that is the way it appears. The name Zechariah is associated with the author of chapters 1–8 and that section ought to be called I Zechariah. The next section, encompassing chapters 9–14, is material added to the scroll of this small work by an unknown writer and it should be designated II Zechariah. This practice, as we have noted, has been followed in the study of Isaiah. Scholarship demands that Zechariah be treated in a similar fashion. Zechariah 1–8 reflects a time after the exile in Babylonia has been ended. Zechariah 9–14 is much later in the period of widespread Persian hegemony.

This book of Zechariah, seemingly so insignificant, has been generally ignored by ordinary Christians and scholars alike. Its importance, therefore, has been minimized. Even those people who claim that the Bible is the inerrant word of God, if asked a question about the message of the book of Zechariah, generally respond with blank looks. If they know anything about this book at all it tends to be the verse that reads: "Rejoice greatly, O daughter of Zion! Shout aloud, O daughter of Jerusalem! Lo, your King comes to you; triumphant and victorious is he, humble and riding on an ass, on a colt, the foal of an ass" (9:9). This verse is familiar because it is regularly read as the Old Testament lesson on Palm Sunday in almost all of those churches that follow a liturgical lectionary. It was also quite clearly the passage on which the Palm Sunday story itself was modeled. Beyond this, however, most Christians would tend to have no knowledge whatsoever about this book.

Yet the fact is that the book of Zechariah is quoted overtly by New Testament writers at least eight times and is alluded to even more frequently than that in the shaping of the gospel tradition. With the exception of a few references in the book of Revelation, every verse in Zechariah to which the New Testament writers point is from II Zechariah—that is, from chapters 9–14. This segment of Zechariah was a remarkably influential book in the formation of the thinking of the early Christians; indeed, it was probably second only to the book of II Isaiah in importance in shaping the portrait of Jesus, an idea that most people would simply not comprehend.

To understand the impact of this statement, it is quite important that we get out of a literal biblical mind-set. Jesus does not fulfill the prophets in the sense that Jesus somehow said and did things that the prophets had predicted the messiah would do. That is patent nonsense, the product of overt biblical ignorance. The gospels are rather interpretive works written two to three generations after the life of Jesus and written in the service of their claim that he was messiah. To underscore this claim, these early Christians searched the scriptures for the content of Israel's messianic hope and expectancy, and then they wrote the story of Jesus to be in accord with these expectations. In the various resurrection narratives, the command to do this kind of interpreting was written into the words and actions attributed to Jesus himself. Listen to Luke where the resurrected Jesus is made to say: "'O foolish men and slow of heart to believe all that the prophets have spoken!' . . . And beginning with Moses and all the prophets, he interpreted to them in all the scriptures the things concerning himself" (Luke 24:25–27). Later Luke has Jesus repeat this theme just for emphasis: "'Everything written about me in the law of Moses and the prophets and the psalms must be fulfilled.' Then he opened their minds to understand the scriptures" (24:44–45). Luke was suggesting that it was the resurrected Christ who had directed the early disciples to find references in the scriptures of the Hebrew people by which they could properly interpret the experience they had had with Jesus of Nazareth. By the time the gospels were written this practice had become their primary interpretive tool. The book of Zechariah and specifically II Zechariah, was in that process among the most influential books in the Hebrew Bible, and the early interpreters of Jesus drew on it heavily to share their understanding of his life.

II Zechariah begins by introducing his readers to one who is, in all probability, intended to be a mythical figure, not unlike the "Suffering Servant" described in II Isaiah. II Zechariah's mythical character is called the "Shepherd King of Israel." It is this king, he says, who will come to Jerusalem not in pomp and splendor, but in humility and lowliness riding upon a donkey, to lay claim to his kingdom. That is the first, but not the last, reference in the gospels from II Zechariah.

When Jesus was arrested, Mark notes that "all of the disciples forsook him and fled" (14:50). By the time the gospels came to be written, however, the twelve disciples had become heroes among the followers of Jesus, so that this story of apostolic abandonment, which was clearly an indelible memory, had to be transformed. That was done by Mark (14:27), who said that the prophets had predicted this abandonment and so the disciples were merely fulfilling the scriptures; thus they were guiltless, and consequently not blameworthy. The text they quoted for this apostolic whitewashing was from II Zechariah: "Strike the Shepherd that the sheep may be scattered" (13:7). Matthew repeats and expands this connection (26:31). Luke assumes it. John alludes to it (16:32).

The "Shepherd King" of II Zechariah was said to be doomed by those who "trafficked in sheep" (11:11), which brings to mind the gospel story of the people who bought and sold animals, primarily sheep, for sacrifice in the Temple. This connection with the story of Jesus cleansing the Temple was made overt and clear when the early churches read the last verse of Zechariah, where the prophet wrote that when the day of the Lord comes, "There shall no longer be a trader in the House of the Lord" (14:21). Was the story of Jesus cleansing the Temple written not to recall an event in history, but rather as an attempt to interpret Jesus as messiah inspired by II Zechariah? I think it is fair to suggest that it was.

The work of the "Shepherd King" was, however, annulled, says II Zechariah, by these "traffickers in sheep," who paid him off to rid themselves of him. The price of his riddance was "thirty pieces of silver." The "Shepherd King" then hurled this money back into the Temple (11:12–13). Matthew is the gospel writer who introduces the thirty pieces of silver into the story of Judas Iscariot and he also has Judas hurl the money back into the Temple. Clearly, Zechariah was his source for this part of his story line (Matt. 26:14–16, 27:3–7).

Later II Zechariah states that God will pour out compassion on the people of Jerusalem "so that when they look upon him whom they have pierced, they will mourn for him as one mourns for an only child and weep bitterly for him as one weeps over a first born" (12:10–11). John used this passage, and gave credit to Zechariah, when he developed the story of the soldier who pierced Jesus' side with his spear (John 19:31–37).

Finally, Zechariah portrays rather dramatically the "day of the Lord," which will come, he says, at the end of time (14:2–11). All of the nations of the world will be gathered in Jerusalem in warfare, says Zechariah, and the Lord will defeat them. The Lord will stand on the Mount of Olives and split the mountain in two. There will be no darkness, only endless light, and finally on that eternal day, living water will flow out of Jerusalem, embracing all of the nations to the east and those to the west and the Lord will become King over all the earth. On that day all will worship the divine King, the Lord of Hosts. It was an incredible mythical portrait of the dawning of the Kingdom of God for which the Jews had been taught to yearn, to pray and to work.

Living water for the Jews is always a symbol of the Holy Spirit. This is thus a Spirit-based portrait on which Luke drew heavily when he wrote the Pentecost story in the book of Acts. The Spirit was poured out on the gathered world, said Luke, and oneness was created, in that they could all speak the language of their hearers (Acts 2).

Once we put all of these pieces together, II Zechariah describes in precise order the pattern that was written into the final week of Jesus' life: the Palm Sunday procession on the donkey, the betrayal, the apostolic abandonment, the crucifixion and the day of Pentecost. It is clear that the little book of II Zechariah exercised vast influence on the way the Jesus story was developed, remembered and told.

One conclusion is obvious. The gospels are neither history nor biography. They are interpretive portraits written by Jewish followers of Jesus, as those followers participated in the worship of the synagogues. Their desire was to portray him as the one who empowered them and who raised them to a new level of consciousness. They saw in Jesus God's living presence and ultimately this is what they began to see in themselves. The messiah had opened to them a doorway into the presence of God. That is how Jesus was identified with the messianic hopes of Israel and that is the basis upon which they made the Christ claim for him, as well as the God claim that would develop over the centuries in the creeds. With newly informed eyes regarding connections such as these, the Bible is fun to read and even more fun to understand.

CHAPTER 20

Malachi

The Dawn of Universalism

Malachi is the last book in the Old Testament as Christians organize the scriptures, and it is the last voice to be heard in the Book of the Twelve, as the Jews organize the scriptures. It will also be the last of the prophetic writings to which I will give major attention in this study. Of the twelve so-called minor prophets we have examined Hosea, Amos, Micah, Jonah, Zechariah and now Malachi. This means that I have determined that Joel, Obadiah, Nahum, Habakkuk, Zephaniah and Haggai are not worthy of our spending much time exploring their message. These books are little read; they do not reach any heights of spirituality and they are filled with images of a vengeful deity who hates the enemies of the Jews. To make this series complete, however, let me say a few words about each of them.

Joel is the most quoted of the remaining books. Joel 1:14 is regularly read on Ash Wednesday in liturgical churches: "Sanctify a fast, call a solemn assembly." Joel 2:13 forms a familiar Lenten theme of repentance: "Rend your hearts and not your garments." Finally, Joel 2:28 is quoted by Luke in Peter's Pentecost sermon

(Acts 2:17): "I will pour out my spirit on all flesh; your sons and daughters will prophesy, your old men will dream dreams and your young men will see visions." Beyond these three verses, however, Joel is little more than a cultic prophet.

Obadiah consists of a series of oracles, none of which are profound, against Israel's enemies. Nahum is a tribal hymn of praise at the destruction of Nineveh; the writer assumes that since Nahum hates the Assyrians, God must also. Habakkuk contents himself to pronounce woes on wicked nations, apparently not able to hear the universal themes of God's unbounded love. Zephaniah is the work of a Jewish puritan and like puritans in all religious traditions he is more self-righteous than helpful. Haggai, a contemporary of Zechariah II, has only one song to sing and that is that the Temple must be rebuilt. If all of these books, which I am for all practical purposes omitting, were lost—and they in fact have always been ignored by the church—the world would not be much poorer for it.

Malachi, however, is different and as such he is a worthy figure to round out our study of the prophets. His major contribution was that he helped move the Jewish consciousness out of its tribal mentality and opened the doors that allowed the Jewish religion to grow to levels of universal understanding.

The first thing that must be noted about Malachi is that Malachi is not the name of the author of this little book. The name comes from the first verse of the third chapter, where we find the words, "Behold, I send my messenger to prepare the way before me and the Lord whom you will seek will suddenly come to his Temple, the messenger of the covenant in whom you delight, behold he is coming, says the Lord of Hosts" (3:1). The Hebrew word for "my messenger" is *mal'akhi* (not dissimilar from the name of the first Prime Minister of Iraq, Nouri al-Maliki, after the second Iraq war), and that is the name by which the book came to be known. It seems to have been the second and last anonymous work that was copied onto the scroll of the Book of the Twelve after Zechariah and thus might be called III Zechariah. Although it was later separated out, the connections are still obvious. Dating this book is easier than most, since it refers to events in history that we can date fairly accurately from other sources. Jerusalem is under the rule of a governor, but both the political and religious lives of the nation are at a low ebb. This book seems not to be aware of the priestly code that was added to the Torah in the late fifth century BCE. It refers to the priests as sons of Levi, rather than sons of Aaron as the priestly code does, and it mentions that the Edomites, their hated foes, have been conquered by the Nabataean Arabs. These things all point to a time before the great reforming governor Nehemiah came into power in 444 BCE, so Malachi is dated somewhere around 450 BCE.

The historical setting is long enough after the original group of returnees from exile arrived in their homeland for a strong sense of disillusionment to have set in among the people. They had clearly believed their own popular propaganda that the return from exile would usher in a glorious messianic age. Hopes had skyrocketed, as they tend to do with a change of circumstances or government, but none of these hopes seemed to find fulfillment. Instead, only a small number of Jews actually returned to their homeland rather than the masses they had dreamed would go, and those who returned soon discovered not the messianic age, but a difficult and dangerous life. There were no walls behind which to seek protection from either enemies or robbers. Despair was heavy and people asked why they should bother to continue to worship when clearly the God of the Jews did not appear to be concerned with the welfare of God's chosen. This little book was thus designed to give hope to these discouraged people. In the process, however, Malachi's message broke the traditional boundaries of Jewish tribal thinking and quite literally redefined the God of the Jews. That is what makes this book so noteworthy and powerful.

Using a question and answer format, this prophet points first to the same issue that we will discover in the book of Job. If you are suffering you must deserve it, you must have acted in a way that precipitated God's wrath, causing God to abandon God's people. Searching for an answer, this writer points to their cultic

sins and offers those as the reason for God's punishment. Yet he
continues to struggle against the limitations of this kind of tribal
thinking, asserting that the God of the Jews is still in control. As
evidence of God's continuing presence he cites the destruction of
the Edomites, suggesting that this was God's punishment of their
traditional enemies, because the Edomites had celebrated the
sack of Jerusalem by the Babylonians. He continues to insist that
the "day of the Lord" will come, which meant to the Jews that
God would yet intervene at the end of history and vindicate the
chosen people. Once again it was tribal religion at its tribal best.

As this unknown messenger wrestled with these realities of
history, however, a crack began to appear in his own tribal mentality. Modern readers need to realize that the world seemed very
small to ancient people. Most of them had never been to sea.
They had no idea what lay beyond their coasts or the boundaries formed by mighty rivers or even mountain ranges. As we saw
earlier, they were certain that the earth was the center of the
universe, that the sun rotated around the earth and that the God
who lived above the sky had the chosen people in the center of the
divine gaze. They believed that this God controlled the weather,
their sicknesses and their plight in history. They had no sense or
understanding of either the size of this planet or the vastness of
the universe. They viewed life from the center of their limited
self-consciousness. The whole world revolved around their lives
and they believed that all of their behavior, whether it was worship related or dealt with human behavior in everyday life, was
judged only on how it pleased God and how God responded to it.

When Malachi finally broke open this mind-set he walked
into a stunning new understanding of both God and the world.
The change began when he observed that all worship, even that
of those he called "heathens," was offered to God. If that is so,
he concluded, then God must be thought of as a heavenly parent,
with all people being God's children. In this patriarchal world, he
articulated this as the "brotherhood" of the human family under
the "fatherhood" of God. The Hebrew scriptures had hinted at
this earlier with the explanations of the origins of other nations

of whom the Jews were aware. Jewish mythology had suggested that the Edomites were the descendants of Esau, Jacob's twin brother, from whom Jacob stole the birthright. The Ammonites and Moabites were the grandchildren of Lot, who was Abraham's nephew. The Arabs were the descendants of Ishmael, Abraham's first son by Hagar, his wife Sarah's handmaid. There was a sense of kinship that bound up the region; indeed, a common DNA permeated them all. This insight is what finally caused Malachi to say: "Have we not all one father, has not God created us all?" (2:10).

As he thought about these things, Malachi appears to have stepped into a new human awareness, and when he did a majestic monotheistic God suddenly came into view and universality finally broke through his tribal mind-set. It was then that Malachi could write these words as if he heard God speaking them: "From the rising of the sun to its setting my name shall be great among the nations" (1:11). Malachi did not realize how wide an arc the sweep of the sun created. He did not know that Europe, China or the Western hemisphere existed, but his mind was expanding nonetheless. He then went on to hear God say, "And in every place incense shall be offered to my name" (1:11). A new realization about the oneness of God had dawned. Tribal thinking was beginning to die.

There is a religious mythology that asserts that God is the same yesterday, today and forever. That may be true, but the human perception of this true God is always changing. We human beings have during human history gone from a multi-spirit-filled, animistic view of God, to identifying God with nature's cycles of fertility, to likening God to the warrior deities of our tribal life and ultimately to a sense of the oneness and universality of God. The biblical story moves from a God who hates the Egyptians so much that God sends multiple plagues on them and even closes the Red Sea so that the Egyptians will drown, and a God who hates the Amorites so much that God stops the sun in the sky to allow more daylight in which Joshua's army can slaughter them, to a place where, through the eyes of Malachi, the Jews begin to see God as one universal reality worshiped by all parts of the human family. That was a step that human beings had to take. Without Malachi's searing insight it would not have been possible for Jesus to take the next step, as he did when he enjoined us to love even our enemies (Matt. 5:44).

Malachi, the unnamed voice, is thus a major person in the evolving definition of the Jewish God and, through the Jews, in the development of our understanding of what it means to be human. He thus becomes a fitting close to that section of the Bible we call the prophets.

PART VI

The Bible's Protest Literature

CHAPTER 21

Job

Icon of a New Consciousness

Three books of the Bible, Jonah, Job and Ruth, are known as "protest literature." They are given that label because they were written to make a specific point, human or political, in a particular moment of history. Because Jonah is also listed among the twelve "minor prophets" we treated him previously in that section. We turn now first to Job and then to Ruth.

To those outside traditional religious circles, Job is probably the best-known book in the Bible. It raises the deepest human questions and deals with the most ancient of human fears. It examines the issue of meaning through the lens of human suffering and the absence in this world of basic fairness and justice. As such the book of Job has a counterpart in every religious tradition of the world. The great twentieth-century psychiatrist Carl Jung used this book as the basis of his probing of the dimensions of human life in what I believe is his most profound work, *The Answer to Job.*[1] Solving the question

---

1   See bibliography for details.

of why there is evil and suffering has been part of the human inquiry forever. It should surprise no one that these themes find a place in the Bible.

The story of Job, in its original oral form, appears to date from about 1000–800 BCE. Versions of that story can be found in the literature of many of the peoples of the world, leading us to suspect that this is a universal human narrative. The biblical version of this story, however, did not get recorded until the 500s BCE. We can date it fairly accurately, since it reflects elements of both Babylonian and Persian religion that came into Jewish awareness during and after the exile of the sixth century BCE. The book of Job introduces the figure of Satan, for example, into the biblical story, but in this account Satan is not yet an evil figure or even a fallen angel. Those features would develop later. In Job Satan is simply a part of the heavenly court who acts on God's command. The prologue to this book sets the stage for the drama.

God and Satan are discussing the faithfulness of God's servant Job. Satan suggests that Job's faithfulness is steady only because he has been blessed with riches and a large family. Why should he not be faithful, Satan asks, since the system of reward and punishment works for him? Would he still be faithful, Satan wonders, if his faithfulness were not so abundantly rewarded? God defends Job's faithfulness as sincere, but agrees to a test to determine whether God or Satan is correct. God thus authorizes Satan to test Job "for a season." Satan will remove the rewards of the good life from Job in order to determine whether his faithfulness would continue. This is when tragedy sweeps down on Job (1:13–22). His flocks are decimated, his wealth is destroyed, his sons, daughters and servants are killed and his health is taken from him. Job then tries to reconcile the established wisdom that God rewards faithfulness and punishes evil with his personal experience. Job is a righteous man. There is no debate about that since even God has certified his goodness in the introduction. Job, however, has now been brought low by these calamities. If calamities result from an evil life, how can the righteous Job explain his misfortunes? The stage is set for the entrance of Job's comforters.

Three of Job's friends, Eliphaz, Zophar and Bildad, hear of Job's tragedies and come to console him. The conversation between Job and his friends goes on for some thirty chapters. Supporting their conclusions, Job's friends have the common wisdom of that age, made up of undoubted "truths." Foremost among them is the assumption that God, as a just deity, punishes evil and rewards righteousness. For God to punish a righteous man would not only be inconceivable, but blasphemous. Job's friends buttress their argument by quoting scripture, since their sacred texts were filled with this traditional interpretation of God. Every defeat that the people of Israel had ever endured was seen by them as God's punishment for their disobedience or unfaithfulness. The message of the scriptures was clear. The Jewish people had been punished with a three-day pestilence when King David conducted a census that displeased God (II Sam. 24). Moses had been punished with death because he had put God to the test in the wilderness at a place called Meribah (Num. 20). God had rewarded the people of Israel with the exodus and the miracle at the Red Sea for the faithful endurance of their sufferings under the oppression of the Egyptians (Exod. 14).

This idea that if one obeyed the law and worshiped God properly one could count on blessings from heaven was a central tenet in popular Jewish religion. If one did not worship properly and live in accord with the revealed law of God, the vengeance of God was said to be sure and swift. Deep down this firmly held belief delivered the Jewish people from the threat of meaninglessness. There was purpose, not chaos, in life. This purpose was best revealed in the concept that human behavior controlled the response of God. Human goodness put God on one's side with personal rewards. Human faithlessness and evil brought God's wrath and divine retribution. Job's friends were confident in the rightness and the righteousness of their convictions.

Given this worldview, when Eliphaz, Zophar and Bildad confronted Job's calamities there was only one possible explanation: Job must be guilty of some unseen, hidden evil. They came to help him come to grips with his secret sinfulness, urging him to beg for forgiveness and to seek the mercy of God. They believed that confession was the only way to bring an end to his tragedy.

Job stood alone against this common theological wisdom. The theological correctness with which he was so familiar was confronted by his own human experience and, as so often is the case, it simply did not fit. He was certain that he was not deserving of these calamities. He could not deny the experience of his own character. He knew himself to be upright and honest, one who not only obeyed the law faithfully, but also paid proper homage to the God of his ancestors. Yet he also knew that he had witnessed the loss of all that he valued—his family, his fortune and his health. In the most dramatic moment in the story, Job is portrayed as sitting on top of a garbage heap, scratching the infected sores of his body with a piece of broken pottery, alone with his inner integrity. None of his calamities made rational sense unless he was deserving of this treatment. He knew this was not true of him, hence his suffering made no sense to him.

The meaning of life itself was thus at stake in this debate. Only by the admission of an evil he did not see within himself could he keep at bay the deep and perennial human fear that maybe there was not a God who was in control. If there was no God, then apparently life was chaotic, ruled only by chance, fate or luck, possessing no purpose, no meaning and no redemptive qualities. If that turned out to be the case, then the only human alternatives were to hope for the chance of blessing, since one could not earn it, or to endure endless suffering (if that was to be a particular human's fate) with no further court of appeal. If the common theological wisdom did not operate, then Job had to figure out whether this meant that God was not just or that there was no God. That either of those conclusions might be correct was the unspoken fear that Job's tormenters were resisting, and that was why they, like all theological fundamentalists, pressed their case with such single-minded fervor.

Job, on the other hand, was willing to run this enormous risk, because the common theological wisdom simply did not interpret properly his experience. With the unprecedented courage of one seeking a new human breakthrough, he stood against the conclusions of his friends, forcing on them a new alternative.

The book of Job ends not with a negotiated settlement of this dispute, but with a new vision of a God who spoke out of the whirlwind to challenge the inadequacy of every human attempt to state how God works and to discredit every human effort to define "the holy." The voice of God reminded Job that the human mind cannot embrace the reality of God. "Where were you when the foundations of the word were laid?" (38:4). The ways of the divine are not the ways of the human. To conclude otherwise is always the fatally wrong theological assumption.

Religion at its core is based on the arrogance of believing that human beings not only can discern the ways of God, but can also act in such a way as to control the actions of God. The human sense of fairness is read into the understanding of God. The human desire to control other people's behavior reinforces the usual theological wisdom that expresses itself in a reward and punishment mentality. Heaven and hell are nothing more than the assertion that the mind of God, as we human beings have created it, is still operating to reward or punish us after our death. Religion almost inevitably creates God in the image of the human being and then tries to force all of reality into that frame of reference, lest it otherwise prove to be inadequate. That is why there is no religious system that is eternal. That is why when human experience can no longer be interpreted adequately inside the traditional religious framework, the framework itself begins to die.

The death of a religious system is never easy. The fear engendered by the loss of religion, or even by what we think of as the death of God, engulfs human life as if it were in a sea of total emptiness. Such a death is conducive to emotional denial, fundamentalist fervor or a killing hostility directed toward that which or those who have shattered our religious delusions. It also, however, produces emancipation from the evils of religion that many people welcome. It is the evils of religion that force us either into a new religious oppression or into the building of a new understanding. This struggle to find a new alternative also stretches our consciousness into new dimensions of what it means to be human, and that is where hope is born.

Job resisted the theological conclusions of his day. He refused to let his experience be interpreted by the categories of the past. He held on until the birth of a new consciousness embraced him. Job is thus an icon through which we can see the meaning of a profound religious paradigm shift.

In this century we are again experiencing exactly that sort of paradigm shift. Our experience and our expanded knowledge have rendered the religious answers of yesterday to be inoperative. The defenders of the inadequate answers of the past are anxious. The critics of those answers feel a new freedom, perhaps to build a new non-religious, secular city.[2] The God of yesterday dies as we struggle to view the birth of the God of tomorrow. Job is thus an eternal symbol of that endless human struggle.

---

2   *The Secular City,* by Harvey Cox. See bibliography for details.

CHAPTER 22

Ruth

The Myth of Racial Purity

We now come to Ruth, the third book written to make a particular point in a particular moment of history. None of these protest books, Jonah, Job and Ruth, ever pretended to be literal history. The central figures in each of these three books are not real people who ever lived; they are literary characters created by their respective authors to allow the drama to unfold and carry a specific narrative message.

The story of Ruth has a "once upon a time" quality about it. It is this quality which signals to the readers that this is a fictional tale with a powerful purpose.

The book of Ruth, a four-chapter narrative hidden away in the Bible between the books of Judges and I Samuel, was written in the post-exilic period of Jewish history, probably near the time of Ezra and Nehemiah, somewhere between 425 and 360 BCE. It received this placement locating it in a time before David became the king, because it purports to tell the story of King David's great-grandmother. That was, indeed, the whole point of the book. Not to get ahead of my story, however, let me set the stage.

During the time of Ezra and Nehemiah, the Jewish nation went through a period of intense negativity to everything that was non-Jewish, which grew out of an enormous fear, one that is always the mother of dislocating prejudices. That fear was grounded in the possibility of their own annihilation. It was the same period that produced the book of Jonah. Despair, defeat and exile had been the Jews' recent history. Their supposedly impenetrable walls around Jerusalem, the city in which their protective God was believed to dwell, had been invaded and destroyed. The Temple, God's earthly dwelling place, had been leveled. These traumatized Jewish people then found themselves removed from that land. According to the book of Psalms, in a text we have referred to earlier, they even wondered if they would ever again sing the Lord's song, since it could not, they believed, be sung in a foreign land (Ps. 137).

When some of them were finally allowed to return from exile two or three generations later, around the year 538 BCE, these newly freed descendants interpreted their restoration to mean that finally God would vindicate them and thus would proceed to establish the long-anticipated Kingdom of God back on Jewish soil. Surely the end of their captivity was the sign that the kingdom was near and that God was back in charge. That, however, was not what happened. This small group was rather subjected to frequent attack, suffering defeat after defeat. A second return around 490 BCE under Zerubbabel also did not give rise to the expected kingdom. A third return under Nehemiah about the year 450 BCE met a similar fate, as did a fourth under Ezra between 400–350 BCE.

With each disappointment the hopelessness of their dreams seemed to be given new confirmation, raising haunting questions. Why was God not protecting them? Why would God allow the chosen people to be so badly treated with first defeat and exile, and then to experience a return made up only of the bitterness of being small, defenseless and continually abused? It was a strange way for God to act, unless God was angry. So, like Job, they sought to determine what they had done to infuriate their God and to bring about their fate. By the time of Ezra they had become convinced that they finally understood the reason for their suffering: They had ceased to be a racially pure people. Intermarriage with unclean Gentiles had corrupted them, and many of them came to believe that nothing would change until the Jewish nation purified itself. A new national strategy was thus adopted. All foreign elements were to be purged. The new Judah was to be for Jews only. All non-Jews and half-breeds were to be expelled. Not surprisingly, xenophobia set in.

This was the context in which another unknown and anonymous author wrote his protest that we today call the book of Ruth. Listen to this story now from this perspective:

A Jewish man named Elimelech and his Jewish wife, Naomi, took their two sons, Mahlon and Chilion, and moved to the land of Moab. Perhaps it was a time of a downturn in the Jewish economy and work was hard to find in Judah. While dwelling in this foreign land, however, Elimelech died and the care of Naomi was left in the hands of their two sons. These sons, living far from Judah, then proceeded to take Moabite wives for themselves, one of whom was named Orpah and the other Ruth. Then tragedy struck again and Mahlon and Chilion died. In that patriarchal society this left a vulnerable and economically non-viable family made up of three single women. Naomi decided that her only choice was to return to Judah, and so she urged her two daughters-in-law to return to their Moabite roots and take their places anew in their fathers' families. It would be a sign of disgrace for them to do so, but an older, widowed mother-in-law without sons had no way to care for these now-single younger women. One of them, Orpah, agreed and did return to her family, but Ruth declined and, in a piece of writing that has been quoted as a mark of fidelity through the ages, said to Naomi: "Entreat me not to leave you. . . . Where you go, I will go; where you lodge, I will lodge; your people shall be my people, and your God my God. Where you die, I will die—there will I be buried" (1:16).

The two of them thus returned to Judah without a male protector. It was a hazardous life in that patriarchal world.

Determined to survive, they settled near the fields of a man named Boaz, who was a distant kinsman of Naomi's deceased husband. Jewish law required that the poor be allowed to glean in the fields of the rich for enough grain to sustain their lives and so each day Ruth brought a sufficient collection of wheat from Boaz's fields to make bread to keep away death by starvation. In the process, Ruth, this foreign woman, won the admiration of her Jewish neighbors, including Boaz, who ordered her to be protected while alone in the fields and to be given access to water.

Naomi, knowing that Boaz was kin to Elimelech, was also aware of the Jewish law requiring the male who was nearest of kin to a deceased husband to take the widow of his departed kinsman into his care as part of his harem, so she devised a plan to confront Boaz with his responsibility for herself and for Ruth. The plan involved seduction.

At the end of the harvest there was to be a celebration at which wine would flow freely. Naomi instructed Ruth to bathe, anoint herself with perfume, put on her best dress and go to the party. Ruth was instructed to see that Boaz's heart was made merry with much wine. When well drunk, Boaz lay down on the floor and went to sleep. Ruth gave him a pillow and covered him with a blanket. Then she crawled under the blanket with him. When Boaz awoke the next morning, he found this woman at his side. He had no idea what he had done. "Who are you?" he asked. "I am Ruth," she responded. "Spread your skirt over me for you are my next of kin" (3:9). What she was saying was, "Marry me!" Boaz demurred, admitting his kinship, but saying there was a nearer kinsman than he who must be given first refusal on this new wife. When this man declined, Boaz did the honorable thing and he and Ruth were married. They had a son, whose name was Obed. He in turn had a son named Jesse and then Jesse had a son named David.

That is where the book of Ruth ends. Ruth was a Moabite. She was David's great-grandmother. David, the hero of the superpatriotic Jews who were at that moment purging from the land all people whose blood lines were compromised, was himself part Moabite! David would have qualified for purging. That is the point of the protest book of Ruth. It was designed to confront the raging xenophobia that was sweeping the land and to reveal its inherent weakness.

As the fear subsided, the xenophobia also faded. It always does. The call of God to human beings is always a call to wholeness. No one is whole when acting out of fear. Fear causes people to diminish the worth and the dignity of another when that other is judged to be somehow impure or inferior by reason of one's very being over which there is no human control: That is for reasons of race, ethnicity, gender, left-handedness or sexual orientation, many of which are regularly reinforced by human religious codes. The book of Ruth, like the book of Jonah, was written to protest all of the limits that human prejudice forever tries to place on the love of God.

How wonderful that such a book was included in the sacred scriptures read and valued by both Jews and Christians! The book of Ruth provides us with a biblical mirror into which we can stare at our own prejudices and then be led to free ourselves from them. That is one good reason why the Bible is called "holy."

PART VII

Liturgical Books and Wisdom Literature

CHAPTER 23

The Book of Psalms

When I was a child growing up in Charlotte, North Carolina, I went with my mother from time to time to Chalmer's Memorial ARP Church, the church which she had attended as a child. Those letters "ARP" identified that church as belonging to the Associate Reformed Presbyterian tradition, an ultra-fundamentalist branch of the most rigid form of Calvinism. What was most unusual to me about this church was that the people did not sing any hymns. Hymns, they argued, were made up of human words written by human authors and as such they were considered unfit for use in worship, where only the "Words of God" were meant to be heard. So instead of using hymns, the members of this church set to music the one hundred and fifty psalms from the Bible, which, they claimed, were "God's Words." In other words, the book of Psalms became the hymnal of this church. For all of the strange, literalistic theology that was reflected in this reasoning process, this church had understood correctly the original purpose of the book of Psalms. It was in fact the hymn book of Judaism, created for use in worship, first in the Temple and later in synagogues. Once this insight is grasped, the language of the book of Psalms makes sense. There are numerous liturgical references and directions found in the psalms: imploring people "to sing to the Lord a new song" (Ps. 33:3), frequently mentioning the choirmaster and referring to a variety of instruments traditionally used in Jewish worship, such as the trumpet, harp and lyre. The psalms also refer to things like sacrifices, processions, altars, burnt offerings, thanksgivings and sacred vows, all of which are liturgical acts.

When one looks at the book of Psalms through the lens of the worship life of the Jews, it also becomes apparent that a number of the psalms were designed for the specific celebrations observed in the annual Jewish liturgical cycle. For example, Psalms 113–118 were used in the three extended festivals that mark the Jewish year: Passover, which was expanded into the Festival of the Unleavened Bread; Sukkoth, also called the Festival of Tabernacles, or Booths, an eight-day harvest celebration in the fall, and Dedication, an eight-day festival of light that comes in the dead of winter, originally marking the return of the light of true worship to the synagogue at the time of the Maccabees, and which today we refer to as Hanukkah. Psalm 118 was particularly adapted to be used in the great procession that accompanied the harvest festival of Sukkoth. In that procession people waved in their right hands bundles of leafy branches called lulabs, made of willow, myrtle and palm, as they recited the words from this psalm: "Hosanna! [Same as] Blessed is the one who comes in the name of the Lord. Hosanna in the highest" (118:26). It is clear to see how the Christian observance of Palm Sunday was influenced by this liturgical observance of the Jews.

Psalm 119 was written originally to be used at the annual Jewish observance of Pentecost, or Shavuot, which celebrated the giving of the law to Moses on Mount Sinai. Shavuot came fifty days after Passover (hence the name Pentecost from the Greek for fifty days) and was observed by a twenty-four-hour vigil. It takes a very long psalm to serve a twenty-four-hour vigil, which is why this is the longest psalm in the Bible. It is also a hymn in praise of the glory and beauty of the Torah, which the Jews believed was God's greatest gift to the world. Psalm 119 is conveniently divided into eight segments of three stanzas each to fit the vigil format of eight three-hour units, thus providing a reading for each part of the vigil. The length of this psalm is consequently not an accident.

Other psalms, especially numbers 102, 120, 130 and 131, were used on days of public penitence and some festivals. They are quite reminiscent of the earliest hymns of the Christian church, which were surely modeled on these psalms. By the phrase "earliest hymns" I have in mind those songs that Luke puts into the mouths of the major characters in the birth narrative: the song of Zechariah, the song of Mary, the song of the angels and the song of Simeon the priest (see Luke 1 and 2). These psalm-like hymns are still used in Christian worship today, though we tend to refer to them by their Latin names: the Benedictus, the Magnificat, the Gloria in Excelsis and the Nunc Dimittis.

Most Christians are not consciously aware of the fact that the gospels themselves were actually born in the synagogue and are largely shaped by the liturgical patterns of the Jews. I shall develop this insight more fully when we get to a consideration of those books. Suffice it for now to say that this is why we find some ninety-three references to the psalms wrapped around the story of Jesus in the gospels alone.

Who wrote the book of Psalms? This question makes no more sense than to ask who wrote the various Christian hymnals. Both are compilations of the worship traditions of the ages. Christian hymnals include the plainsong words and settings of the thirteenth century, the Reformation words of the sixteenth century, the social gospel message of the nineteenth century, the pious evangelical words of the late nineteenth and early twentieth centuries, the modern futuristic hymns of the late twentieth century and in hymnal supplements even the words that express the hopes of the twenty-first century. Likewise, the book of Psalms reflects the long religious history and pilgrimage of the Jews and thus has no single author. There are psalms dedicated to the beauty of creation, psalms that extol the virtues of the king, psalms that bewail the human condition and psalms that express both the despair of the exile and the joy and hope connected with the return from the exile. Just as our hymnals contain some of the dreadful theology espoused in Christian history that speaks of blood and sacrifice and the wrath of God, so in the book of Psalms we are frequently embarrassed by the theology of yesterday. We meet in the psalms, for example, some of the worst aspects of a tribal deity. Contrary to what my mother's ARP church thought, the psalms are hardly the "Words of God," unless you want to attribute to God some dreadful aspects of depraved behavior. The psalms are made up of uniquely human words addressed to God, expressing uniquely human emotions and feelings.

We have no idea how or when the book of Psalms arrived at the number of one hundred and fifty as the totality of the psalms that merited inclusion in the sacred text of the people. In one of our earliest complete versions of the Bible, a fourth-century work known as the Codex Sinaiticus, the whole set of one hundred and fifty psalms as we know them today are present. Yet another somewhat later fourth-century work, known as Codex Vaticanus, lacks Psalms 49–79. We do know that at some point in Jewish history an order was imposed on the book of Psalms. From the earliest time they seem to have been divided into five books, each ending with a doxology in the final verse of the last psalm in each section. Book I includes Psalms 1–41; Book II, Psalms 42–72; Book III, Psalms 73–89; Book IV, Psalms 90–106; Book V, Psalms 107–150. That probably represented, once again, a Jewish liturgical adaptation of the use of the psalter to accompany the five books of the Torah—Genesis, Exodus, Leviticus, Numbers and Deuteronomy—the annual reading of which organized the yearly liturgical calendar in many of the more traditional synagogues of antiquity.

There are other things in the psalter pointing to a long development over time. The name of God is spelled two ways, reflecting the two centers of Jewish life and history: Jerusalem, where the name Yahweh was primary, as we have seen, and the Northern Kingdom, where the name Elohim was preferred. In the last verse of Psalm 79, we are told, "Here, the prayers of David are ended," as if to say that an incorporated section has come to an end. Verbatim duplications in some of the psalms reflect the fact that they were from more than one source. We now believe the psalms were compiled into more or less their present form by the

Jews somewhere in the time span 400–200 BCE. They reflect various aspects of Jewish history and obviously various authors. For the record, the authorship of any of the psalms by King David is pious myth, not a fact of history.

Much more could be said about the book of Psalms. Many of its entries are etched into our memories by the sheer beauty of the words. One thinks of the familiar Psalm 23, "The Lord is my shepherd, I shall not want," or of Psalm 19, a hymn to creation that Joseph Addison turned into a poem that begins "The spacious firmament on high with all the blue ethereal sky," which was set to music by Franz Joseph Haydn in 1798, or John Milton's poem "The Lord will come and not be slow, his footsteps cannot err," which was based on Psalms 82, 85 and 86.

The psalms have also played a prominent role in funeral services during Christian history. In this context one thinks of Psalm 42, "Like as the hart desireth the water brooks, so longest my soul after thee, O God," and Psalm 46, "God is our life and strength, a very present help in trouble." There is even the thought frequently voiced at funerals from Psalm 130: "If thou Lord will be extreme to mark what is done amiss, O Lord who may abide?"[1]

Many people wonder if perhaps the psalms should not be used so heavily in Christian worship. Certainly some of their words do violate our sensitivities. Time does "make ancient good uncouth," noted the poet James Russell Lowell.[2] Nowhere is that truth better seen than in the book of Psalms. At best they are a mixed blessing!

---

1   All of the psalm quotations are taken from the 1979 Episcopal *Book of Common Prayer*. See bibliography for details.
2   These words are from a poem that begins "Once to every man and nation comes the moment to decide." They are quoted from the 1940 Episcopal Hymnal, number 518. See bibliography for details.

CHAPTER 24

Wisdom Literature

Proverbs, Ecclesiastes and the Song of Solomon

hree books of the Old Testament are generally regarded as being the constituent parts of what has been called "wisdom literature." They are Proverbs, Ecclesiastes and the Song of Solomon, sometimes entitled the "Song of Songs."[1] In this chapter I will focus on these wisdom books, all of which are attributed in the mythology of the Jews to King Solomon, who was regarded as the wisest of all of the Jewish kings. That reputation is based primarily on a story found in the first book of Kings, chapter 3, which portrays Solomon as asking God not for wealth or long life, but for the gift of wisdom to enable him to be a good king and to judge his people properly. When one reads what the rest of the Bible says about Solomon, however, the idea that his life was marked by wisdom appears to be a very strange claim. He had a harem of a thousand wives. He quite literally dissipated during his reign the enormous goodwill built up by his father, King David. Finally,

---

1   Sometimes the book of Job is also considered to be part of the wisdom tradition. Because we have treated Job in our section on protest literature, I will not return to it here.

his unwise policies produced a rebellion at the time of his death which resulted in the secession of ten tribes from his kingdom to form the Northern Kingdom. For Jews to be willing to give up their ties with Jerusalem and the Temple and to break forever the sense of Jewish unity, which was later a factor contributing over the centuries both to a sense of Jewish weakness and to a history of persecution, means that they must have found the rule of Solomon to be oppressive. None of these results could have arisen from the acts of a wise ruler! Mythology, however, has strange power and the image of wise King Solomon has hung on despite the witness of history. The wisdom literature of the Bible claims King Solomon for its founder in the same way that, as we noted earlier, the book of Psalms has claimed King David as its author. In neither affirmation is history well served.

Turning first to the book of Proverbs, one discovers quickly that this work is really divided into four books to which a few appendices have been added. Book I includes Proverbs 1:1–9:18 and consists of ten extended discourses containing admonitions and warnings, plus two poems in which wisdom is personified. One of these poems (8:1–36) appears to have influenced the prologue to the Fourth Gospel, in which the Logos ("Word") is personified in quite similar language. This first book appears to have been composed in the late fourth or early third century BCE, some six hundred years at least after Solomon's death.

Book II, which includes Proverbs 10:1–22:16, and Book IV, which includes 25:1–29:27, are the two places which make the overt claim that their words are "the proverbs of Solomon." That claim is strange on many levels, but it should be noted that even the book of I Kings indicates that Solomon's wisdom did not cover all aspects of human behavior.

Book III is composed of 22:17–24:42 and appears to have been based on a much earlier Egyptian book of wisdom, which is dated about 1000 BCE and is entitled the "Instruction of Amen-em-ope." To this book is attached the first of five appendices, 24:23–34. The others, which were attached to Book IV, constitute (1) a dialogue between a skeptic and a believer (30:1–9),

(2) proverbs of a numerical type (30:10–33), (3) the counsel of a queen mother to a young monarch (31:1–9), and (4) a portrait of an ideal wife of a prominent man (31:10–31). I have taken these divisions from the *New Oxford Annotated Bible,* but one can get them from almost any study of the book of Proverbs.[2]

The content of the book of Proverbs has insinuated itself into the common wisdom of our society far more deeply than most people imagine. One has only to recall such familiar sayings as "The fear of the Lord is the beginning of wisdom" (Prov. 1:7), "He who troubles the household will inherit the wind" (Prov. 11:29), "A soft answer turns away wrath" (Prov. 15:1), "A good name is to be chosen above great riches" (Prov. 22:1), "Spare the rod and spoil the child" (Prov. 13:24—not an exact quote from Proverbs, but close, and the adage is most often repeated in this form), and "Train up a child in the way he [or she] should go and when he [or she] is old he [or she] will not depart from it" (Prov. 27:6). Many people, including prominent politicians, repeat these phrases with little knowledge that they originate in the book of Proverbs.

Wisdom literature became popular among the Jews in the fifth and fourth centuries BCE, following the return from exile that began around 540. The cultural assumption was that the time of the prophets had passed. Divine revelation could no longer be anticipated and the voice of God was no longer heard, so people searched for guidance in life in the accumulated experience of human wisdom. The wisdom message, cited time after time, was that good living would be rewarded, not in some afterlife, which at this time hardly existed as a concept in Judaism, but in the quality and integrity of one's present life. When that did not seem to work out, as was the case in the story of Job, there was a sense of religious disillusionment. It was that feeling of disillusionment that became particularly apparent in the second major work in the wisdom section of the Jewish Bible to which I now turn.

---

2   See bibliography for details.

Ecclesiastes

The book of Ecclesiastes, or "Qoheleth the Preacher," a title by which this book is also known, is far more a philosophical treatise on the meaning of life than it is a testimony to belief. It even expresses despair about the reality of God and raises troubling questions about the primary and traditional beliefs of the Hebrew religion. Portraying God as the "inscrutable" originator of the world and the "determiner" of human fate, Ecclesiastes is skeptical of the human ability to make change, finally declaring that no human accomplishments make any difference in determining one's ultimate fate. Thus, for this author, there is no clear meaning in life and no ultimate purpose. This means, says this book in its recurring theme, "All is vanity." There is also no hope for life beyond this life in Ecclesiastes, for it asserts that death brings only oblivion.

One wonders how a fourth-century BCE work of this nature managed to get accepted into the Hebrew canon of scripture, since it appears to be at odds with the usual stated Jewish understanding of God. Two reasons are traditionally cited. First, in the first two verses, the book is attributed to the son of King David, an attribution that was interpreted to imply authorship by King Solomon. The second is that an orthodox postscript was added in 12:9–14 that concludes with the admonition that "we are to fear God and keep God's commandments knowing that God will bring every deed into judgment." That is a strange ending for a very different book with a very different message and undoubtedly comes from the pen of a later editor, but this ending probably allowed the book to gain entrance into the sacred text.

I have always liked the honesty of Ecclesiastes and the fact that this book's almost nihilistic writing could find a place in the scriptures of my faith tradition. I suspect, however, that those who claim a magical, revelatory source for the Bible always skip this faithless, despairing work.[3]

---

3   Professor Lloyd G. Geering of New Zealand has recently published a book on a conversation with Ecclesiastes. See bibliography for details.

Song of Solomon

The final book in the wisdom section is entitled the Song of Solomon. This is a book of lyric poems or fragments of poems about courtship and human love. One commentator suggested that these poems were really bawdy songs sung in a Jewish pub by males lusting after the body of a female. Others have said that they are courtship songs written to be sung at weddings. Still others have suggested that these narratives portray a god and goddess in love. Whatever the explanation, the fact remains that the Song of Solomon is erotic, extolling the beauty and wonder of physical love and sexual attraction. It is quite obvious when reading this book that Israel never produced a Queen Victoria!

This writing also made it into the canon of scripture, first by claiming, as it does in the first verse, that it was the work of wise King Solomon, and second by being allegorized. Hosea, the eighth-century BCE prophet whose story we previously chronicled, had understood God as the husband of Israel (Hos. 7:16–19) and so these love songs were often said to have been between God and God's bride, the Jewish people. In the Christian era, disciples of Jesus continued to find allegorical interpretations by playing on the metaphor of the church as the bride of Christ, a theme stated most overtly in the book of Revelation (21:2, 9). The Song of Solomon has also been interpreted through the ages as describing the intimate experience of divine love in the individual soul. The wisdom literature, taken as a whole, formed another movement, another emphasis, in the unfolding life of the Jewish people, and in order to present this dimension it was accorded its own place in the biblical narrative.

One other note of some historical interest is that the concept of "wisdom" and the word itself in the Hebrew language was feminine in form. This was also true in the Greek language into which these Hebrew scriptures were destined to be translated some two hundred and fifty years before the Common Era in a form we call the Septuagint. So it was that appeals to the "divine sophia" (the Greek word for "wisdom") helped to temper the heavily patriarchal character of biblical thinking about God. Many people would in time see "wisdom" as an aspect of the Holy Spirit and thus advocates for the feminine in the definition of God for the first time found in the wisdom literature a scriptural basis to support their gender in their claims of divinity. That concept, once so foreign in our faith story, has now moved to the place where more and more of us are willing to see God as both mother and father, and to recognize that whoever God ultimately is, God is finally beyond the limited language of human gender divisions.

In time, with our sexist preconceptions opened up, scholars began to discover in the biblical text ideas that moved us beyond seeing God as an enlarged and unlimited being like ourselves. Then we found other divine images that were transpersonal, viewing God after the analogy of the wind, or the power of love or even a rock.[4] In each of these metaphors we began to see how it is that most of our God talk is not really about who or what God is, but about making sense of the human experience of the "holy." There is a difference. So embrace the truth found in the biblical wisdom literature, savor it and transform it into the symbols of your own experience. That is finally the only way to read this ancient, sacred and mythological book we call the Bible.

---

4   Val Webb, an Australian theologian, in her book *Like Catching Water in a Net,* develops many biblical images of God that are not gender-specific and are transpersonal—images such as "consuming fire" and "thirst-quenching water." In the Bible God is referred to as an eagle who will cover us with its wings, a high tower, a hiding place, a fortress. We have made religion quite sterile by limiting our image of God to patriarchal, male symbols. Val Webb's second book, *Stepping Out with the Sacred,* is equally provocative. See bibliography for details.

CHAPTER 25

Lamentations and Esther

Books Designed for Liturgical Observances

Many parts of the Bible were written to be used on occasions of public worship. They were never intended to be read as history or biography. We have seen evidence of this a number of times on this journey through the scriptures. The Bible itself was used as a liturgical book by the Jewish worshiping community. We shall soon document in much more detail that the Christian gospels were created in a liturgical context and were designed to be read in worship while the Christians were still part of the synagogue and were thus still observing the feasts and fasts of the synagogue. Christians adapted many of these feasts and fasts for their own use and in the process gave them new meanings. So it was that the Eucharist was an adaptation of the Passover meal, baptism was a Christianized version of the ceremonial bath of the Jews and Lent was born as a preparation for baptism that would occur at Easter in the same way that the Jewish converts had a period of preparation before being inducted into Judaism at Passover. No book of the Bible was far removed from the ongoing liturgy of the people.

We have already noted that Psalm 119 was composed to be read at the Jewish Festival of Shavuot, or Pentecost, when the giving of the law to Moses on Mount Sinai was being celebrated, and that Zechariah 9–14 has a particular connection to the eight-day fall harvest festival known as Sukkoth.

This same pattern is apparent once more in two other little-known books of the Bible. Only when the liturgical themes that lie in the background are made conscious do these two books really make much sense. I refer to the book of Lamentations, found immediately after the book of Jeremiah, and the book of Esther, found after the book of Nehemiah.

Lamentations was a book written to be read on the Jewish observance of a holy day known as the Ninth of Ab, which came generally in our month of August. It is a series of laments over Jerusalem, designed both to recall and to bewail the fall of that city to the Babylonians in the sixth century BCE, an event that we have noted many times as crucial in Jewish self-identity. The Ninth of Ab was the day chosen to mark this ultimate national tragedy in every generation. People once attributed this book to Jeremiah, and that probably accounts for its placement in the Bible just before that prophetic work, but Jeremiah had been dead for hundreds of years before Lamentations was written. This book was recited liturgically on this day of public fasting and mourning. Four of its chapters follow a form we know as the alphabetical acrostic—that is, they each have twenty-two verses, one for each of the twenty-two letters in the Hebrew alphabet. The book was a series of dirges to allow the defeats of history to be recalled and then to focus on the lessons learned in those defeats for Jewish people.

Most Christians are familiar with this book only because it has been adapted for Christian use on Good Friday. Many Good Friday liturgies begin with these words from Lamentations: "Is it nothing to you all ye who pass by? Behold and see if there is any sorrow like my sorrow with which the Lord has afflicted me" (1:12). By using these words on Good Friday, Christians were likening the death of Jesus liturgically to the death of the Jewish nation at the time of their defeat by the Babylonians and their enforced exile.

Other words from Lamentations that have found their way into Christian worship include those used in the 1822 hymn by John Keble, "New Every Morning Is the Love" (based on 3:22); the phrase used in Christian prayers to a God who has "taught us in thy holy word that thou dost not willingly grieve or afflict the sons of man" (3:32), and the secular phrase that something is "worth its weight in gold" (4:2). This little book, which can be read in five minutes, constantly surprises the reader with its message.

A second little-known liturgical work in the Bible is the book of Esther. Like Lamentations this book was also written to be read in synagogue worship on a particular Jewish holiday. Esther is attached to the Jewish Festival of Purim, which normally comes in February or March in our calendar. It is a charming and purely secular story in which no Jewish religious practice is mentioned and the name of God is never used. I recall meeting a musician from New York, while we were both walking the Milford Track on the beautiful South Island of New Zealand, whose ambition it was to turn the story of Esther into a modern opera. I hope he has done so, for this narrative lends itself to that medium with great power.

The story line of the book of Esther is fascinating. A Persian king named Ahasuerus, who ruled a kingdom that stretched from Ethiopia to India, was drinking with some royal guests and some of the leading citizens in the city of Susa. He decided to invite his queen, Vashti, into the feast so that these guests could stare with envy at her beauty. Vashti, however, refused to come, which created an embarrassing moment. If the king's wife could defy her husband, then any wife could defy any husband and the power of patriarchy would be over. All women must obey the command of their husbands, the text says, for this is "the law of the Medes and the Persians" (1:19). So in response to the queen's disobedience, the order was sent across the land that "all women shall give honor to their husbands" (1:20)—or, as it was popularly interpreted then and much later, "every man shall be king of his own home." Queen Vashti was banished and a contest was set up to pick the most beautiful virgin in the land to be the new queen. The choice fell on Esther, the cousin of a Jewish man named Mordecai, who had raised her as his daughter when her parents died. It appears that her Jewish identity was unknown to the king. Later two of the king's eunuchs conspired to remove the king from the throne, but their scheme was discovered by Mordecai and reported to the king, who had the eunuchs hanged and who then placed the good deed done by Mordecai—that is, informing the king of this danger—into the Book of Memorable Deeds. Meanwhile, the king reorganized his administration and appointed a man named Haman to be over all his affairs. Haman, drunk with his new authority, required the populace to bow down before him. They all did so except for one man, Mordecai the Jew, who, because of his religious convictions bowed his head to no human being. This so infuriated Haman that he initiated a plan to have Mordecai hanged and to destroy all the Jews in the realm. When notice of this intention became public, Mordecai asked Esther, now the queen of the land, to intercede with the king on behalf of her people. She did so even though it identified her as a Jew and placed her in mortal danger by demanding the king's attention.

Still smitten by her charms, the king allowed this intrusion on his royal dignity and agreed to hear her request. She invited him to come with Haman alone to a dinner she would prepare and at which she would make her petition known. They came, but Esther now said she would not make her request known until a second dinner that again only Haman and the king would attend.

Haman was quite pleased to be included in these dinners along with the king and the queen, and he began to fantasize about his increasing power. He proceeded in his campaign against the Jews by building a gallows on which to hang Mordecai the Jew, his major nemesis. Before they attended the second dinner, however, the king had a restless night, and in his sleeplessness he read from the Book of Memorable Deeds where Mordecai's act in saving the king's life was recorded. The next day he inquired of Haman as to what should be done for a man the king wanted to honor. Haman, assuming that he was to be the honoree, spelled out a list of public honors to be bestowed upon this fortunate man. The king agreed to every detail and directed Haman to do all of the things he had just outlined—but to Mordecai the Jew. To his chagrin, Haman had to carry out this order on the one he considered his most bitter enemy.

Things got even worse for Haman when he accompanied the king to the second dinner with Queen Esther to hear her petition. She asked that the law designed to annihilate the Jews be rescinded and that Haman, the author of this law, be executed. The king did as Esther had requested. The Jewish people were saved and Haman was hanged on the same gallows that he had erected for Mordecai. This escape from the peril of genocide on the part of the Jews was then ordered to be celebrated annually on the Feast of Purim so that, in observing this day, the Jews could recall the time when Queen Esther saved them from annihilation.

It is an exciting story, but it hardly qualifies as the "Word of God," especially when the text of this book goes on to say that the Jews, now freed from annihilation, responded by slaying five hundred of their tormentors, including the ten sons of Haman.

There is so much in the Bible that is lively and insightful to read, once we crack the pious framework and remove the outrageous claims to literal authority that have been placed into and around these ancient words. Human beings almost inevitably and intuitively seek the truth of God and it comes through many sources, of which the Bible is certainly one. The truth of God, however, cannot ever be captured in propositional form, for it is always bigger than the human mind can embrace. Our perception of truth evolves as human consciousness expands. We claim no finite book as the literal source of truth without becoming idolaters. All literalists in every religious system, certainly including many Christians around the world, need to face the fact that the biblical books of Lamentations and Esther point to this truth and bring readers to this realization in a very obvious way.

CHAPTER 26

The Chronicler, Ezra and Nehemiah

National Mythmakers

The Old Testament, as we Christians organize it, closes in the post-exilic period. That would date its final works in the mid to late 300s BCE. The biblical story thus comes to a conclusion in a very difficult period of Jewish history. The Jews were a defeated nation returning from exile and trying to lay claim to their former country, which had now been settled by other people for several generations. Those settlers, whose ancestors had come, sometimes forcibly, from other nations several generations earlier were not happy to welcome the returning Jews, whom they saw as invading their land, nor did they recognize the overt Jewish claim to ownership. So it was that resistance against the Jews was high and hostility toward them was intense. This was twenty-three hundred or so years ago, though it sounds very much like the modern story of Jews in the Middle East.

Jewish survival in this land required then, as it does now, that the Jews erect symbols of their permanence. This meant

rebuilding the protective walls around Jerusalem, rebuilding the
city itself and ultimately rebuilding their Temple, which was an
outward symbol of their claim to live in and possess this land.
The Temple itself seemed to announce that this land belonged
to the God of the Jews, who had given it to them. Some of the
less inspired minor prophets such as Haggai, Nahum, Zephaniah
and Obadiah, whom we treated with only a brief sentence or two
in this book, spoke for this nationalistic fervor. They were tribal
figures in the service of a tribal religion. The four final books that
I will cover to complete our study of the origins of the Old Testament are also products of this period and reflect a similar mentality. They are I and II Chronicles, Ezra and Nehemiah.

Most people are not familiar with the books of the so-called
Chronicler at all. Much of the material in them is also contained,
sometimes verbatim, in the books of I and II Kings. Ezra and
Nehemiah were originally part of the corpus of the Chronicler,
so all of these books are deeply interrelated. The Chronicler,
however, was not a historian, at least not in the modern sense. He
made no effort to discover the facts of history or to establish a
firm basis for his conclusions. The Chronicler was rather a theologian whose primary purpose was to retell Jewish history from
his particular theological perspective. He wanted to inform the
Jews of his generation of what it would be like for them to be,
in a proper fashion, the people of God. He did this by describing
the reigns of Kings David and Solomon, not as they were, but as
they ought to have been. So in the two books of Chronicles we
get idealized kings who are not really human.

Nowhere is this idealized theme better noted than in the
Chronicler's description of King David's final sickness, in which
the king is portrayed as laying out in minute detail the plans
for the building of the Temple. This was the Chronicler's way
of suggesting that the Temple, or at least the idea and the plan
for the Temple, was the product of David's reign rather than of
Solomon's. Compare that with the story of King David's final
days as told by the much earlier book of Kings. In the narrative
found in the first chapter of I Kings, David was a sick and inca-

pacitated old man who could not govern in his weakness, so a court intrigue developed around him as to who would be his heir. Solomon, who was certainly not the firstborn son of King David, became the eventual winner of this struggle. His claim to the throne was modest to say the least. He was the second child of the adulterous relationship between King David and Bathsheba, the wife of Uriah the Hittite, whom David had had murdered. You may remember their story from our earlier discussion of the prophetic principle.

David had many older and more nobly born sons than Solomon who might have succeeded to his throne. The most obvious candidate was Adonijah, who was backed by both Abiathar the priest and Joab, David's military chief of staff. Solomon, however, aided by his mother, who had become as close to a queen as David ever had, joined with Zadok the priest, Nathan the prophet and Benaiah the military leader, to pull off the coup that had Solomon crowned king with David's blessing even prior to David's death, dashing the hopes of all his potential challengers.

It was also suggested in that first chapter of I Kings that as King David neared death he was suffering from chills that could not be overcome even with many blankets. His attendants decided on a new strategy. They would conduct a "Miss Israel" contest to determine the most beautiful woman in the land. The winner's prize would be to lie with the sick king to warm his chilled body with her own. When Abishag the Shunammite was chosen, she immediately entered Jewish folklore and was said to have been the inspiration for the romantic material in the biblical book known as the Song of Solomon, which we recently considered. I submit that this is a rather different end-of-life story from contemplating the dimensions of the yet to be built Temple!

While the books of Ezra and Nehemiah appear to be part of the work of the Chronicler, there are some details of history on which these narratives are based. Of the later returning groups from captivity one of them appears to have been led by a governor named Nehemiah and another by a priest named Ezra. Interestingly, one learns more about Ezra by reading the book of

Nehemiah than one learns about Nehemiah. Two things, however, occur in these last two books in our consideration of the Old Testament that shape later history. The first is a story we have noted earlier in which a new and expanded law, or Torah, was brought to Ezra the priest to be read in its entirety to the gathered assembly of the people. After this reading, the people covenanted with God to obey this law and to enjoin its precepts on the common life of the newly established Jewish nation. This is thought to be, as we mentioned previously, the only biblical reference to the Yahwist-Elohist-Deuteronomic-Priestly version of the Torah that came into its more or less present form out of the exile.

The second is that as we come to the close of the Hebrew scriptures—what we might call the First Testament—we find the narrative suggesting that the completed Torah was now being read to the people. It was a fixed part of Jewish liturgy. Sacred stories all find liturgical outlets. The circle is being closed in a very dramatic way. The Bible, both testaments, emerged and evolved through the history of the Jewish people, which we have now traced, and was the means of recalling liturgically that history. As we bring this study of the Hebrew scriptures to a close, we bring that history, very briefly, back into our awareness: The writing of the most sacred part of the Hebrew scriptures, the Torah, began, probably in the middle years of the tenth century BCE, as a tribal document to justify the major institutions in the land of Judah. A second version was written to justify the secession of the northern tribes from Judah. The two stories were merged following the defeat of the Northern Kingdom at the hands of Assyria in 721 BCE. Later this narrative was expanded by a group of seventh-century BCE reformers, who are called the Deuteronomists. Finally it was thoroughly re-edited and increased to almost twice its original size over more than a century during and after the Babylonian exile by a group of people we know today as the priestly writers. This revised document formed the content of the covenant by which the Jewish people agreed to live, which was thus based upon this version of the law. The

Torah then shaped the continued history of these same Jewish people.

During these same years the history of the Jewish nation after the death of Moses was also written, and these history books take us from Joshua and the judges, through the establishment of the monarchy, the division of the Jewish nation, the destruction of the Northern Kingdom and finally the defeat, exile and return of the people of Judah to what they were convinced was their God-given sacred soil. Into that history the writing prophets wove their insights. Next the wisdom literature was incorporated. Then the liturgical books were added. Occasional protest books arose when someone found the conflict between his or her understanding of God and the practices of the people's religion to be in severe tension. This is how the sacred story of the Jews came into being. In time that Jewish story became the foundation on which the sacred story of the Christians was written. That is why Christian Bibles all contain two testaments. Added to the foundational testament of the Jewish people—the First Testament—the New Testament containing the life of Jesus was understood in combination as a new and transformative expression of the ongoing Jewish story.

History reveals that instead of this entire sacred story evolving into a new whole at the dawn of the first century, it became first filled with threat and pain between those Jews who believed the Torah was complete, and those Jewish followers of Jesus who would later be called Christians, who believed that Jesus, like the prophets of old, represented a new experience of God that had to be incorporated into the ongoing faith story of the Jewish people. By the end of the first century CE those tensions led to a separation between church and synagogue and began a history of what we today call anti-Semitism, reflecting a hostility that has darkened the reputation of the Christian church. Today there are many reasons to suggest that a new and rational understanding between Jew and Christian is being born and is growing. To demonstrate the truth of that statement, I will make rapprochement between Jews and Christians a major theme when I begin our journey through the New Testament.

Before turning to the New Testament, I need to note, just for the record, that a series of books that we now call the Apocrypha, which are dated between 200 BCE and the birth of Jesus, are present in many versions of the Bible. These require at least a word of explanation. The books of the Apocrypha, though beyond the scope of this volume, are important in that they inform us of many of the details of that inter-testament period and illumine many aspects of the New Testament. Many of these are like the wisdom books in the Bible itself. One thinks of works such as the Wisdom of Ben Sirach and the Wisdom of Solomon. Others are akin to the history books of Samuel and Kings. In that regard one thinks of I, II, III and IV Maccabees. Some are wonderful stories, like Bel and the Dragon and Susannah—accounts that are as vivid and as make-believe as the story of Jonah and the great fish.

Christians debate to this day what the value of these books is and what their authority in the life of the church is or should be. For me they are of inestimable cultural and historical value, but they do not offer a great source for insight or heightened spirituality. So I close our study of the books of the First Testament by tipping my hat ever so briefly to the Apocrypha, and I prepare to look anew at the twenty-seven books that form the New Testament, which I believe to be the second great covenant that arose out of Jewish history.

PART VIII

Introducing the Christian Scriptures, Commonly Called the New Testament

CHAPTER 27

A New Beginning—
An Old Theme

I turn our attention now to a collection of writings called the
"Second Covenant" or the "New Testament." My purpose
in this section continues to be the same as I outlined at the
beginning of this book. I will explore the profound truths
that I find beneath the literal words of the text. I will do this
by taking you, my readers, deeply into each of the books that
constitute the Christian scriptures. The New Testament consists
of twenty-seven separate works written over a period of some
eighty-five years. The earliest book of the New Testament is
probably I Thessalonians, generally dated around the year 51 CE,
while the latest is probably II Peter, generally dated around the
year 135 CE. The influence of the New Testament on Christian
history has certainly been powerful and dramatic, but we need to
escape the excessive claims of religious piety and embrace the fact
that this influence has been both positive and negative.

On the positive side it is clear that the institution called the
Christian church, which both produced and grew out of these
twenty-seven books, has inspired quite literally millions, even
billions, of people in many ways. Most of the great universities
of the world were begun as part of the Christian church's commitment to knowledge and, in particular, to imparting the saving

knowledge of the sacred scriptures. Most of our healing institutions, from hospitals to hospices, arose out of the Christian sense that every human life is of infinite worth, which carried with it the compelling need to alleviate suffering insofar as that was possible. Most of the great art of the ages, at least up until the seventeenth century, had as its content scenes primarily derived from these twenty-seven books. These art treasures are of such immense value today that, for the most part, they are stored in the world's greatest museums and guarded rigorously, for they are recognized as a valuable and constant source of enrichment for the people. Most of the great music of the ages, at least up until the dawn of modernity, was an attempt to put the primary themes of the New Testament into the indelible sounds that we today still recognize and sing. One thinks of the *St. Matthew Passion* and the *St. John Passion* by Johann Sebastian Bach, which put the Bible's portrayal of the last moments in Jesus' life to the profound music that only Bach could compose, and of the Christmas oratorio *Messiah* by George Frideric Handel, which interpreted Jesus primarily in the light of the book of II Isaiah. These works and many others of similar vintage are today familiar and much-loved cultural treasures. One cannot understand the history of the Western world or explore these cultural artifacts without becoming deeply aware of the impact that the New Testament has had on the life of our civilization.

There is, however, also the dark side of the New Testament that must be faced and lifted beyond the stained-glass accents of antiquity into full consciousness. The New Testament has created victims whose lives have been diminished at best and destroyed at worst by the direct impact of reading from this "sacred" source. I think of the Jewish people who have suffered so deeply throughout Christian history because of this book. The words attributed to the Jewish crowd by Matthew in his narrative of the crucifixion, "his blood be upon us and upon our children" (Matt. 27:25), have caused much Jewish blood to flow quite literally in everything from individual acts of anti-Semitic violence to the Crusades and the Holocaust. The Fourth Gospel's use of the phrase "the Jews," spoken, or at least largely interpreted as being spoken, through clenched teeth, helped legitimize anti-Semitism. The portrayal of a man called Judas, a name that is nothing but the Greek spelling of the name for the entire Jewish nation of Judah, as the anti-hero of the Jesus story served to give permission to Christians through the ages to justify their feeling of revenge against those members of this ethnic group of people, whom the Christians falsely held to be responsible for the death of Jesus.

Lost in all of this hostile passion is the truth that Jesus was a Jew, his disciples were all Jews and the writers of the twenty-seven books of the New Testament were also Jews! The only possible exception is Luke, the person thought to be the author of both the gospel that bears his name and the book of Acts, who is believed to have been born a Gentile but to have converted to Judaism and thus to have come through the synagogue into the church. This means that when we read the New Testament, we are reading the words of Jewish writers, interpreting the experience and impact of the Jewish Jesus primarily in the light of the Jewish scriptures and under the ongoing influence of the synagogue traditions of the Jews. Yet these books have fueled over the centuries a killing frenzy of anti-Semitism. The single greatest carrier of this hostility has been nothing less than our Christian Sunday school curricula and materials. Jewish people thus have a hard time seeing these twenty-seven books as "sacred scriptures."

Continuing with the negative side of the ledger, the institution of slavery was affirmed throughout history from words in the New Testament. Slavery was practiced for centuries in the Western world by God-fearing, Bible-reading Christians. Even the popes at various times owned slaves! The section of the United States that fought so fiercely to preserve this evil institution was also known as the Bible Belt; it was the Bible-reading people of the South who made lynching legal, who replaced slavery with segregation and who resisted every effort to keep racial justice from being achieved. Much of their justification for this behavior came from quoting St. Paul, who in his letter to Philemon urged the runaway slave Onesimus to return to his master, while simultaneously urging Philemon, his master, to be forgiving to his slave. In the epistle to the Colossians, the writer instructed slaves to be obedient and masters to be kind. Perhaps it could be said that a kinder and gentler slavery is better than a cruel and harsh one, but it is to be noted that both Paul and ordinary members of the early Christian church clearly accepted the legitimacy of this cruel institution, making no effort to abolish it and thus legitimizing it in the minds of others for centuries. One wonders then today how those who were enslaved and their descendants might view the New Testament, from which texts were cited to justify slavery, segregation and second-class citizenship for people of color. These scriptures were clearly not sources of life to these victims of our prejudice.

Women have also not fared well at the hands of these male-written and for the most part male-read and male-interpreted books of the New Testament. Rather, the New Testament has fed the deep-seated cultural misogyny of the ages with such admonitions as those found in Ephesians for wives to obey their husbands, in Corinthians for women to keep quiet in church, and in Timothy, where women are forbidden to exercise authority over men. Under the influence of the New Testament women in the Christian world were denied higher education for centuries. As a direct result of this lack of education they were also denied entrance into the professions, denied the right to vote, denied the ability to own property in their own name and denied leadership roles not only in the Christian world but in the Christian church until well into the twentieth century. When progress did come for women it was driven primarily by the secular spirit, while organized religion, as expressed in the Christian church, resisted these changes with scripture-quoting vehemence. In major sections of the world today this anti-feminist, Bible-laced rhetoric continues to be articulated both officially through ecclesiastical bodies and by individual believers. In the light of this treatment one wonders how women would ever be drawn to the texts of the New Testament or be able to view them as sacred or even inspired.

The same could also be said for the ecclesiastical and cultural victimization of the gay, lesbian, bisexual and transgender people in our population. They too have lived throughout history with Bible-fueled hostility that has manifested itself in gay bashing and in actual murder. Texts have been quoted from Romans that called homosexuality "unnatural" and condemned it, and from other epistles that mistranslated the Greek word *arcenokoitus,* which refers to a passive male, but which has generally been translated as one who is deviant, a sodomite or a pervert (even though the word's original meaning was probably a reference to male prostitutes, possibly even Temple prostitutes). There is no doubt that the center of homophobia in the Western world today remains inside the Christian church, now ghettoized from the mainstream of society, and this homophobia is regularly articulated by Christian voices from the pope to evangelical Protestant leaders. In the light of these realities one wonders how homosexual people could ever appreciate the message of the New Testament.

In my experience it is not possible to overestimate the levels of biblical ignorance present today inside the Christian population. Most of the above-cited abuses rise out of that ignorance of scripture. Much preaching that emanates from both Catholic and Protestant pulpits not only reflects that ignorance, but also continues to spread it.

In this study of the New Testament I will attempt to counter this biblical ignorance and to break the grip that it continues to have on much of our population. Using the resources of contemporary biblical scholarship, I will, in this section of this book, seek to articulate clearly how these various books came to be written and in that process endeavor to oppose the rampant literal misunderstanding that is entrenched in so much of our culture today in regard to the Bible. I will go into both the meaning and the key points of each New Testament book just as I have done with the books of the Old Testament. I will try to show the differences among the four gospels that reveal more contradictions than most people believe to be possible. I hope you, my readers, will enjoy the journey. I know I will.

At the very least I hope people find through this book a richness in the Bible that small ecclesiastical minds have tried for centuries to hide from the average pew-sitter. I know that this has been my experience as a student of the Bible and I hope I can make evident through this book both my intense love and my boundless enthusiasm for the New Testament. The Bible has been my companion for a lifetime of study. I began reading this book on Christmas day when I was twelve years old. My father had died in September of that year and my religious interest must have been visible to my mother, who gave me that Christmas my own personal Bible. It was a large, leather-bound volume with gilt-edged, tissue-thin pages on which the words of Jesus were printed in red. That night I began a lifelong love affair that sometimes was a love/hate affair with the Bible. I continue to study it daily. It is that study which will be evident as these pages are turned.

CHAPTER 28

Dating the Historical Jesus

I n order to understand the New Testament with any real integrity, that document must also, as we have just demonstrated with the Old Testament, be placed into its historical setting. The events in the life of Jesus of Nazareth did not happen in a vacuum, nor are these biblically described events necessarily history, as history is now defined. Understanding the New Testament requires both of these realities to be embraced. Not only was Jesus born in, shaped by and interpreted through a particular period of history, but the narrative details of his life found in the gospels were not recorded until somewhere between two and three generations after his life had come to its end. Both of these facts are ignored in many church circles today.

First we need to seek to fix the dates around the life of Jesus. That is accomplished by an appeal to both the remembered story of his life and the secular records that we can locate, which date other people who appear in his story. It is not an exact science, but it is the best we have and is, I believe, in general a trustworthy guide.

Accounts of Jesus' birth are recorded in only two of the gospels, Matthew and Luke. While no reputable scholar today thinks of these stories as literal history, we do find some historical links in the stories that we can use for dating purposes. Both gospels associate the birth of Jesus with the reign of King Herod, who was known as Herod the Great. Matthew, the earlier of these two sources, weaves his story of the wise men around references to the reign of Herod. He also casts Herod in the familiar Jewish role of the wicked king who sought to destroy God's promised deliverer. Matthew, in effect, retells the story of Moses as if it were a Jesus story, simply substituting Herod for the pharaoh. While these human stories are messianic interpretations and not remembered history, there is no reason to suggest that this means the anchoring of the birth of Jesus to the reign of Herod was itself fanciful. Matthew is even more specific than this, suggesting that the birth of Jesus took place near the end of Herod's reign, just prior to his death. When we turn to secular records, we learn that Herod reigned in this Jewish nation from 37 BCE until his death in 4 BCE.

We also know from historical records that, at the time of Herod's death, the Jewish nation was subdivided into three provinces, each ruled first by the sons of Herod and later, at least in the case of the province known as Judea, which was the partial successor to the nation of Judah, by an appointed Roman procurator.

Luke confirms this tradition when he dates the births of both John the Baptist and Jesus as occurring when Herod was king of Judea. Luke adds that this was also when Caesar Augustus was on the throne of the Roman Empire and Quirinius was governor of Syria. Secular records, however, reveal that Quirinius, who did not come to power until 6–7 CE, does not fit well into this historical reconstruction. Luke appears to have inserted Quirinius into his story to support his idea that a general taxation or enrollment was ordered in which people had to return to their family's ancestral home, a device Luke uses to explain how Jesus' birth happened to occur in Bethlehem. The association of the birth of Jesus with the last year or years of Herod's reign is, however, fairly clear in Luke, and we can assume that both this reference to Herod and Matthew's reference to Herod got fixed in the memory of the Christian community. It is for these reasons that most scholars today date the birth of Jesus no later than 4 BCE, the date of the death of King Herod, and probably no earlier than 6 BCE. I tend to share in that bit of historic reconstruction and have adopted as my "best guess" the year 4 BCE as the time when Jesus was born. I am fairly certain, however, that his birth took place in Nazareth, as the first gospel of Mark and the last gospel of John both assume, and not in Bethlehem, as Matthew and Luke seek to defend. The pressure to transfer his birth to Bethlehem is a clear bow to later messianic development. It was Paul, writing to the Romans around the year 58 CE, who first claimed that Jesus was in the Davidic line and thus heir to his throne (Rom. 1:3). This was the reference, I believe, that ultimately gave rise to a Bethlehem birth story.

So, with the birth date fairly accurately set, we search for a way to determine the date on which the end of the life of Jesus occurred. Once again we discover that the gospel tradition is clear in one historical association. It connects the crucifixion of Jesus with the procuratorship of a Roman official known as Pontius Pilate. Although Pilate is not mentioned in Paul's writings, the first gospel of Mark, written in the early years of the eighth decade of the Common Era, anchors the passion and death of Jesus during the reign of Pilate so deeply that it would be hard to suggest that these two things were not significantly linked.

Pilate enters Mark's gospel when the arrested Jesus, having been interrogated by the Jewish authorities, is delivered to Pilate early in the morning of the day of the crucifixion. Pilate receives ten other mentions in Mark's gospel, all associated with the passion story, the last one occurring when Pilate allows the body, now confirmed to be dead, to be delivered to Joseph of Arimathea for burial. While the historicity of this burial narrative in the newly hewn tomb in the garden of Joseph is largely doubted, the connection between the crucifixion and Pilate is not. Matthew refers to Pilate nine times, all in connection with the story of the crucifixion. Luke has twelve such references, but Luke has included two pre-crucifixion mentions, one to date the beginning of Jesus' public ministry (3:1), and the other to chronicle Pilate's role in a previous Galilean uprising (13:1). John raises the number of Pilate references to twenty-one. It is also worth noting that, in these two later gospels of Luke and John, Pilate grows into a more and more sympathetic figure, while Judas and the Jewish leadership appear to turn more and more negative. We thus can see in the texts themselves traditions and memories changing and developing. To complete the biblical record, Pilate is mentioned three times in the book of Acts (which is really a second volume of Luke), always in speeches attributed to the apostles Peter and Paul. There is only one reference to Pilate in the epistles. It occurs in I Timothy, an epistle whose Pauline authorship is universally denied and is dated to a much later period of Christian history. So, once again, without claiming more than history can validate, we can conclude that the crucifixion of Jesus was connected to the reign of a man named Pontius Pilate as Roman procurator.

If we accept that fact as being settled, we can then go to Roman records to learn that Pilate served in this post in Judea from 26–36 CE, which gives us the limits within which to locate the crucifixion. Through other means, too lengthy to go into here, but leaning on narratives about Pilate's removal from office recorded by Josephus, a first-century Jewish historian, we can narrow that eleven-year span and state the high probability that the crucifixion happened at some time near the year 30 CE. This guess could be off by some two years on either side, but it still remains the closest on which we can come to consensus. Our conclusion, then, is that Jesus lived between 6 BCE and 32 CE at the outside and, to focus it a little more narrowly, our best guess would be between 4 BCE and 30 CE. The range of the life of Jesus, according to our most informed estimate, would thus have been between thirty-four and thirty-eight years.

I have no doubt that Jesus was a figure of history and am completely unimpressed by those recent writers who have tried to prove that he was a mythological figure of Jewish or early Christian fantasy based on Egyptian sources.[1] I think the biographical

---

1   I refer to two books that have gained significant popularity in the last decade. One is *The Jesus Mysteries* by Timothy Freke and Peter Gandy, and the other is *The Pagan Christ* by Canadian author Tom Harpur. I enjoyed both books and have great appreciation for Tom Harpur, whom I know personally, but I do not think either book succeeds in making its case. The two books are interdependent since Harpur leans heavily on Freke and Gandy. See bibliography for details on both.

notes recorded in one of Paul's earliest and most surely authentic epistles (Gal.1:18–24) are determinative. Paul relates a conversation that he had with Peter and James, whom he identified as "the Lord's brother," some three years after his conversion. According to our best historical analysis this conversation would have occurred no less than four and no more than nine years after the death of Jesus. That is far too short a span of time for mythology to develop. This means that while not all the details of the Jesus story are certifiably historical, Jesus himself is. So, again, we locate Jesus in human history as having lived between roughly 4 BCE and 30 CE.

Two things become obvious immediately from this dating exercise. First, Jesus' entire life was lived as a Jew under the domination of the Roman Empire. He was part of a conquered and oppressed people.[2] Rome first took over the rule of this land in 65 BCE in an alliance with the successors of the Maccabees and ruled it with an iron hand until the fall of the Roman Empire. In a war during the years 66–73 CE the Romans forcefully stamped out a rebellion by the Jewish zealots, which resulted in the destruction of Jerusalem and the Temple. While that destruction happened well after the life of Jesus, it did occur before any of the gospels were written, and scholars now believe that this destruction of Jerusalem shaped the memory of Jesus in the gospels far more than was once recognized. We will look at this assertion later.

The second conclusion that this dating analysis makes obvious is that the earliest records we have of anyone writing anything about Jesus are the works of Paul, who did his writing between 51 and 64 CE, or twenty-one to thirty-four years after the death of Jesus. That means that there is a total absence of information and thus a total silence for at least twenty years after the life of Jesus ended in crucifixion before a single detail about Jesus was written down by anyone anywhere in a form that has endured to this day. Even then, we need to note that Paul tells us very little about the day-to-day life and actions of Jesus and that

---

2   The best analysis of this reality of which I am aware is in the work of John Dominic Crossan. See bibliography for details.

Paul died before any gospel had been written. The gospels, from which we get most of our image of Jesus, were written between the early 70s and the late 90s, or some forty to almost seventy years after his death. This means that the gospels are not eyewitness accounts, but are rather the products of the second and even the third generation of Christians. The gospels were also written in Greek, a language that neither Jesus nor his disciples spoke or wrote. Given all these facts, we need to dispense with the idea that these books were intended to be either history or biography. They clearly had a very different purpose.

That introductory discussion should be enough to destabilize many of the assumptions that faithful, but not necessarily well-informed, people have made over the centuries about the New Testament. It also sets the stage for us to begin to examine these Christian scriptures with fresh eyes and open minds. That is my purpose as we enter this section of our analysis of the Bible.

CHAPTER 29

Dating the New Testament in Relation to the Life of Jesus

As was noted previously, the books of the New Testament were written, according to our best scholarship, between the years 51 CE at the earliest and 135 CE at the latest. During these approximately eighty-four years the Middle East, the region out of which these books emerged, was undergoing constant turmoil and change. Those tensions inevitably find expression throughout these writings, and they lead us to a series of almost incontrovertible conclusions, which I will begin stating in this chapter with little or no explanation. The explanations will come later, so listen closely.

We have no original words of Jesus in the language in which he spoke in the entire New Testament. We have no firsthand accounts of the things he is supposed to have done. Even the earliest narrative describing the crucifixion (Mark 14:17–15:47) is a creation of at least the second generation of Jesus' disciples, and it is constructed not on eyewitness testimony, but on the interpretive use of the Hebrew scriptures to portray Jesus as the fulfillment of Jewish expectations. Having established the dates for Jesus' life, we now must line up the books of the New Testament on the time grid of the first century so that we can discern how the various books included therein are related to history. By doing that we can trace such things as when various new claims for Jesus arose and why, when heightened accounts of the miraculous were added to his life and memory and how developing layers and traditions of the Jesus story became part of the Jesus narrative.

The first written source to interrupt the silence following the death of Jesus is Paul. Most Pauline scholars would date his work between 51 at the earliest and 64 CE, when he appears to have died. Yet not all of the books that bear Paul's name were written by him. New Testament scholarship is generally convinced that only I Thessalonians, Galatians, I and II Corinthians, Romans, Philemon and Philippians were actually authored by the apostle Paul. II Thessalonians, Colossians and Ephesians appear to be post-Pauline works written by some of his disciples from the late 60s to the early 80s. That narrows the sources from which we can comfortably gather our factual material.[1]

Next we place the four gospels onto this grid of history. All four appear to have been written between 70 and 100. The book of Acts, the so-called pastoral epistles (I and II Timothy and Titus), the general epistles (I Peter; I, II and III John; James, and Jude) and the book of Revelation would all be dated generally inside the ninth and tenth decades (80–100). II Peter is the only work clearly dated in the second century of the Common Era. With that dating system in mind, let me now go back and chronicle how the story developed between Paul, our earliest New Testament writer, and John, the last gospel writer. Then we will see what light we can cast on the silent years of the oral period.

Paul is the first person to give us any written details about the life of Jesus, but these details are scanty indeed. Letter-writer that Paul was, it was not his agenda to relate the words

---

1   When I get to the study of Paul I will be much more specific as to how decisions about their authorship have been made. For now I just want us to embrace the fact that there are only seven epistles that are all but universally attributed to Paul.

of Jesus, stories about Jesus or even major events of Jesus' life, except inadvertently. Paul reveals no sense, for example, of Jesus having had a miraculous birth. He says of Jesus only that he was "born of a woman" like all human beings and that he was "born under the law" like all Jews. Paul also indicates that he knows James, the brother of Jesus, but he never mentions the names of Jesus' parents, nor does he tell us anything about them. That is only the first of many ideas that will challenge our traditional assumptions.

When we come to examine the Pauline corpus we will spend considerable time distinguishing between the few things that Paul appears to know about the life of Jesus of Nazareth and the more numerous traditions that developed by the time the gospels were written. Suffice it now simply to list the things of which Paul does not seem to be aware. They include such things as: any miracle story associated with Jesus or any parable associated with Jesus; the role of Jesus as teacher; the idea that one of the disciples was a traitor; every detail associated with the narrative of the passion, from the Palm Sunday procession through the details of the crucifixion, and any of the content that we now associate with the narrative accounts of the first Easter. Paul simply never refers to these things. How are we to account for this? Did he simply omit them? Did he not know about them? Had they not yet been developed? If the last alternative turns out to be correct, can we have confidence in the historicity of any of the gospel details? For most people this possibility will challenge deeply and emotionally their understanding, not only of Jesus, but of almost everything they have ever learned about Christianity. Yet no one can today study the New Testament with any integrity and not raise these issues. I file them now with the promise that I will come back and discuss them in greater detail later in this volume. For the moment just embrace the sweep of the way the Christian story developed as it traveled through history. It was not born as a fully developed religious system. Many things that we think of as essential to the Jesus story were in fact added to the tradition well after the life of Jesus had come to its earthly end.

Turning away now from Paul, the inaugural New Testament writer, and toward the familiar four gospels, we first line them up in the order in which they were written historically. That order is not the way they appear in the Bible today.

The first gospel was Mark, probably written in the early 70s, followed next by Matthew in the early 80s, then by Luke in the late 80s or possibly even the early 90s, and finally by John near the turn of the first century. The first three gospels, omitting John for the moment, are not three separate witnesses, since Matthew and Luke copied large portions of Mark into their works. John may or may not have been aware of the first three gospels. I believe he was and I can make the strongest case for his familiarity with both Mark and Luke, but what is clear is that he was not dependent on any of them. So when we line up the books of the New Testament and read them in the order of their writing, we can see the developing story line quite clearly.

Mark, in the eighth decade, was the first to introduce John the Baptist (1:4), the first to say that Jesus performed miracles and the first to suggest that Jesus' mother was named Mary (6:3).[2] None of those things had ever been mentioned in any written source before. Mark did not refer to a father figure in Jesus' life at all, much less one named Joseph. In Mark it was Jesus who was called the carpenter, not Joseph, since there is no mention of Joseph in the earliest gospels (6:3). Mark is the first writer to introduce Judas as the traitor (3:19) and the first to write a narrative of the cross (14:17–15:47). In that narrative, such now-familiar details as Peter's denial, the crown of thorns, the crucified thieves and the cry of dereliction, "My God, why have you forsaken me?" (15:34) entered the tradition. Mark is also the first to introduce Joseph of Arimathea and to relate a story of Jesus' burial (15:42ff). When Mark got to the Easter event, he portrayed only an empty tomb and a messenger who made a resurrection announcement (16:1–8). Mark has no angel and the raised Christ

---

2   That is the single shred of evidence on which the tradition developed that the mother of Jesus was named Mary, at least until the birth narrative entered the tradition in the ninth decade.

appears to no one. That is all we have of the Christian story until the ninth decade.[3]

Matthew, writing about a decade after Mark, added other unique touches. He was the first to provide a genealogy (1:1–17), the first to introduce the virgin birth story of Jesus (1:18–26) and the first to weave the story of Jesus around the narrative of Moses. I will develop that emphasis in detail later. Matthew is the only gospel writer to suggest that Jesus ever preached something called the Sermon on the Mount, in which Jesus reinterpreted the law of Moses from on top of a new mountain (5–7). Matthew adds to the developing Jesus tradition the parable of the sheep and the goats found nowhere else in the Bible (25:31–46). He copies all of Mark's miracles, while adding none of his own. Finally, Matthew is the first gospel to portray the Jesus of Easter as one who had been physically raised from the dead, though it must be said that on this point Matthew is quite ambivalent. The raised Christ is physical with the women in the garden (28:9–10), but specifically not physical with the disciples in Galilee (28:16–20).

Luke, writing a little less than a decade after Matthew, builds on the miraculous birth story, adding a number of details that do not harmonize with Matthew. In Luke, for example, angels have replaced the star and shepherds have replaced the magi (2:1–8). Luke adds two new miracle stories to the expanding tradition: the raising from the dead of the widow's son at Nain (7:1ff) and the healing of the ten lepers (17:18–19). Luke is also the source of the best known of Jesus' parables: the good Samaritan (10:25), the prodigal son (15:11ff) and Lazarus and the rich man (16:19ff), none of which appears in any other gospel. Luke specifically omits the cry of dereliction from the story of the crucifixion— the cry that Mark and Matthew state was his only utterance from the cross. He then proceeds to add three new words from the cross that had never before been mentioned (23:34, 43, 45). Luke also makes the resurrection quite physical (24:39), and adds

---

3   Readers need to be aware that Mark's gospel ends at verse 8 of chapter 16. All material that appears in some texts (such as the King James Version) after verse 8 is an early-second-century addition to Mark's gospel.

to the tradition the stories of both the ascension and Pentecost, never mentioned before (Luke 24:50–53, Acts 1–2).

John, writing his gospel in the final years of the tenth decade, adds two new miracle stories to the Jesus tradition: the turning of water into wine in Cana of Galilee (2:1–11) and the raising of Lazarus from the dead (11:1–44). He expands the teaching of Jesus, frequently turning that teaching into long, highly developed theological monologues that seem quite foreign to the Jesus of history. John prefers to use the word "sign" instead of the word "miracle," and he makes the ascension something that occurred not after but before Jesus appeared for the first time to the disciples (20:11–18), violating the order that Luke has suggested (Luke 24 and Acts 1).

This very brief analysis gives us a sense of how the Jesus story unfolded in the writing of the gospels. We will fill in the details later. For now, however, I simply want my readers to be aware that scholarly analysis suggests a dramatic expansion of the Jesus story in the written records that we possess and which we can date quite accurately between 70 and 100. With that insight clearly in mind, I ask you to wonder with me about how the story might have grown from 30 to 70, a time-span for which we have little or no data for comparison. That exercise will prepare us to look at the New Testament in a different way from the one with which most of us are familiar. So we turn now and try first to walk through that dark tunnel where oral data was once available, but is no longer.

CHAPTER 30

The Oral Period

Where did the story of Jesus reside in that oral period of time I have described as a "dark tunnel"? The years between the date of the crucifixion and the first epistle written by Paul are years of absolute silence, from which we have nothing that has survived in writing to this day. From the years 51–64, we have available to us Paul alone, but, as we have noted, he relates very little about what Jesus actually said or did. It is not until we get to the gospels, which were written forty to seventy years after the end of Jesus' life, that we receive a consistent story, but what increasingly we have to face is that few of the details of that story can be looked at as history. In the previous chapter we noted when various aspects of the Jesus story entered the tradition. If the tradition grew between the earliest gospel, Mark, and the latest gospel, John, in ways that we can now document, then how much did it grow and change between the end of Jesus' life and the first gospel? In this chapter, I will seek to muster whatever light we can find to explore this tunnel of darkness.

Where does one go to look for clues? I know of only one possible place. If a subject is filtered through any vehicle—by that I mean any institution or societal system—for a significant number of years, that vehicle ought to show an imprint. So we study the gospels looking for signs that identify how the Jesus material was preserved. Such signs are not hard to find in the gospels.

The first clue comes when we examine how often the word "synagogue" appears in those gospels. One finds a reference to the synagogue or to synagogues eleven times in Mark, nine times in Matthew, sixteen times in Luke and five times in John. Historically we know that the Christian movement was expelled from the synagogue about the year 88 CE and that John's gospel is the only one of the four that reflects that expulsion, which is perhaps why synagogue references drop off in John. The fact remains that deep into the fabric of the Jesus story, as we have that story in the gospels, a very significant connection is observable between people's memory of Jesus and the synagogue life of the Jews.

The second clue is to note that by the time the gospels came to be written, the memory of Jesus had already been interpreted through the Jewish scriptures; indeed, Jesus had already come to be understood as the fulfillment of the Jewish scriptures. There are references to these scriptures in almost every account of the four gospels. Indeed, the gospel writers assume that their readers or listeners already possess a deep familiarity with the Hebrew scriptures, since they make no effort to explain such references. In the opening verse of the first gospel, for example, the author, Mark, wrote these words: "The beginning of the gospel of Jesus Christ; as it is written in the prophets." He then proceeded to quote both Malachi and Isaiah. Mark then moved on quickly to introduce John the Baptist and to recount the story of Jesus' baptism by John. Anyone familiar with the Hebrew scriptures will recognize immediately that John the Baptist has already been interpreted as the forerunner of the messiah, a role that Jewish messianic thinking assigned to Elijah. Mark has clothed John with camel's hair and a leather girdle (1:6), which was reminiscent of the clothing in which Elijah was portrayed in the Old Testament (II Kings 1:8). Mark has suggested that John's diet consisted of "locusts and wild honey" (1:6), the food of the wilderness in which Elijah lived. Only those familiar with the Jewish scriptures would understand the level of communication that was going on here.

The feeding of the multitude by Jesus with five loaves and two fish in Mark (6:30–44) is reminiscent of the story in the Hebrew scriptures of Moses providing bread to feed the multitude in the wilderness, which is described in the book of Exodus (16:46ff). The miracles that Mark is the first to tie to the story of Jesus are closely identified with the miracles attributed to Old Testament heroes Moses, Elijah and Elisha, or with the miraculous cures that Isaiah said would accompany the coming of the messiah (Isa. 35).[1] Once again only an audience familiar with these sources would know their original form and what it was that Mark was trying to communicate.

When we turn to the second gospel, Matthew, we find that in his opening chapters, everything that happened to the infant Jesus was said to be a fulfillment of the prophets.

When we turn to Luke, this pattern continues. Luke, like Matthew, simply copied much of his narrative from Mark, but when he added material, it was often out of the Hebrew scriptures. The two miracle stories mentioned earlier that are unique to Luke's gospel both turn out to be Elijah and Elisha stories being retold, but this time about Jesus.

There are countless other illustrations of the fact that the memory of Jesus had, by the time the gospels were written, become so deeply wrapped inside the Jewish scriptures that this integrative process had to stretch backward in time. The question thus becomes: Where could this coalescing of the memory of the life of Jesus with the scriptures of the Jewish people have happened? The answer is: Only in the synagogue! Why is that so obvious, you might wonder? Because only in the synagogue did people ever hear the scriptures read, taught, discussed or expounded. Only in the synagogue was there any familiarity with the Hebrew sacred story, so only in the synagogue could these Jewish stories have been applied to and retold about Jesus.

The next step in this discovery process comes when we place ourselves inside the experience of the people who lived in the

---

1   I document both of these connections in detail in my book *Jesus for the Non-Religious*. See bibliography for details.

first-century world. In that setting alone does this insight become
almost undebatable. The vast majority of first-century people
could not read. The printing press had not yet been invented.
Books were rare because they were expensive, since every book
had to be hand-copied. Therefore, individuals did not own personal Bibles. There was no Gideon Society to place the Hebrew
scriptures in your motel or hotel room. The only way that first-
century people could possibly have become familiar with the
Jewish sacred story was by attending the synagogue, where the
scriptures were read to the people. Using these scriptures to
interpret Jesus' life was, therefore, an activity that could have
happened only in the synagogue. For this reason, we can be
fairly certain that in those silent, dark years that we call the oral
period, the memory of Jesus—including the things he said, the
things he did and the narratives told about him—could have been
recalled, restated and passed on only in the synagogue.

We add to this knowledge the insight conveyed in the gospels
that the life of Jesus was lived inside and interpreted through the
great events of the Jewish liturgy. When that connection is made,
we have another major clue. All of the gospels, for example, tell
the story of Jesus' crucifixion against the background of the
Jewish observance of the Passover. In the story of Jesus' transfiguration there are echoes of the Jewish observance of the Festival
of Dedication, or Hanukkah. In the narrative of John the Baptist
with which Mark opens his gospel, there are numerous notes that
are reminiscent of the Jewish observance of Rosh Hashanah.

The memory of Jesus was clearly not transmitted through
individuals. The gospels reflect rather the corporate presence of
the synagogue community gathered in worship. In the liturgy of
the first-century synagogue, described rather accurately in Acts
(13:15–16), there would be a long reading from the Torah, the
books of Moses; then a reading from what the Jews called the
former prophets (Joshua through Kings), and finally a reading
from what they called the latter prophets (Isaiah through Malachi).
At that point, the synagogue leader would ask if anyone wanted
to bring a message or to relate an experience that might illumine

these readings. Followers of Jesus would stand and recall their memories of Jesus as the readings for that Sabbath elicited such memories. That is exactly what Paul has done in a narrative told in the book of Acts (13:16b–41), and this clearly was the context in which the stories of Jesus were passed on during the oral period. Sabbath by Sabbath, year by year, in synagogue after synagogue the stories of Jesus were related to the Jewish scriptures read in worship, and this was the process in which the gospels were formed, orally at first, but later written down, to be used in the synagogues in which the followers of Jesus had continued to worship for some forty to almost sixty years after the earthly life of Jesus had come to an end.

Thus we shine the light from the synagogue into the dark, mysterious oral period of Christian history, and suddenly the darkness of the unknown fades and we begin to see that the gospels are the product of the synagogue. That clue will open a rich interpretive vein, which we will mine again and again as our study of the New Testament unfolds.[2]

---

2   This analysis is spelled out in much more detail in my book *Liberating the Gospels: Reading the Bible with Jewish Eyes*. See bibliography for details.

Part IX

Paul: The First New Testament Writer

CHAPTER 31

The Witness of Paul

The first person to crack the silence and write anything that we still possess about Jesus of Nazareth was the man known as Saul of Tarsus, who later changed his name to Paul. His conversion to being a believer in and a disciple of Jesus occurred, according to the work of the twentieth-century church historian Adolf Harnack, between one and six years after Jesus' crucifixion.[1] If we adopt the date of 30 CE for the crucifixion, then Paul's conversion would be located between the years 31 and 36.

The familiar story of that conversion is hardly history, since it was written by the author of the book of Acts more than thirty years after Paul's death and perhaps sixty years after his conversion. I doubt that Paul would have recognized any of the details recorded. In his own authentic writings Paul never refers to the life-changing experience that occurred on the road to Damascus, the bright light that supposedly rendered him temporarily blind, the vision he was supposed to have had, which involved a conversation with Jesus, or even his baptism at the hands of Ananias. I suspect that the narrative in Acts was a fantasy created by Luke to give content to what Paul does share about his pre-Christian life. In his epistle to the Galatians, written in the early

---

[1]   From his book *The Mission and Expansion of Christianity in the First Three Centuries*. See bibliography for details.

50s, Paul writes, "You have heard of my former life in Judaism, how I persecuted the church of God violently and tried to destroy it" (1:13). Perhaps the closest Paul ever came to describing his conversion experience occurred when writing to the church in Corinth: "I know a man in Christ," he says, "who fourteen years ago was caught up to the third heaven—whether in the body or out of the body, I do not know, God knows. And I know that this man was caught up into paradise . . . and he heard things that cannot be told, which man may not utter" (II Cor. 12:1–6). Whenever there is a conflict between an account of Paul's activity as recorded in the book of Acts and the authentic writings of Paul himself, the weight of scholarship always comes down on the side of Paul's own work.

From autobiographical notes found in his epistles we get the picture of Paul as a zealously religious student, devoted to the Torah and proud of his Jewish heritage. It was this Jewish faith tradition into which he was born and which in his mind he never left, since he saw Jesus as the fulfillment of both the law and the prophets. He presents himself in his writings as the star pupil in the rabbinical school, so it should surprise no one that he came to understand Jesus by applying familiar Jewish symbols to him. By studying Paul carefully we can begin to regain the perspective that Paul had—namely, that Jesus was a Jew, and that Judaism was the frame of reference in which Jesus was originally understood and interpreted. The followers of Jesus were at the time of Paul still practicing Jews, still regular worshipers in the synagogue. To say it bluntly, Paul was not a Christian and neither was Jesus! Christianity did not become a religion separate from Judaism until the latter years of the ninth decade, by which time Paul had died and all of the gospels except John had been written. In this proposed time scheme there may be some question about Luke, but even if Luke is dated after the synagogue-church split, it is nonetheless significantly based on Mark, which pushes Luke's content into that earlier time zone. John is thus the only gospel clearly written after the church had separated from the synagogue. So we need to embrace, both intellectually and emotionally, the fact that during the years in which Paul was writing, the disciples of Jesus were not called Christians, but "followers of the way," and they were still members of the synagogue. Paul can thus be understood properly only when we hear his words in this Jewish context.

In I Corinthians Paul writes that the two fundamental and defining moments in the Christian tradition, the crucifixion and the resurrection of Jesus, happened "in accordance with the scriptures." That could only have meant the Jewish scriptures, for when Paul wrote there were no others. As we journeyed through these Jewish scriptures in the first part of this book, we noted various messianic images that the early Christians would later use as the lens through which they would understand the Jesus experience. The most popular of these images was that of the "Servant" or "Suffering Servant" drawn in what we called II Isaiah (Isa. 40–55). Other images out of the Jewish scriptures, however, are also identifiable, as the early disciples of Jesus, all of whom were Jews, sought to portray Jesus as the fulfillment of all Jewish expectations. The words Paul used about the crucifixion in I Corinthians were quite clear: "Jesus died," he said, "for our sins" (15:3). In all probability this phrase was a direct reference to the Jewish liturgical observance called Yom Kippur, or the Day of Atonement, in which a physically perfect and presumably morally perfect animal was sacrificed for the sins of the people. This sacrifice enabled people on that one day of the year to feel that they could come to God despite their sinfulness, since they came, Yom Kippur proclaimed, through the cleansing blood of the "lamb of God." In time this connection would give rise to some gross theories that theologians came to call "substitutionary theories of the atonement," which portrayed God as punishing the innocent Jesus for our sinfulness and gave rise to the Protestant mantra "Jesus died for my sins." The same idea was present in Catholic piety, since the Catholic Church taught that in the Eucharist the sacrifice of Jesus for the sins of the world was reenacted in each mass.

While Paul does not, as the early gospels do, think of the Last Supper as a Passover meal, he is the first person we can identify who suggested that Jesus could be understood as "the new paschal lamb" (I Cor. 5:7). By the time the gospels were written, however, this connection had come to be treated as history, and the crucifixion and the Passover season had become inextricably bound up together. I believe, however, that this was an interpretive, liturgical connection and not a historical memory. From other evidence that I cited in a previous book and will not repeat here, my sense is that the crucifixion actually occurred in the fall of the year, not in the spring.[2]

It is easy for me, however, to understand why the death of Jesus and the death of the Passover lamb came to be thought of together. Paul saw in the death of Jesus an action in which the power of death itself was broken. Recall that, according to the book of Exodus (11–12), this was also the meaning of the death of the paschal lamb. It was when the people of Israel placed the blood of the paschal lamb on the doorposts of their homes that the angel of death "passed over" those houses, banishing death from their households. Paul was suggesting, I believe—long before the crucifixion story had ever come to be located in the Passover season and become identified with Passover, as it is in the gospels—that the death of Jesus on the cross had turned the cross similarly into a symbolic doorpost of the world and that the blood of Jesus, the new paschal lamb on that cross, had broken the power of death for all who came to God through the life and death of this Jesus.

So in the writings of Paul we get the sense that the memory of Jesus was primarily interpreted through the Jewish scriptures and was also related to the synagogue's liturgical cycle, with special attention being paid to the holy days like Yom Kippur and Passover. That identification will expand greatly with the passing years. By the time the gospels were written, the other Jewish holy days seemed to come into interpretive play, as we will see when we get to the consideration of those texts.

There is one other detail in Paul that we need to examine before we begin to look at his writings in their specificity. That

---

2   *Liberating the Gospels: Reading the Bible with Jewish Eyes.* See bibliography for details.

detail becomes apparent in the constant self-denigration found throughout his epistles. I refer to such words as "O, wretched man that I am, who will deliver me from this body of death?" (Rom. 7:24), or "While we were living in the flesh, our sinful passions, aroused by the law were at work in our members to bear fruit for death" (Rom. 7:5).

Do these words and others like them fit a pattern? If so, what do they reveal? We turn next to address those questions.

CHAPTER 32

Paul's Secret Thorn

Have you ever wondered what Paul's deepest secret was? Surely he had one. If you listen to his words, an agony of spirit is easily recognized, perhaps even a deep strain of self-hatred. How else can we read these words: "I was once alive apart from the law, but when the commandment came, sin revived and I died. The very commandment which promised life proved to be death to me" (Rom. 7:9–10). He goes on to say of himself, "I am carnal, sold under sin. I do not understand my own actions. For I do not do what I want, but I do the very thing that I hate" (Rom. 7:14–15). Having thus indicted himself, he offers a rather self-serving explanation, which is little more than a feeble attempt at exoneration. "It is no longer I that do it," he says, seeking a satisfying explanation, "but sin that dwells in me" (Rom. 7:20). Don't blame me, he is arguing; blame sin! It is like saying, "It's not my fault; the devil made me do it!"

Next Paul offers what might be a clue: "Nothing good dwells within me, that is, in my flesh" (Rom. 7:18). What do you suppose it is that tortures Paul? It is clearly something inside him. Once Paul spoke of "fighting without and fear within" (II Cor. 7:5), but while he described the external threats, he never identified the "fear within." Now he seems to locate that fear "in my flesh," and clearly he believes that this fear has power over him to the point that he feels powerless against it. "I can will what is right," he laments, "but I cannot do it" (Rom. 7:18). Once more he tries to find something outside himself to blame and so he repeats his previous idea: "If I do what I do not want [to do], it is no longer I that do it, but sin that dwells within me" (Rom. 7:20). Still writing introspectively he states, "I see in my members another law at war with the law of my mind and making me captive to the law of sin, which dwells in my members" (Rom. 7:23). The word translated as "member" is a strange word, at least as Paul uses it. The Greek word for "member" is *melos,* which literally means "bodily appendage"—like an arm or a leg. How could sin dwell in one's arms and legs? How could one's arms and legs be in warfare against one's mind? Males, however, have another appendage, called euphemistically "the male organ." While being an appendage, it is also a gland that does not always obey the mind of the person to whom it belongs. This gland is stimulated on some occasions when it is quite inconvenient. On other occasions, it is not stimulated when one desires it to be. If that were not so, there would be no market for Viagra or Cialis! Since Paul is constantly suggesting that evil, or sin, dwells in his flesh, can we not conclude that whatever disturbs him so deeply is somehow connected to his sexuality? It seems apparent that such a connection is real, for he concludes this series of self-accusatory phrases with an outburst that demands some explanation: "Wretched man that I am, who will deliver me from this *body* of death?" (Rom. 7:34, italics added).

Elsewhere in Paul's epistles he says, "What return did you get for the things of which you are now ashamed? The end of those things is death" (Rom. 6:21). Paul seems to feel that his life is lived under the sentence of death. He has a deep-seated sense of shame. Paul also reveals that he has a hidden aspect to his life. He calls himself an imposter "who yearns to be" true, one who is "unknown," and one who "though dying yearns to be alive" (II Cor. 6:8–10).

Paul is also a religious zealot, perhaps a fanatic. He is a strict adherent of the Torah, in which he has obviously bound himself tightly. He describes himself as one who obeys every requirement of the law (Phil. 3:6). We looked earlier at some of these writings, but they bear repeating in this new context. I was, he says, "circumcised on the eighth day, of the people of Israel, of the tribe of Benjamin, a Hebrew born of Hebrews; as to the law, a Pharisee, as to zeal, a persecutor of the church, as to righteousness under the law, blameless!" (Phil. 3:5). He even says of himself, "I advanced in Judaism beyond many of my own age. . . so extremely zealous was I for the tradition of my fathers" (Gal. 1:14).

Given that self-description, one must now ask what there was about the Jesus movement that threatened Paul so deeply that he was moved to try to stamp it out, as he did before his conversion. Religious zealotry always says more about the zealot than it does about the cause he opposes. Again, Paul says of himself: "I persecuted the church of God violently and tried to destroy it" (Gal. 1:13). One does not attack Muslims in the Crusades unless something about Islam itself is seen as an imminent danger to the Christian claims that are being made. One does not burn heretics at the stake unless the lives of the heretics threaten something deep within their persecutors. One does not oppress and murder Jews, as Christians have done through the centuries, unless Christians fear that the very existence of the Jews causes that which is basic to them to collapse. One does not fly airplanes into the World Trade Center and the Pentagon to "kill the infidels" unless those infidels call into question the truth by which Islamic fundamentalists live. That is the nature of religious fanaticism and persecution historically, including the torture and death that often flow out of such fanaticism. Since Paul persecuted the Christians, we need to ask what there was about the Christian movement that caused him to believe that if the Christian movement survived, he might not. That is the question that fanaticism in any form asks. So our search continues.

Another autobiographical detail appears in his epistles when Paul counsels those who are not married "to remain as I am"—that is, single (I Cor. 7:8). So we know that Paul was not married. He also counseled those who could not control their sexual desires to marry, since as he stated, "It is better to marry than to be aflame with passion" (I Cor. 7:9). Paul, however, never sought to alleviate his internal pressures by following his own advice. Paul actually seemed to have negativity toward women. Women do not like him to this day, especially women priests. He warned his readers against even touching a woman, yet he seemed to have a peculiar attraction for a woman's hair, about which he made overt references (I Cor. 11:6, 14, 15).

Paul also shared with his readers that he possessed a "thorn in his flesh," which he never defined, but which he prayed for God to take away (II Cor. 12:7–9). It appears that the removal of this thorn was beyond God's power, which meant that it was a given and not the result of Paul's doing. It was of Paul's very being. There is finally one other revealing passage in the Pauline corpus that, for me, pulls this investigation together. In the first chapter of Romans, a text frequently cited to uphold the deep prejudice in the Christian church against homosexuality, Paul suggests that homosexuality is actually a punishment inflicted by God on those who do not worship God properly (1:21–27). In other words, Paul argues that God, as a punishment for not paying attention to the intimate details of worship, confuses human sexuality so that men are attracted to men and women to women. It was and is a strange argument, but one perhaps understandable to a religious person who feels driven to obey every jot and tittle of the law.

Some years ago, while studying at Yale Divinity School, I came across a 1930s book written by Arthur Darby Nock in which this author raised for me for the first time the possibility that Paul might have been a deeply repressed gay man.[1] He would have been taught by his religion that his possible homosexuality placed him under a death sentence according to the law of God as recorded in Leviticus 18 and 20. Paul would also have been aware of the books of the Maccabees, which were very popular among Jews in Paul's time. IV Maccabees states that if one worships God properly and with consuming intensity, "all desire can be overcome" (IV Macc. 2:2, 3:17–18).

---

1   See bibliography for details of this work, titled simply *St. Paul*.

When I put all of these things together a pattern emerges. Paul was a zealot who tried with all his might to worship God properly. He bound the desires that he found natural within himself, but nonetheless deeply troubling and intensely negative, so tightly inside the laws of the Jews that he was able, at least partially, to suppress those desires.

This was the internal pressure that caused Paul to view his body quite negatively. The promise of death, said the Torah, was the end result of the sin that Paul appears to have felt sure lived in his uncontrollable "member." He experienced the Christian movement to be one that relativized the power of the law to control evil desires in the name of something the Christians called "grace," which they defined as the infinite and undeserved gift of love. He heard Christians telling people that they did not have to struggle as he had struggled to be righteous, but they had only to trust this divine love that accepted them "just as I am," as the evangelical hymn has it. Freedom always frightens people who are hiding from themselves inside a rigid religious practice. So it was that Paul appears to have determined that if Christianity succeeded, his security system built on years of binding repression would fall apart. That is, I believe, what led him to persecute. That is also what led Paul to exclaim, in the new awareness after his conversion, that "nothing can separate me from the love of God," not even, as he said, "my own nakedness" (Rom. 8:35, 38–39).

Was his thorn in the flesh his deeply repressed homosexuality? Other theories have been offered: malaria, epilepsy, a chronic eye disease, diabetes, perhaps even an abusive and distorting childhood sexual experience. None, however, fits the details we know of Paul's life so totally as the suggestion that he was a gay man. Christians could not listen to this possibility so long as they were in the power of a definition of homosexuality as something evil. That definition, however, has died under the influence of modern science and medicine. So the idea of Paul as gay, but still a good Jew, is not now incompatible. Imagine rather the power of the realization that we Christians have received our primary definition of grace from a gay man who accepted his world's judgment and condemnation until he was embraced by the Jesus experience and came to the realization that nothing any of us can say, do or be can place us outside the love of God. Paul, a deeply repressed gay man, is the one who made that message clear.

CHAPTER 33

Paul's Early Epistles

I Thessalonians and Galatians

I now turn to the actual content of the epistles of Paul. My plan is to divide the authentic writings of Paul into three broad categories. There is what I call "the early Paul," best seen through his first two epistles, I Thessalonians and Galatians; then there is "the middle Paul," best illustrated through his most familiar works, I and II Corinthians and Romans, and finally there is "the late Paul," best observed through the epistles known as Philemon and Philippians. Please note that these seven epistles constitute what scholars all but universally agree are the authentic letters of Paul. I will examine Paul in his various roles as pastor and as theologian. This Pauline segment of our larger task of examining the origins and makeup of the New Testament will then conclude with a brief analysis of the disputed epistles, the dispute being whether or not they are genuine works of Paul. That list includes Colossians and II Thessalonians, which very few scholars still contend are Pauline, and Ephesians, about

which there is almost no dispute at all, since it appears to have
been written well after Paul's death.[1]

Most of us Christians are unable to discern any differences
in voice, tone or content in the entire body of work that we now
call the epistles, whether written by Paul or not. That is probably
because we never read them as a whole and thus never get a sense
of Paul's specific thinking. We tend to hear them instead only in
small snatches being read as lessons in church and with no context. My hope is that in this section on Paul I will be able to provide my readers with sufficient knowledge of the distinctiveness
of each epistle that the differences between them will become
obvious.

The first epistle that Paul wrote, most scholars agree, was
I Thessalonians. It is, however, placed sixth in the epistle section
of the Bible, because these letters were put into the canon of
scripture according to their length. Romans, Paul's longest letter,
is thus first, and Philemon, Paul's shortest letter, is last. If they
had been listed chronologically I Thessalonians would be first,
Galatians second, I and II Corinthians third and fourth, Romans
fifth, Philemon sixth and Philippians seventh. Following that
chronology, we begin our study of Paul's content with I Thessalonians, and then we will move to Galatians.

In the first decades of Christianity Thessalonica was the capital of Macedonia and Galatia was located in Asia Minor. The
book of Acts tells us that Paul visited both of these towns on his
early missionary journeys. He wrote these two epistles in the first
few years of the sixth decade, probably between the years 51 and
53. Keep in mind the fact, stressed earlier, that at this time Christianity was a revisionist movement within Judaism. Paul went
to each town as a traveling evangelist who also happened to be
a rabbi. The venue for his words was thus the Sabbath service in
the synagogue, though we need to recognize that in both I Thessalonians and Galatians these synagogues were far removed, both

---

[1]   We will take up in a later chapter the pastoral epistles I and II Timothy and
Titus, which are also attributed to Paul, but obviously they are not Pauline since
they reflect a period of history well after his death.

physically and emotionally, from the strictness of the more ortho-dox Judean synagogues.

Members of these synagogues were Greek-speaking, Hel-lenized Jews who lived as members of the Jewish Diaspora. The synagogue was thus not only a worship center for them, it was also their cultural center. Diaspora synagogues had also by this time begun to attract Gentile worshipers. This was an era of great religious ferment in the Greek-speaking Roman Empire. The gods of the Olympus had lost most of their credibility and appeal. The mystery cults seemed too bizarre and had not yet become established. This meant that the synagogue was more and more a place to which serious worshipers of many varieties turned. In the synagogue there was a firm conviction that God was one. The Torah of the Jews portrayed this one God as con-cerned about life and ethics, as well as about patterns of worship. As the Jews moved further away from their homeland many of them began to shed the more rigid aspects of their patterns of worship, and Judaism became for them more ethically oriented, more abstract, more spiritual and less definably Jewish. Gentile worshipers were not drawn to the cultic aspects of Judaism, like kosher dietary rules, circumcision and Sabbath day observance, so these changes made the Jewish religion even more attractive to them.

Paul, as a Greek-thinking, Hellenized Jew, was thus frequently more appealing to these modernizing Jews and the Gentile visi-tors than he was to the stricter Jewish members of the audience, who viewed the synagogue as their last attachment to their an-cestry and homeland. In Thessalonica Paul clearly emphasized in his preaching the messianic claim for Jesus. That role had many connotations for the Jews, but among the most compelling was that the messiah, when he came, would establish God's eternal kingdom and inaugurate God's earthly rule. In the service of this idea the early disciples of Jesus had been consumed with the task of connecting the life of Jesus to the messianic promises found in their scriptures. They thus searched their sacred writ-ings for hints and clues to prove that Jesus was "the expected one." Sometimes they stretched these texts beyond the breaking point. At the heart of the Jesus message was the claim that death had been conquered and that his followers would be transported into eternal life very soon. These Jewish disciples of Jesus, along with many of the Gentile visitors to the synagogue, connected with this aspect of the Jesus message and as a consequence began to form themselves into a separate community of believers, but still within the life of the synagogue. They attended Sabbath day services regularly, but they also began to gather on the first day of the week in one another's homes for the Christian liturgy that they called "the breaking of the bread," at which time they prayed "thy kingdom come."

This obvious desire by Gentiles to be in the synagogue, but not of the synagogue, was more than some traditional Orthodox Jews could tolerate, so Paul and his teaching became a source of divisiveness in the various synagogues of the empire. The Orthodox Jewish believers began to attack Paul's credentials and his reputation. The Gentile worshipers had turned from idols to the one God of the Jews, but Paul had located this God in the life of Jesus and had so deeply convinced them of this that they too had begun to wait for Jesus' promised return from heaven. Clearly this second coming was the message they had heard from Paul.

As time passed, however, the Kingdom of God did not arrive and they began to waver. When Thessalonian family members began to die, the worshipers' despair increased. Something was clearly wrong if their loved ones died before the kingdom arrived. The bulk of Paul's message in this first epistle was designed to assure these troubled worshipers that the dead would rejoin the living when that second coming arrived. No one knows, he assured them, either the time or the season when that second coming will occur (I Thess. 5:12). Paul, the pastor, thus urged them to be vigilant, to keep awake, to be sober and to put on "the armor of God" (I Thess. 5:8ff), an image that he would expand in later works.

In Galatia, the pastoral issue was quite different. The content of Paul's message in this second epistle was the affirmation that in Christ alone believers' salvation was assured. The centrality of Jesus in Paul's earlier preaching had apparently caused those who responded to that message to move dramatically away from the Jewish Torah. Keeping the cultic rules of Judaism lost its urgency in Paul's proclamation of the infinite love of God, which he believed had been revealed in the life of Jesus. This seemed to Orthodox Jews to be nothing less than a prescription for moral anarchy and the obliteration of the Torah itself. So they struck back at Paul and were supported by the heavy guns of the more traditional Jewish Christians from Jerusalem, including Peter and James, the Lord's brother. This tension erupted into the first major division in Christian history. Was the Christ figure merely a new chapter in Judaism? Was he another prophet in a long line of Jewish prophets waiting to be incorporated into the ongoing Jewish story? Did believers in Jesus have to come through the rituals and rites of Judaism in order to be Christians? The answer to these questions was yes for the more traditional Jewish Christians, and Peter and James spoke for that constituency.

For Paul that stance was a violation of everything his Christian experience had taught him. Paul had found in Jesus a love sufficient to embrace him just as he was. Paul had tried the other way, seeking to obey every commandment of the law in order to win salvation. That had not proved to be a path that led him toward wholeness. Religious observance never is. It was and is just another form of human slavery, another attempt to win divine favor, to manipulate the deity with good behavior. At best that approach produces religious self-centeredness, not what Paul would later call "the glorious liberty of the children of God" (Rom. 8:21). For Paul the battle he was fighting in this epistle was for the heart of what he believed was the Christ experience. In defense of his understanding of Christ he mounted a strong counterattack, dismissing Peter's behavior as unworthy of the gospel and expressing a strong dislike for James, the Lord's brother (Gal. 2:11ff). He berated those in the congregation in Galatia who had so quickly abandoned his gospel for this new religious bondage (1:6). Galatians reveals Paul not only at his most passionate, but also at his angriest and his most human. Defending his claim to be an apostle, Paul tells us more in this epistle than anywhere else about his conversion experience, and the meaning he found in Jesus that had been the source of his conversion (1:11–24). When the smoke of battle cleared, Paul stood victorious. The book of Acts would later relate the story of Peter's conversion to Paul's inclusive understanding (see Acts 10).

It is also in Galatians that Paul first articulated the unity that he found in Christ, who obliterates the human security boundaries between Jews and Gentiles, males and females, bond and free (3:27–29). All are one in Christ, he asserted. Paul, in the power of an all-consuming love that was beyond anything he had imagined possible, was now determined not to allow that single message to be compromised. He won this battle, but it was one that Christians would fight again and again throughout history. Perhaps it was that this message of unqualified love seemed too good to be true. Imagine a God who knows the secrets of our hearts, but who loves us anyway! That is the meaning of the Christ story for Paul, and as such it would represent for all believers a major step into what it means to be human.

CHAPTER 34

The Corinthian Letters

Paul was a complicated mixture of many things. He was a missionary who traveled hundreds of miles by foot and by boat to tell his story. He was an intense zealot who would fight vigorously to defend his understanding of the gospel. He was a theologian who sought to put his experience of God into rational thought-forms so that they could be passed on to others. Perhaps above all things, however, Paul was a pastor who sought to smooth out disputes, confront evil and ease hurt feelings in the congregations that he founded and served. When we examine his correspondence with the church in Corinth, it is this pastoral side that dominates. Even when he discusses issues like the resurrection, his discussion is pastorally oriented: He seeks to ease the anxiety in the people of the Corinthian church connected with mortality.

The first thing to note about the two Corinthian letters is that they appear to be composites of a more extensive correspondence that perhaps reached a total of four or even five Pauline letters. By a careful analysis of these two remaining epistles to the Corinthians, scholars have come to the conclusion that portions of these "lost letters," to which Paul actually refers in the epistles that we do have, have been included in what we call II Corinthians. These scholars point to such passages as II Corinthians 6:1–7:1 and II Corinthians 10–13, which seem to contain extraneous verses at places where it appears that inserts have been made into the texts—inserts that actually break the flow of Paul's argument. Despite this strange construction, however, scholars find no evidence to suggest that any portion of II Corinthians is not the authentic work of Paul.

We need to remember that preserving letters in the first century was an inexact and costly procedure of hand-copying, and that no one had yet assigned the status of "sacred scripture" to the writings of Paul. Maybe then his congregations in effect edited those writings, preserving from some letters only those parts they believed were most important.

When we turn to the content of these two Corinthian epistles, we find Paul dealing with human beings who are acting very much like human beings. Paul knows what every pastor knows—namely, that congregations are not made up of angels. At the same time congregations learn very quickly that ordination does not bestow perfection on their ordained leader. Pastoral care is the sensitive attempt to bring wholeness out of an exchange between human passion and human insecurity. It is a delicately nuanced balancing act, the purpose of which is to enhance the humanity of all who are involved. If we need a text to describe what I believe is the goal of all pastoral activity, it would be the Fourth Gospel's definition of Jesus' purpose: "I have come," John has Jesus say, "that they might have life and have it abundantly" (10:10). That is finally both the mission of the Christian church and the hoped-for outcome in every pastoral relationship. Abundant life, please note, does not always mean happiness or even the easing of pain. Many people seek wholeness in quite destructive ways, with addiction to drugs, alcohol, sex and even success being just a few of them. Sometimes abundant life becomes possible only in confrontation and brokenness. Real pastoral care is not about helping another to feel good; it is about helping wholeness to be created. Paul understood that and every pastor must learn it sooner or later. Wholeness is seen in the freedom to be and in the ability to escape the survival mentality that inevitably locks us into self-centeredness. Wholeness is found in the maturity of being able to live for another by giving our love away. It is through that understanding of pastoral care that we will explore the issues found in the epistles to the Corinthians.

The Corinthian congregation appears to have had more than its share of human needs and even to have exasperated Paul on more than one occasion. Some of the issues to which he refers primarily in I Corinthians are simply human divisions among the people—party-line divisions, one might say. Some people claimed loyalty to Paul, some to Apollos and still others to Peter (I Cor. 1:11ff). Beyond that, their rowdy behavior had begun to distort the worship life of the whole people. In that early part of Christian history the Eucharist was started with a community meal called "the agape feast." The Corinthians, however, had turned this common meal into a gluttonous orgy that left some of the poor hungry. Then they had turned the Eucharistic wine into an occasion of public drunkenness. Paul obviously needed to speak to this behavior (I Cor. 1:29ff).

There was also a dispute in the congregation about the meat served at this agape feast (I Cor. 8:1ff). It was always bought at a local butcher shop where, in this pagan society, it had been slaughtered in ceremonial offerings to the idols of the people. Could Christians eat meat that had been offered to idols? Some Corinthian followers of Jesus were offended by this idea. Still others had become enamored with Paul's message of salvation as the ultimate expression of God's grace and the conviction that this grace, so abundantly and freely given, was not dependent on their personal behavior. This meant that they had now become participants in what the church came to call "antinomianism"— that is, some were suggesting that the more they sinned, the more God's grace abounded. This stance appeared to render any sense of personal, ethical responsibility completely meaningless. Still others seemed to have a hierarchy of values associated with certain activities of the synagogue. Prophets who shared their prophetic words with the congregation were deemed to be of less value than those who claimed the gift of "glossolalia," or "speaking in tongues"—that is, the ability to utter words that only God could understand! This was, they seemed to think, the highest gift of all and thus the most to be honored (I Cor. 12:4ff).

If this were not enough for one pastor to deal with, there was also a gender dispute going on. Some Corinthian women seemed to take seriously Paul's words, in his earlier letter to the Galatians (3:28), that "in Christ there is neither male nor female." This new freedom and equality for women obviously challenged the patriarchal value system of that ancient world. Some women, quite clearly, were pushing these boundaries well beyond even Paul's comfort level. No one, not even Paul, escapes his or her cultural prejudices completely. The extent of this boundary-pushing becomes obvious when Paul argues for male "headship." The head of a woman is her husband (I Cor. 11:5), he asserts. He supports his argument by referring to his literal reading of the creation story: "Man was not made from woman, but woman from man" (I Cor. 11:18). It was strange biology, but prejudice always has difficulty negotiating facts.

While Paul's prejudiced humanity is in full display in this last conflict, on most of the others he rises to the pastoral challenge. Paul begins by telling the people that Christ alone is their foundation and that any division of loyalties among the followers of various leaders is based on the inability to understand that these leaders are simply "servants through which you believed—I planted, Apollos watered, but only God gave the increase" (I Cor. 3:6). In regard to the Eucharist, Paul upbraids the members of this congregation for eating and drinking in such a way that some are hungry while others are drunk. He urges them to eat and drink in their own homes and to recognize that the act of breaking bread and drinking wine in the Eucharistic feast is "a participation in the body of Christ" and what Christ's life of love and sacrifice was all about (I Cor. 11:27–32). The Eucharist, he proclaims, is a liturgical way in which they participate in Christ's wholeness.

Paul takes antinomianism on directly, reminding his readers of their mutual responsibility to one another. He suggests that immorality, at its heart, is to treat another human being as a thing to be used rather than as a person to be loved. He defuses the debate about meat offered to idols by saying that since idols are nothing, meat offered to idols is meat offered to nothing, so there is no prohibition as to its use. He continues, however, by stating that this stance misses the point of this dispute. "All things are lawful, but not all things are helpful. All things are lawful but not all things build up" (I Cor. 10:23). It is a subtle, but powerful, distinction. The evil in this debate, he continues, is the lack of sensitivity on the part of some to the feelings of others. Candy by itself is not evil, was his analogy, but to offer candy to one battling with obesity or diabetes is not loving. It does not build up the person or fulfill the goal of Christ.

Finally, Paul gets into the debate on spiritual gifts (I Cor. 12). There is no hierarchy of gifts, he argues, for all gifts are in the service of the same spirit and are expressions of the same God who inspires us all. The gifts of all the people offered in worship are necessary to the building up of all, he suggests. Every gift is for the benefit of the whole community, which he calls "the body of Christ." Following this analogy of the body, he moves on to suggest that their bickering as to whose gift is the most important makes as much sense as a debate among the eye, the ear, the hand and the foot as to which part of the body has the higher value.

This sets the stage for Paul's writing of what is surely the most beautiful, the most memorable and the most quoted passage in the entire Pauline corpus. After describing the body, in which the various organs and parts work together for the good of the whole, Paul says, "I will show you a more excellent way." Then he begins his famous ode to love. "Though I speak with the tongues of men and of angels, but have not love, I am a noisy gong or a clanging cymbal" (I Cor. 13:1ff). He continues by defining love as patient, kind, not boastful or jealous, and never-ending. He recognizes that all human knowledge is partial. No one sees God face to face; we all see "through a glass darkly" (I Cor. 13:12). He urges the Corinthians to put away childish things and to grow up. Finally, he concludes "that faith, hope and love abide, these three, but the greatest of these is love" (I Cor. 13:13). It is Paul at his insightful best.

CHAPTER 35

Resurrection
According to Paul

In I Corinthians 15 we have the first account of the Easter event that is found in the Bible. It was written around the years 54–55 CE, or twenty-four to twenty-five years after the crucifixion and sixteen to seventeen years before the first gospel was composed. The details are scanty and provocative. In order to get inside Paul's understanding of the central narrative in the Christian story, we need first to cleanse our minds of the traditional Easter content found in the later gospels. To go where I need to go in this book requires that I not allow myself to be influenced by gospel ideas written well after Paul's death. So in this chapter I will seek to put myself and you, my readers, into the actual frame of reference that was present a generation before any gospel had entered history.

There is in Paul, for example, no hint of a special tomb in a special garden or of a stone that had been placed against the mouth of this tomb. There is no mention of either a messenger or an angel making the resurrection announcement. There is no reference to women coming to the tomb at dawn on the first day of the week, bringing spices to anoint Jesus' body. Paul does not appear to know of the story that Matthew includes of a mountaintop in Galilee (Matt. 28:16–20), from which the raised

Jesus gave the divine commission. He reveals no knowledge of Luke's account of the two disciples walking to the village of Emmaus who are overtaken by a stranger, who turns out to be Jesus (Luke 24:13–35). In Paul's narrative there is no hint of the account recorded by John focusing on a resurrection appearance with Thomas absent, Thomas's subsequent doubt and his later ecstatic words, "My Lord and my God" (John 20:19–30). All that Paul relates in this Corinthian letter is a list of those to whom the raised Christ appeared or was made manifest (1 Cor. 15:3–8). He leaves it quite ambivalent as to what the content of those appearances was. When Paul speaks about either the crucifixion or the resurrection he employs no supernatural signs. There is no darkness that covers the earth from noon to 3:00 P.M. on the day of the crucifixion, of which all the gospels seem to take notice. There are no earthquakes, no touching of the wounds in his hands and no cosmic ascension into heaven. If these things were part of the original Easter story, then we must conclude that Paul either was not interested in or was unaware of them, raising the distinct possibility that these traditions were not original, but were developed after Paul's death. As these realizations dawn, the traditional way in which the resurrection stories found in the gospels have been understood as literal possibilities begins to fade. This glimpse from Paul into his understanding of primitive Christianity is thus quite revealing, sometimes even troubling, since it challenges what has come to be called "original" Christianity. It was not as "original" as we have imagined.

When Paul names the key witnesses to whom, he asserts, the raised Christ has appeared, or been made manifest, we enter an ever-deeper world of mystery and intrigue. Even Paul's list calls what most of us have been taught to think of as traditional Easter conclusions into question (I Cor. 15:5–9).

Was the resurrection of Jesus a physical event that took place within the boundaries of time, an event that could be documented as a literal, observable, historical occurrence? I do not think so. Paul actually asserts in his later letter to the Romans (written some four years after I Corinthians) that it was in the resurrection that God "designated" Jesus to be "the Son of God" (Rom. 1:1–4). By the standards of the Nicene theology of the fourth century, Paul was thus a heretic, for he asserts that God raised Jesus into the status of being the divine son only at the resurrection. This attitude, which would later be called "adoptionism," was condemned by a future church council as an "impaired" understanding of Jesus. Our study, therefore, begins to force us to probe a far deeper mystery—that is, the nature of Jesus himself.

Paul lists his witnesses, beginning with Simon, whom he calls Cephas. There is nothing unusual about Cephas being listed first in this I Corinthians account. Simon, nicknamed Cephas or Peter, was generally regarded as the head of the disciple band, but one wonders whether this was an historical memory or a reading back into history of the role that Simon played in the life of the early church and thus in the resurrection drama. We will never know for sure, but the primacy of Peter is a note present through-out the gospel-writing period. In Mark, the messenger of the resurrection says to the women, "Go tell the disciples *and Peter*" (16:7, emphasis added). Peter is the one portrayed as making the confession that Jesus is the Christ at Caesarea Philippi (Mark 8:27–30). Peter is the one for whom Jesus says he will pray that "when you are converted, you will strengthen the brethren" (Luke 22:32).

Next on Paul's list is "the twelve." The designation "the twelve" is fascinating for two reasons. First, while the number twelve for the disciples is a constant in the tradition, the gospel writers do not agree on who constituted that body. Mark and Matthew have one list. Luke and Acts have another. John refers to "the twelve" but provides no list at all, yet he refers to people such as Nathaniel, whom he portrays as clearly at the center of the Jesus movement, who is on no one's list. Is it possible that the number twelve was a more important symbol than were the actual people who constituted the twelve? The evidence seems to point in that direction.

The second fascinating thing about Paul's use of the designation "the twelve" is that it is quite obvious that Judas Iscariot is still one of them. Paul had apparently never heard of the tradition that one of the twelve was a traitor. The betrayal involving Judas Iscariot thus also appears not to have been an original part of the Christian story. When Judas does appear in the gospels, he gives every evidence of being a literary composite of all of the traitors in Jewish scriptures, which hardly suggests that he was himself a person of history.[1]

Next Paul says that the raised Jesus appeared to "five hundred brethren at once." There is nothing in any later gospel that provides any clue as to the content of this claim. A few early-twentieth-century New Testament scholars sought to establish a connection between the appearance to these five hundred brethren and the Pentecost experience described only in the book of Acts, but that is a huge stretch! Paul's strange list will get even stranger as it gets longer.

Paul moves on to say that next the raised Jesus appeared to James. Who is this James? Is he James, the son of Zebedee; James, the son of Alphaeus; or James, the brother of the Lord? Those are the three Jameses included in the pages of early Christian history. By a process of elimination, James, the brother of the Lord, appears to be the probable one. James, the son of Zebedee, was killed by King Herod in the early years of the Christian movement, according to the book of Acts (12:1). James, the son of Alphaeus, is a total unknown, never mentioned again in any Christian writing that we can locate beyond his inclusion on a list of twelve disciples (Luke 6:13–16). James, the brother of Jesus, however, was a major player in early Christian history. It is this James about whom Paul expressed his anger in the epistle to the Galatians. It is this James who appears to have been the leader of the Christians in Jerusalem when Peter departed on his missionary journeys. It is this James who insisted that Gentiles had to become Jews first before they could become Christians. The weight of scholarship suggests that this is the James, the brother

---

1   I developed this point quite fully in my book *Liberating the Gospels: Reading the Bible with Jewish Eyes,* pp. 251–76. See bibliography for details.

of Jesus, to whom Paul is referring. The idea that Jesus had no brothers and sisters was born in a much later period of Christian history, when the attempt was being made to prove that the mother of Jesus was a "perpetual virgin." That was an unknown idea when the New Testament was written. Mark refers to Jesus as having had four brothers and he even names them: James, Joses, Judas and Simon. Mark further states in this same text that Jesus had at least two sisters, neither of whom in that patriarchal world was deemed worthy of naming (Mark 6:3). So the intrigue deepens.

The next reference on Paul's list only heightens the mystery. "Then," says Paul, he appeared to "all the apostles." Who are they? He has already mentioned "the twelve." This must be a different group; Paul was not given to vain repetition. A distinction between "the twelve" and "the apostles" was clear to Paul, but it had disappeared by the time the gospels were written.

The final name on the list is the most fascinating of all. "Last of all," Paul writes, "as to one untimely born, he appeared also to me" (I Cor. 15:8). Paul was making the startling claim that he too had been a witness to the post-resurrection Jesus and that his experience of the resurrected Jesus was identical with the experience that everyone else on his list had, except that his was last.

How much later would "last" be? As we have noted earlier, Paul's conversion appears to have come no less than one year and no more than six years following the crucifixion. If that is accurate, as I believe it is, then we have to conclude that Paul understood the resurrection very differently from the way it is portrayed in the later gospels. For Paul, the resurrection was not the act of a dead man walking out of a tomb and back into the world. It was not the physical resuscitation of a three-days-deceased body. A resuscitated formerly deceased body does not wait around for one to six years to make another dramatic appearance. Even Luke recognized this when he placed the ascension of Jesus forty days after the first Easter, at which time, he states, all resurrection appearances ceased. The experience that Paul had on the road to Damascus (Acts 9) was not, according to Luke, a resurrection appearance at all, but some kind of numinous vision. Resurrection thus clearly meant something quite different to Paul in the early years of the Christian church than it came to mean by the time the gospels were written. By that time (70–100 CE) the idea of resurrection had evolved until, at least in the later gospels (Luke and John), it had become something quite physical and stories developed about the resurrected Jesus walking, talking, eating, drinking and interpreting scripture in a physically functioning, resuscitated body. That, however, was clearly not Paul's understanding. What, then, did the resurrection mean to Paul? Can we, by looking deeply at Paul, ever recover that original meaning of Easter? We can try, and I will seek to do that in the next chapter.

CHAPTER 36

Resurrection Through Jewish Eyes

The most cursory look at Paul's understanding of the meaning of Easter reveals something dramatically different from the images in the gospels, with which most of us are more familiar. Even at the risk of being repetitive in some details, let me assemble those data that point one in a different direction. In Romans (1:1–4) Paul writes that God declared (or designated) Jesus "to be the Son of God" by raising him from the dead. That does not mean physically resuscitating him back into the life of this world, as many have argued. If it did, Paul's later words in that same epistle would become nonsensical: "Who will bring any charge against God's elect? Is it Christ . . . who was raised from the dead and who is at the right hand of God?" (8:34). We cannot read these words as a reference to the ascension, for no story of Jesus' ascension had yet been written. That comes in Luke, who will not write for another thirty years. "Raised" for Paul appears to mean not resurrected from the dead, but raised into the life of God. This same theme also finds expression in the epistle to the Colossians, which most scholars believe to have been written by one of Paul's associates within a decade after Paul's death, but once again before any story of Jesus' ascension had entered the tradition. Here the words say, "If you have then been raised with Christ, seek those things which are above, where Christ is seated at the right hand of God" (Col. 3:1). This is clearly another early reference to Paul's understanding of resurrection. The word "raised" in Paul's mind embraced dimensions of being both raised from death and raised into God. Later in Christian history these two dimensions of the same concept would be separated into the dual activities of "resurrection"—that is, being raised from death and the grave—and "ascension," which meant being raised into union with God in heaven. It is clear, however, that for Paul those two actions were one and the same thing. Jesus for Paul was not resuscitated back into the life of this world; he was raised into being part of who God is. It was not resuscitation; it was transformation.

This interpretation is confirmed in another text from Romans, where Paul writes: "Christ being raised from the dead, will never die again, death has no more dominion over him—the life he lives, he lives to God" (6:9). A person raised physically back into the life of this world would surely have to die again. That is the universal law of life—all living things ultimately die. It is quite clear in this epistle that resuscitation back into the physical life of this world is not what Paul had in mind when he spoke of Jesus "being raised." Again in Romans, Paul suggests that "as Christ was raised from the dead by the glory of the father, we too might walk in newness of life" (6:4). In other words, in this Christ figure a new dimension has been added to our lives that is not subject to death. Paul then asks his Roman readers how it could be that if Christ is at the right hand of God, we can ever be separated from this Christ. Jesus, for Paul, appears to have been raised into the meaning of God who is love, not into the presence of an external being who lives above the sky. Still later Paul writes again in Romans: "Who shall separate us from the love of Christ?" (8:35). Then he proceeds to answer his own question by saying that nothing in human existence is now capable of doing this. Paul argues in I Corinthians that "flesh and blood cannot inherit the Kingdom of Heaven" (15:50). He is so obviously not talking about the physical resuscitation of the body of Jesus, which would have enabled Jesus to return to his former earthly life. It is not for this life that we have hope, was Paul's message. Resurrection was the transformation of who Jesus was into a realm or into a state of consciousness beyond the boundaries of time and space. That is why Paul goes to such lengths to make a distinction between our natural bodies and something he calls "a spiritual body" (I Cor. 15:44).

We have trouble envisioning what this is all about for two primary reasons. The first is that we are using human words that are bound by both time and space to describe an experience that, if it is real, is beyond time and space. Second, our minds have been corrupted by later understandings of resurrection that involve appearance stories in which Jesus seems to come and go at will. By the time the gospels are written, the physicality of the resurrected Jesus grows more with each passing year. The portrait of the raised Jesus drawn in the later gospels of Luke and John, products of the late ninth and tenth decades of the Christian era, are those of a physical body in which the processes of death have been miraculously reversed. This resuscitated Jesus asks for food to demonstrate that his gastrointestinal system is functioning (Luke 24:4). He is portrayed as both walking and talking to demonstrate that his skeletal system, his vocal chords and his larynx are functioning (Luke 24:13ff). He is interpreted as teaching and opening the minds of his followers to the meaning of scripture, which serves to demonstrate that his brain is functioning (Luke 24:44ff). He is said to argue that he is not a ghost and to urge the disciples to touch his very physical body to demonstrate that he is in fact fleshly (Luke 24:40). In John he is pictured as inviting Thomas to examine his physical wounds (20:27ff). Of note is the fact that only in these last two gospels of Luke and John are the two events that we call resurrection and ascension portrayed as separate events (Luke 24:1–12, 50–53; John 20:11–18). Resurrection, as it is later interpreted in Luke and John, gets Jesus physically back into the life of the world; ascension gets him back to his origins, which were thought to be beyond this world, as part of the being of God.

We need to embrace once more the fact that Paul was a Jew and that he thus processed everything that he experienced in and through the life of Jesus in terms of Jewish traditions. So to hear Paul's words in their proper Jewish context, we have to look at the traditions of the Jews for examples of people being raised into God either by avoiding death or by being "translated" from death into God's presence. In none of these cases was this act conceived of as a physical resuscitation back into the life of this world. There are three such episodes in the Hebrew scriptures and there are references to each of them in the Christian story. It is clear that these Jewish stories served as the examples that were destined not only to shape Paul's thought on the resurrection, but also to inform all early Christian thinking.

The first one of these Jewish "translations" involved a man named Enoch, whose story is told in a single verse in the fifth chapter of Genesis (5:24). He is identified simply as the father of Methuselah, who is presumed to be the oldest person in the Bible, having reached, we are told, the ripe old age of nine hundred and sixty-nine years. Of Enoch it was said that he "walked with God and was not, for God took him." Enoch was considered to have lived a life of such goodness and holiness that his virtue was rewarded by his being lifted beyond death into the immediate presence of God. Later much mythology gathered around the figure of Enoch, and during the inter-testament years he was said to have authored a book that described the realm of God as only an eyewitness could do. This book of Enoch found a place in those writings that are non-canonical but influential, and it is actually quoted in the New Testament book of Jude (1:14–15).

The second of these Jewish stories described the final events in the life of Moses, the greatest of all the Jewish heroes, the founder of Israel and the father of the law. The death of Moses is recorded in Deuteronomy 34 with great care, but also with much mystery. Moses was said to have died in the wilderness of the land of Moab with only God present. God was said to have buried him in a grave that God had prepared, the location of which is "unknown from that day to this" (34:6). God was portrayed as writing an epitaph that presumably was designed to eulogize this gigantic figure.[1] It was not long, however, before the tradition began to grow that Moses had not actually died, but had been transformed and transported into God's presence and was now himself an inhabitant in the dwelling place of God.

The final figure in this Jewish trilogy was Elijah, probably second to Moses in the hierarchy of Jewish heroes. Elijah was deemed to be the father of the prophetic movement in Judaism. As we saw earlier, when the Jews defined Judaism, it was in terms of its twin towers—the law and the prophets, or Moses and Elijah.

The story of Elijah's death is told in the opening chapter of II Kings, again with details that are full of wonder and mystery. In effect the narrative says that Elijah did not really die at all. He was rather transported into the presence of the living God by a magical, fiery chariot drawn by magical, fiery horses and propelled heavenward by a God-sent whirlwind. In that new status, as one who shares in the presence of God, Elijah was portrayed as dispensing a double portion of his spirit onto his single disciple, Elisha, who had been chosen to be his successor. We shall see when we get to the writings of Luke in the book of Acts (chapters 1–2) that when Luke wrote the story of Jesus' ascension and the sending of the Holy Spirit, he borrowed many of the details from this story of the ascension of Elijah. In a revealing interpretive clue Mark, Matthew and Luke all relate the story of the "transfiguration" of Jesus, in which it was said that Jesus was seen conferring with Moses and Elijah, both of whom had transcended the limits of death and were already dwelling in the presence of the God of life (Mark 9:2–8, Matt. 17:1–8, Luke 9:28–36). In whatever the experience of Easter was, in the minds of the gospel writers Jesus was destined to join these two heroes, Moses and Elijah.

These were the things that the Jewish Paul had in mind when he said that Jesus had been raised from the dead. The resurrec-

---

1   The epitaph praised Moses for living to age one hundred and twenty without the need for glasses or Viagra! The text actually says that his eyes were not dimmed and his natural force was not abated, but the meaning is quite clear.

tion was, for Paul, the act by which God affirmed the life of Jesus as holy by raising him at death into the eternal life of God. The raised Jesus was thus the one who could mediate this access— that is, he was the way into the eternal life of God for all who came through him. John's gospel would later refer to him as "the gate" (or the door) (10:9). The resurrection of Jesus in its earliest biblical formulation thus had nothing to do with empty tombs, physical resuscitations and appearing apparitions. Those expansions would all come later in the developing Christian traditions. This is, however, where Paul was, and this is what the resurrection of Jesus meant in the primitive Christian community that Paul represented.

CHAPTER 37

Romans

The Gospel of Paul

I
f there is one book in the New Testament that might be
called "the gospel of Paul," it is the epistle to the Romans.
This letter is different from all of Paul's other work in several ways. First, Paul had never been to Rome and so he
had no relationship whatsoever with the members of the Roman
church. He was not unknown to these Roman Christians, but
they did not view him as the founder of their congregation or
as related to them in any special way. He was thus not in charge
of the congregation's ongoing life and it was not his responsibility to adjudicate their disputes or to solve their problems. These
were the things that had in large measure framed the context of
Paul's other letters. Second, and as a direct consequence of this
first distinguishing mark, this letter was a reasoned theological
treatise with universal themes, rather than a response to critical
but nonetheless local issues. Third, Paul was a supplicant in this
letter to Rome. He was in the position of asking a favor from
these Christians, so he was eager to ingratiate himself to them
in order to win their approval. Paul wanted this congregation in
Rome to assist his missionary endeavors by providing him with a

base of support, so that he might expand his journeys to places as far away as Spain. To gain their trust, Paul was concerned to put his theological understanding of the Christian faith unambiguously before them and to minimize the negativity that had grown up around him from the conservative parts of his worshiping community. For these reasons, Paul's epistle to the Romans reflects a clear and concise statement of Paul's conception of Jesus, the meaning of salvation as he understood it and his version of the overall meaning of Christianity. The epistle to the Romans is thus Paul at his studied best.

This epistle is also the longest and most carefully organized piece of Paul's writing that we possess. In this logical, orderly and systematic treatise, Paul moves from his introductory and salutary opening verses (1:1–15) to the statement of the theme basic in all of Paul's work: Salvation, he argues, is the gift of God and it is available to all people. This theme is overtly stated in 1:16–17.

Next, he proceeds to build his case by articulating his perception of the need present in both the Gentile world and the Jewish world for the Christian gift (1:18–3:30). Then he spells out his understanding of the messiah, the Christ (3:21–4:25). Paul concludes this section of the epistle with what is probably the most crucial and carefully stated passage of his career, describing his understanding of what life in Christ is and can be (5:1–8:39). Bringing his basic theological argument to its climax and conclusion, he pens these climactic words: "For I am sure that neither death, nor life, nor angels, nor principalities, nor things present, nor things to come, nor powers, nor height, nor depth, nor anything in all creation will be able to separate us from the love of God in Christ Jesus our Lord" (8:38–39). We will return to the fullness of this Pauline argument in a subsequent chapter in order to explicate the earliest understanding we have of the role of Christ in the drama of human salvation. For now, however, I want to move quickly in an effort to create a clear picture of the totality of this epistle.

Having come to his powerful conclusion at the end of chapter 8, Paul next moves on to what can only be understood as a large

parenthesis, which consumes him in chapters 9 through 11. Here
he addresses a question that is close to his heart as a Jew, and
about which the Christian movement was at that time still torn
in conflict: Why was it that the people of his Jewish nation as a
whole appeared to be rejecting the promised gift of salvation that
Christ came to bring—a gift which Paul believed had been promised to the Jews and for which, in Paul's mind, the Jewish scriptures and indeed all of Jewish history had been preparing them?
So deeply did the Jesus message resonate with the Jewish Paul
that he found it all but unfathomable that not all Jewish people
saw it as he did. We see him wrestling with that question in this
great parenthesis in a very public way.

Paul introduces chapter 9 with assertions that cause us to recognize how painful this dilemma was for him. "I am speaking the
truth in Christ," he begins. "I am not lying," he assures his readers. "My conscience bears me witness in the Holy Spirit" (9:1).
Only someone who is quite apprehensive as to whether his argu-
ments would prevail would use those particular phrases. Then
Paul goes on, with much emotion, to express the "great sorrow
and increasing anguish" in his heart (9:2ff). He would rather, he
says, find himself accursed and cut off from Christ forever than
to find his people, his tribe, in their present negative position.
He argues that the people of Israel are the recipients of a special
relationship with God, which he characterizes with the word
"sonship" (9:4). In that same verse he recites the treasures found
in Judaism: "The glory of the covenants, the giving of the law,
the worship in the Temple and the promises of God." He traces
this Jewish heritage as it flowed down the centuries from the patriarchs Abraham, Isaac, Jacob and Joseph until it came to what
Paul believes is God's ultimate gift of salvation found in Christ
Jesus. Yet he is aware that the majority of his own kin stand apart
from and are even negative to that gift. "Has the word of God
failed?" he asks (9:6). He finds some consolation in that part
of biblical history that suggests that not all the descendants of
Abraham were destined to share in the promise. God had chosen
Isaac, Abraham's second-born son, over Ishmael, the firstborn.

God had chosen Jacob, the younger twin, over Esau, the older twin. These were not examples of God's injustice, he argues, but a recognition of the fact that no one receives the promise of God as a birthright, but only as a gift of grace. It is, he argues, God's prerogative to have mercy on those on whom God decides to have mercy (9:6–18). It is a matter of being receptive. The clay, he states, does not tell the potter what the potter can mold the clay into being (9:21). He quotes first from Hosea and then from Isaiah to fortify his argument (9:25–29). He also calls on Moses to validate this argument. He suggests that Israel is still caught in its tribal identity and does not yet recognize that there is no distinction between the Jew and the Greek since God is Lord of all and God does not limit divine grace by nationality or even by religion (10:13).

Paul wants no one to suggest that God has rejected the chosen ones. It is in this context that he reminds his readers of his Jewish origins and background (11:1). He then recalls that the Jewish scriptures inform us that both Elijah and Elisha were sent to others beyond the boundaries of Israel, not just to the Jewish people (11:2ff).

Finally, as if the answer he was seeking dawned on him as he wrote, Paul came to a new insight, a new conclusion. The rejection of Jesus by the Jews was simply part of God's plan. Because of Israel's apparent inability to hear or to see, the door to salvation had been opened for the Gentiles to enter the Kingdom of God, and thus the message of salvation could reach the entire world. Israel's negativity must be seen as playing a role in the divine drama (11:13–16). The hardness of heart that he believed his fellow Jews to be now displaying toward the gift of salvation was itself an act of divine providence, since it was the means whereby God would offer salvation to the entire world.

In many ways this was a strange argument, but it managed to bring resolution to what was for Paul an enormous conflict. Salvation was God's free gift to all beyond every human division, and even Jewish rejection was destined to serve that purpose. So Paul, greatly relieved by this new insight, brings this segment of his letter to the Romans to an end with a doxology: "O the depth of the riches and the wisdom and knowledge of God! How unsearchable are his judgments and how inscrutable his ways" (11:33). This was Paul's explanation of how the mind of God works.

Having completed this long parenthesis, Paul now employs the word "therefore" to hook the theological argument of his first eight chapters together with the ethical implications of that argument, to which he now turns in chapter 12:1–21. He reminds his Roman readers that they are to treat their bodies as a living sacrifice, "acceptable to God." He urges them not to be conformed to the world, but to be transformed so that they do not "think of themselves more highly than they ought to think." He repeats his analogy that the church must be like the human body, a single whole but with many members. Christians are to rejoice in the gifts of all the members. He urges them to let their love be genuine, to hold fast to what is good, to contribute to the needs of the saints and to practice hospitality. Followers of Jesus are not to be overcome with evil, but to overcome evil with God.

Next, in chapter 13, Paul addresses the responsibility of Christians to the civil authorities. He suggests that all authority comes from God, so the Romans Christians are not to resist those who exercise political power. All earthly rulers, he declares, are "God's servants on earth." It is Paul's variation of the later "divine right of kings" argument. We might note in passing that this and similar texts have been used throughout history against all revolutionary movements. The British used it against the Americans in 1776 and the North used it against the South in America's Civil War in 1861–1865. Martin Luther King, Jr. had to set these words by Paul aside in order to carry out his role as the leader of the Civil Rights Movement. Paul reflects here the perennial tactic that the established authority always uses against the rising tide of a new consciousness.

Paul finally introduces relativity into things when he says that nothing is unclean in and of itself, but it is unclean for those who think it unclean (14:5ff). This idea is contained in Paul's plea for followers of Jesus to be sensitive to the values of one another. Christ, he concludes, was even willing to become a servant to the circumcised in order that through them the Gentiles might also come to glorify God.

Having glimpsed the sweep of Paul's argument in this magnificent epistle, we now turn to examine Romans in greater detail and, through this letter, the core of Paul's thought.

CHAPTER 38

The Theology of Paul as Revealed in Romans

Paul of Tarsus was quite obviously a first-century man. We forget that when we use his words as literal proof texts. He thought in categories consistent with the worldview of his time. He believed that he lived in a three-tiered universe over which God reigned from a heavenly throne just above the sky. Like his Jewish ancestors, Paul had never heard of a weather front, a germ or a virus. He viewed both the weather patterns and human sickness as divine punishment sent from this external, supernatural God and based on human deserving. One cannot, therefore, read the first-century Paul as if he spoke from the vantage point of eternal truth. The epistle to the Romans and other Pauline works are simply letters that Paul wrote about very real first-century congregational issues. These letters are personal, passionate, argumentative and sometimes even vindictive. Paul would probably be the most surprised person in the world, and the most disturbed, to learn that the words in his letters had been elevated by the people of the Christian church to a position of such authority that his voice is actually confused with the voice of God.

Paul was both a keen observer of human life and a perceptive human being; he was, however, also an introverted examiner of his own inner thought and being. Our task as modern interpreters of Paul is to separate Paul's incredible insights into human life from the dated and thus distorting worldview of his day. It is not an easy task, but it is possible to do it.

Paul was first of all a human being with intense human feelings. Prior to his conversion experience he had been a fiercely loyal Jewish zealot, which led him to be an uncompromising persecutor of the Christian movement. Following his conversion he was still uncompromising, even if now as an advocate for the Christian faith. While the object of his passion shifted dramatically, his personality remained quite constant. Almost inevitably he interpreted both what he believed was the meaning of the claim of Jesus' divinity and what he believed was the meaning of salvation out of his first-century understanding of human life, and in the process he always universalized the particular lens through which he viewed his world and himself. One must, therefore, never forget the fact that the insights of Paul are highly subjective.

Paul was also a Jew. I have said that before, but it is so vital a part of Paul's makeup that it needs to be repeated again and again. Judaism framed the thoughts in his mind before he spoke them. He had studied under the great rabbi Gamaliel. He identified himself in his writing as a thoroughgoing Hebrew, passionate for the Torah. Paul's personality was such that he did nothing, certainly no expression of his religious life, in a halfway or lukewarm fashion.

We start to unravel this Pauline viewpoint first by looking at his understanding of the human situation. What does it mean to Paul to be human? From where do the pain, the fear and the insecurity come that mark human life? Paul was quite sure, out of his Jewish background, that human life was created in God's image with God's law written across the human heart. This human creature, who was in Paul's mind almost divine, had fallen from that lofty status into what he called "sin." It was, he believed, a cosmic fall that affected every human being and it doomed all people to a life in bondage to the incalculable power that he believed sin possessed. Paul defined himself and all others through his own understanding of human life. Sin for Paul was an alien power. We are not now and we cannot ever be, he stated, what we were created to be. The human impulse toward sin was, for Paul, so deep that it actually prompted the act of sinning. This impulse cannot be part of nature, lest God be blamed for it, but it none-theless holds human life in its power. When we listen to Paul's words we hear tones of pathos, almost approaching schizophre-nia, but that agonized duality reflects how Paul perceived him-self. When he writes we hear his yearning to be freed from his sinful state, yearning to be able to direct his own life toward the purpose for which he believed he was created. To find the ability to do just that was for him the meaning of salvation, and it was this gift of salvation that he believed he had experienced in Jesus. Human life, which was, he thought, created for fellowship with God, instead has been estranged from God, divided within itself and separated from all others. His dream was to be made whole, to be at one with God. He sought a biblical explanation for this human reality in the creation story that, true to the mind-set of his day, he assumed to be history and thus a divinely inspired analysis of the human condition.

St. Augustine, a fourth-century bishop of Hippo and the pri-mary theologian in the first thousand years of Christian history, would take this Pauline insight and make it the basis for what is still called "traditional Christianity." It was because of this Paul/ Augustine line of thought that Christianity today still wallows in sin. The cross became the place where the cost of sin was paid. It was out of this mentality that guilt became the coin of the realm in institutional Christianity and that is how and why be-havior control has become the primary activity of the Christian church. When this "original sin" was related by Augustine to sex and reproduction, the repression of sex became in Christianity an aspect of salvation. Celibacy and virginity became the higher paths. Repression, however, including sexual repression, never gives life. It rather creates new victims. Christianity has become the major religion of victimization in the Western world. Bad anthropology, an incorrect understanding of humans, inevitably creates bad theology, an incorrect understanding of God.

Paul, perceiving what he believed was this fatal flaw in human nature, saw Jesus ultimately as the rescuer of the flawed ones. Since all human life shared in that flaw, salvation was a universal gift given to all, "to the Jew first but also to the Gentiles" (Rom. 1:16). In this gift Paul believed that Christianity had the power to transcend all human divisions, including religious divisions—indeed, even the divisions created by the holiness of the Torah, the Jewish law, which, like most religious systems, excluded all who were not bound to the Torah. Salvation in his mind was that process in which human wholeness is offered to all. In Christ, he believed, all human boundaries disappeared. Salvation was a call to a new humanity. It was this vision that compelled Paul to become the missionary to the Gentiles, the one charged with turning the message of the Jewish Jesus into the gift of salvation offered to the entire world. When he wrote his letter to the church of Rome, he spelled out this point of view, hoping that the Roman Christians would feel as strongly about this vocation as he did and would thus be willing to provide him with the means that he hoped would carry him and his missionary activities to Spain (Rom. 15:28) and thus to what the book of Acts referred to as the ends of the earth (1:8).

Paul's message was in this sense profoundly true: There is about human life a sense of separation, a loneliness and a drive for survival that do indeed make us chronically self-centered, at war with our higher instincts. Paul's way of understanding and dealing with that humanity was and is, however, profoundly mistaken. Indeed, it is today inoperative, and by literalizing this mistaken understanding Christianity is now all but threatened with extinction.

As post-Darwinians we now know that there never was a perfect creation.[1] All life has evolved from a single cell into our

---

1   Darwin's monumental and life-changing book *On the Origin of Species by Means of Natural Selection* was first published in 1859. See bibliography for details.

present self-conscious, enormously complex human life, which is, for the time being at least, at the top of the evolutionary ladder. Since there was no perfect creation, then there could not have been a "fall" from perfection. One cannot fall from a status one has never possessed. If we have not fallen from perfection, we do not need to be saved, redeemed or rescued. So the way Jesus has traditionally been interpreted vanishes into irrelevance. One can artificially resuscitate a dying form only as long as the presuppositions undergirding that form are still believable. The human experience, however, still cries out for some other explanation of this experience. What is it?

We are self-conscious creatures. All living things are survival-oriented. Plants stretch to receive the light of the sun in order to live. Animals fight for life or flee danger in order to survive. Neither plant life nor animal life, however, is aware of its survival drive. Human beings are. When self-conscious creatures make their own survival their highest goal, they then organize their world around that need.

Paul's experience of human life was correct. His explanation was wrong. His experience of Christ as life-giving love was correct. His explanation of how that love was manifested in Jesus' life was wrong.

Can one find salvation by being rescued from this fatal flaw in our humanity, as Paul seemed to believe? I do not think so. We can, however, find wholeness in the experience of being lifted beyond these boundaries. I am now convinced that this experience of being lifted into a new consciousness was the heart of what the Jesus experience was and it is this experience alone to which Christians must witness.

CHAPTER 39

Who Is Christ for Paul?

The Gospel in Romans

I t was Paul's experience-based conviction that somehow and in some way everything that he meant by the word "God" had been met and was present in the life of the one he called Christ Jesus. "God was in Christ" was the way he expressed it rather ecstatically in one of his earlier epistles (II Cor. 5:19), and the role of Jesus was to mediate this God presence to us, which would cause us to become "a new creation." In Christ we would transcend the deep-seated human sense of being separated, alone, broken and in need of restoration or healing. In Paul's mind, only God could do this act of healing or bring about this sense of a new wholeness. Because Paul believed that he found this healing in Jesus, he was driven to the obvious conclusion that through some process God must be uniquely present in this Christ. This was in a nutshell Paul's thinking process.

How did the holy God, believed by Paul to be external and above the sky, become present in Jesus so that this gift of salvation in Jesus could be offered? That was not so clear in Paul. He gave no evidence that he had ever heard of the late-developing story of Jesus' birth to a virgin, who had conceived this child by the Holy Spirit. For Paul, Jesus was not a deity masquerading as a human being or a divine visitor to earth; he was rather a human life in whom God had been experienced as present. Paul did speak in Philippians, in a passage that I will develop later, about God somehow emptying the divine presence into Jesus of Nazareth, but the words there do not mean "preexistence," as they are so often interpreted to suggest. There was, however, a God presence that was in Christ of which Paul was certain, and in that God presence he rested his claim for the salvation that he was certain Jesus came to bring.

Can we translate Paul's experience of being made whole in Christ Jesus into an explanation that is appropriate to our time, when to speak about God as dwelling above the sky violates everything we have learned since the days of Copernicus and Galileo in the sixteenth and seventeenth centuries? Can we speak of God as intervening in life and history in a supernatural way without violating everything we have learned about how the universe operates since the days of Isaac Newton? Can we still speak of the original perfection of human life and its subsequent fall into sin without violating everything we have learned about human origins from the time of Charles Darwin? That is our task as we seek to bring the epistle to the Romans to a conclusion.

We begin by turning the religious question around: What was there about Jesus that caused the people who had experienced his presence to explain it in supernatural terms? What was there about him that caused people to assert that human life alone could never have produced what it was they had met in Jesus? That was what virgin birth traditions were designed to do, after all. What was there about Jesus' life that caused people to attribute miracles to him—nature miracles, healing miracles, raising of the dead miracles? In the climax of the Jesus story, what was there about Jesus' life that caused his followers to believe that death itself, what Paul called the last enemy, was overcome by him? Paul was certain that wholeness was the gift of Christ. He was convinced that in this Jesus the world, which had long been separated from God, was now reconciled; humanity and divinity, the eternal and the temporal, had somehow in the life of Jesus touched each other.

In seeking to understand how not just Paul, but the other disciples of Jesus too, tried to communicate this truth we have to look at the way the Jesus experience was described in the later gospel tradition. Let us glimpse the gospels now, but we will do so through the thought of Paul and not the other way around, as the Christian church has tended to do.

First, in Christ tribal boundaries were transcended. The call of Christ was to a new humanity in which tribal identity mattered not at all. We see this throughout Mark's gospel, as he has Jesus heal the daughter of a Syrophoenician Gentile woman (7:24–30) and then raise back to life the daughter of a Gentile named Jairus (5:35–43). It is Mark who has Jesus feed a Jewish crowd of five thousand people with five loaves and two fish on the Jewish side of the lake and then feed a Gentile crowd of four thousand with seven loaves and a few fish on the Gentile side of the lake (6:30–44, 8:1–10). It is Mark who puts a Gentile soldier underneath the cross to watch Jesus draw his final breath and then to make the profound pronouncement that truly God was present in this life. "Surely this man was the Son of God" (15:39), the man is quoted as saying. This soldier was not engaged in a fourth-century Christological debate, as he is so often interpreted to have been. He was rather describing the new God-filled humanity found in the human ability he saw in Jesus to give life away, to escape the survival-oriented reality of humanity.

Matthew also addresses the issue of boundaries. He has Jesus' final words be the divine commission to carry the meaning of Jesus, the life-giving love of God, beyond the boundaries of our tribal security into all the world—to those who are different, unbaptized, uncircumcised, unclean, but still not beyond the love of God that this Jesus had revealed (Matt. 28:16–20). It was Luke, writing in the book of Acts, who suggested that the story of Jesus was not complete until it had rolled from Galilee, where it began; to Samaria, the home of those who were the objects of the deepest Jewish prejudice in the first century; then on to Jerusalem, the center of the Jewish world, and finally to Rome, which was then the center of the world itself (Acts 1:8ff). It was John who had Jesus say, "Other sheep have I who are not of this flock, them too I must bring" (10:16).

The Jesus experience that would ultimately dominate the gospels would set aside human prejudice—against Samaritans, against lepers, against women—because human wholeness can never be found in the denigration of another. The Jesus of the gospels would transcend the boundaries of religion in the name of humanity, best symbolized in the words attributed to him that all religious rules are finally in the service of expanded humanity. Even the Sabbath day laws must be set aside if they ever diminish human life (Mark 2:27).

These were the things that seemed to flow from the life of this Jesus, bearing witness to the fact that his humanity was full, complete and free. He did not need the sweet narcotic of human praise in order to be whole. He did not have to build himself up by tearing down another or even by lording it over another. He embraced everyone just as he or she was, from the man known as the rich young ruler (Mark 10:17–22) to the leper, called unclean by the assumption of his religion expressed throughout the gospels, to the woman caught in the act of adultery (John 8:1–11).[1] He loved them into being all that they could be.

This quality of the life of Jesus is more profoundly painted in the story of his crucifixion than anywhere else. Jesus was betrayed and yet he loved his betrayer. Jesus was denied and he loved his denier. Jesus was forsaken and yet he loved his forsakers. Jesus was judged worthy of being condemned, mocked, persecuted and murdered and yet he loved those who condemned, mocked, persecuted and killed him. That is not the picture of a broken human life, but of a whole life, a complete life, of one who is free to give life away because that one possesses life so fully.

The quintessence of his life, as depicted in the gospels, is

---

[1]   We need to observe that scholars do not believe this story of the woman taken in the act of adultery is an original part of John's gospel, but they do think it is a story true to the message of Jesus.

best seen in his death. Jesus is not pictured as grasping at life or seeking to extend it another minute; rather, as his life is draining away, he is still portrayed as giving life and love to others. As he dies, he is pictured as speaking a word of forgiveness to the soldiers (Luke 23:34), a word of hope to the penitent thief (Luke 23:43) and words of consolation to a grieving mother (John 19:25–27). It matters not whether these are the descriptions of an event that happened in human history; they are certainly the corporate memory of a life that no longer installed survival as its highest value. Jesus was bearing witness to a life power present in him that death could not overcome. Those who do not know how to live cling to life with a desperation born out of fear, but those who possess life are free to lay it down because death no longer has dominion over them. That is what people saw in Jesus.

These were also the things about Jesus of Nazareth that tugged at the heart of the fragile, self-denigrating Paul, the Paul who felt fragmented, who experienced a war between the law that governed his body and the law that governed his mind, the Paul who cried out in anguish, "Wretched man that I am, who shall deliver me from this body of death?" (Rom. 7:24). In and through Jesus, as Jesus had been presented to him, Paul experienced the healing presence of the love of God, a love that accepted him as he was and called him to be all that he could be. That was the meaning of salvation for Paul, and since only God could bring that salvation, Paul concluded Jesus must be of God. That is how the mind of Paul processed the Jesus experience. Paul opened himself to that experience and lived into it. That is why he could write that nothing could separate him from the love of God. It was out of Paul's sense of having found wholeness, reconciliation and atonement in Jesus that he wanted to bear the Jesus message to the world. All human life, he believed, must find a way to be lifted beyond its survival mentality into the ability to live for another, to give life away to another. Paul found that power in Jesus.

The Christian church lives today for but one reason: to make people aware of the love of God that accepts us as we are and then calls us to live fully and to be all that each of us can be. Then we give that gift away to others, freely and without prejudice. That is what it meant to Paul when he wrote that God was in Christ. It was not theology; it was experience. Theology explains experience, but experience gives life.

CHAPTER 40

The Elder Paul

Philemon and Philippians

The process of aging works wonders on the human spirit. Even battles once so emotional that they felt as ultimate as pitting life against death lose their rancor in time, and the differences that once divided people so deeply lose their potency. Age brings both mellowing and perspective. That was surely true of Paul. In this book I have tried to read Paul chronologically—that is, in the order of his writings. It is an inexact science, but I am comfortable with the order I have adopted. In that way we can see the changes taking place before our eyes. In Paul's first epistle, I Thessalonians, written about the year 51, he was concerned about the fact that the second coming of Christ had not yet happened. Why, people wondered, had Jesus not returned by now to inaugurate the desired Kingdom of God on earth? Paul tried anxiously to explain the delay. In Galatians, his second epistle, we see the white-hot anger that separated Paul from those he called "the Judaizers," symbolized in Galatians by James, the Lord's brother, and by Peter, both of whom were demanding that all converts keep the Torah and come into Christianity only by way of Judaism. Paul, deeply touched by what he came to call "grace," would not submit to this legalistic point of view from which he had fled—namely, that salvation came through one's deeds, one's obedience to the Torah.

The Paul of the middle years of his career was thoughtful, systematic and good at problem solving. In this phase of his life, he penned his letters to the Corinthians and his masterpiece, his epistle to the Romans. In the Corinthian letters, he was majestic in spelling out the meaning of love, and in the first of those two epistles he wrote the earliest understanding of Jesus' resurrection that we still possess. In Romans he came as close as he ever would to systematizing the meaning of Christ in beautiful words that still ring across the ages.

The years rolled on for Paul, however, as they do for all of us. As he began to age, a note of tranquility entered his writing. He was no longer convinced that Jesus would come again in his life-time, so he settled into long-range plans and even began to con-template his own death. In this phase of his life, again like most of us, he lived more in the "now" and less in the future, and so relationships grew in importance for him. It was at this time that he wrote his two final epistles, which we now turn to consider. Both epistles, Philemon and Philippians, reflect the older, more contemplative Paul. Both were written, according to a major-ity (but certainly not the totality) of the most reputable biblical scholars, while he was imprisoned in Rome only a couple of years before his martyrdom.

Philemon is fascinating in that one wonders why it was pre-served at all, and why it was placed in the collection of Paul's letters that circulated among the churches before the first gospel was written. It is so different in essential ways from every other epistle. Philemon is a personal letter, less than one page in length. It is addressed to an individual, not to the church community. It has to do with a request made by Paul to have a runaway slave named Onesimus set free. Paul makes this request even as he re-turns Onesimus to his master because, in the culture of that day, that was the "right" thing to do. Paul hopes that because he has obeyed the rules, his request to allow Onesimus to come back to him will be granted. Paul tells his friend Philemon, to whom he writes this letter, of Onesimus' conversion and of his indispensable faithfulness in Paul's service. Paul wants Onesimus pardoned for running away and then freed so that he can return to continue his work as Paul's assistant. It is hardly the kind of letter that would normally be included in a group of epistles written to various churches and containing the carefully reasoned argument of the epistle to the Romans. Yet here it is.

John Knox, a top-tier twentieth-century Pauline scholar, offers a fascinating explanation as to why Philemon was included. Basing his argument on an epistle written by one of the church "fathers," Ignatius, in the early years of the second century, which indicates that a man named Onesimus had become the bishop of Ephesus after Paul's death, Knox suggests the possibility that this was the same Onesimus about whom Paul was concerned in the epistle to Philemon. The reason it might have been added to this collection of Paul's letters, says Knox, is that it contained significant material that was important to the church in Ephesus, which scholars now believe was to have been the destination of this first collection of Paul's epistles. It is an interesting speculation and worthy of being passed on, so long as it is clear that it is just a speculation. There seems to be no other plausible argument as to why this private and very short letter became treasured church property.[1]

When we move on to Philippians, we come to the most affectionate letter we have of Paul's and also to the picture of a man who knows that his life is nearing its end. The Philippian congregation clearly cares for Paul and Paul clearly cares for them. He addresses them as "saints" for whom he gives thanks "upon every remembrance" of them (1:3). Philippi was, according to the book of Acts, the first city in Europe that Paul had visited and was

---

1   I read this in Knox's introduction to Philemon in *The Interpreter's Bible*. The scholarship in that Bible is uneven and in some cases dated, but it remains a favorite source for many preachers who work each week on a sermon based on a specific text. See bibliography for details.

where his first European church had been planted. The Philippians had sent him gifts in prison and they were clearly worried about both his safety and his health. Paul's agenda in this letter is first to thank them and then to comfort them about his situation. He fears he may never see them again. He promises to send Timothy to assure them of his well-being. He fills the epistle with words of joy, hope and consolation. He no longer expects the return of Christ in his lifetime and so he wrestles with his own death, which he assumes to be imminent. He wonders out loud whether it is better "to depart this life to be with Christ" (1:23) or to persevere for the sake of his churches. He suggests that when one stands at last in the presence of Christ, this earthly life will be seen as being of no great value. "To live is Christ, to die is gain" (1:21) is his conclusion. There is a deep-seated contentment in Paul that finds expression in this epistle. "I have learned," he says, "to be content in whatever state I find myself" (4:11). I can do all things, he assures his readers, through Christ who strengthens me (4:13). In his conclusion to this letter, he does not go into a long ethical treatise as he does in so many of his earlier epistles, where he moves from spelling out his understanding of Christ to drawing from that the implications for those who seek to live out the Christ life. In Philippians his ethical teaching is one single verse: "Whatever is true, whatever is honorable, whatever is just, whatever is pure, whatever is lovely, whatever is gracious, if there is any excellence, if there is anything worthy of praise, think about these things" (4:8).

The most memorable passage in Philippians, and one of the most mysterious and oft-quoted of all Paul's work, is found in 2:5–11. It is called the "self-emptying" passage. In these words there is a powerful affirmation that, for Paul, all we mean by "God" has been experienced in Christ. When these words were later translated into English, they reflected the ancient battles from the time in which the church sought to determine how it was that Jesus could have been both human and divine, battles that consumed the Christian church until the fifth century. I do not think that the Jewish Paul ever thought in those categories.

The way this passage is read today is that Christ did not grasp after his pre-existent divinity, but rather emptied himself, taking the form of a servant, and he was, therefore, exalted by God to the status which was originally his. Some scholars believe that Paul is quoting in these "self-emptying" verses an early Christian hymn. That may be so, but I believe the passage also reflects Paul's vision of Jesus as "the new Adam." The first Adam did grasp after the dignity of God. The serpent's temptation in the Garden of Eden story was that if Adam would but eat the forbidden fruit, he would "be like God" (Gen. 3:5). The people in the church at Philippi had tensions in their lives over how to worship, what to believe and how to act. Each side in each debate claimed superiority. Paul urged them to let the mind of Christ be their mind. Then he explained that Christ did not grasp after a superior status, but emptied himself. It was in the fullness of his humanity that he found the freedom to give his life to others, and that was how God was seen in him and why "at the name of Jesus, every knee shall bow" (2:10).

The ultimate purpose of human life is to love in the face of hatred, to forgive in the face of pain, to live in the face of death. In doing those things one must be free of the need for self-exaltation. That is what it means to reveal the divine in the human. It was this concept that convinced Paul that the God presence had been experienced in Jesus. The pathway into divinity is through humanity. The pathway into eternity is through time. This is the closing theme in what we now believe was the final authentic letter of the apostle Paul.

CHAPTER 41

Post-Pauline Epistles

II Thessalonians, Colossians and Ephesians

W e have now completed our look at the seven epistles that are all but universally acknowledged as the authentic works of the apostle Paul. There are, however, six other epistles that claim Pauline authorship. Three of them, II Thessalonians, Colossians and Ephesians, are Pauline in nature, but appear to have been written within a decade after Paul's death (65–75 CE). The other three, known as the pastoral epistles (I and II Timothy and Titus) are much later in time and reflect far less the imprint of Paul, despite their claims. So these six epistles fall into two distinct groups. Because II Thessalonians, Colossians and Ephesians all seem to predate the gospels, I will treat them before we begin our study of the gospels. Since the pastoral epistles, on the other hand, seem to postdate at least the synoptic gospels, I will look at them following our consideration of Luke, so that we can continue our attempt to watch the Christian story evolve in history. So before bringing Mark and the other gospels into focus, I want to say some brief words about these three post-Pauline works in order to make our study of the Bible complete. All three, II Thessalonians, Colossians and Ephesians, appear to bear some connection at least to the memory of Paul if not to Paul himself.

We see the contrast between Paul and the author of II Thessalonians almost immediately. Could the same person who wrote the ode to love in I Corinthians 13 have also written these words: "God deems it just to repay with affliction those who afflict you. . . . They shall suffer the punishment of eternal destruction and exclusion from the presence of the Lord and from the glory of his might" (II Thess. 1:6, 9–10)? Those words have a vindictive quality about them, which makes them seem alien from the one who said that without love his words were little more than "a noisy gong or a clanging symbol" (I Cor. 13:1).

Later in II Thessalonians we read words that strike out with a vehemence against those who suggest that the second coming has already occurred, while Paul as he grew older appears to have come to peace about the delay of the second coming. He carries with him no anticipation that it is still a viable possibility and thus feels no anxiety at its slowness in arriving. Yet the author of II Thessalonians argues against this conclusion, writing that the Thessalonians are deceived, since "that day will not come unless the rebellion comes" and the "man of lawlessness is revealed, the son of perdition, who opposes and exalts himself against every so-called god or object of worship so that he takes his seat in the Temple proclaiming himself to be God" (2:3–4). Once more the words of this epistle are so out of character for Paul that they argue against his authorship. They reflect a later time in the life of the church in which intra-community battles were being fought in the Christian churches. About the various combatants in these battles the author of II Thessalonians says that God "sends upon them a strong delusion to make them believe what is false" (2:11). Paul was not likely to have spoken that way in the closing years of his life.

This brief epistle closes with an admonishment about those who are idle and who nonetheless expect to be taken care of by the community. This author writes, "If anyone will not work, let him not eat!" (3:10). Those words have been used through the centuries to condemn the poor and to suggest that they deserve their poverty because of their laziness. It is hardly compatible with the words of Paul, expressed elsewhere in the authentic Pauline corpus. II Thessalonians sounds much more like institutional strife in a community that has wandered far off the path in the next generation. It is not Pauline.

In the epistle to the Colossians the author is clearly in conflict with those who claim that they possess superior knowledge. Some of the mystery cults and the Gnostics made such a claim, but there is little reason to believe that the Paul of history interacted with them in this way. This author also admonishes against the observance of "the festivals and the Sabbaths" as if they had substance, and he says that in Christ you have "died to the elemental spirits of the universe" (2:20).

Both the epistle to the Colossians and the epistle to the Ephesians advise against any rebellion against authority. Both give admonitions about obedience or speak about the need for children to obey their parents, slaves to obey their masters and wives to obey their husbands. Colossians also ends with a note referring to the church that meets in the house of a woman, whose name is Nympha (4:15), which suggests a new stage in gender sensitivity. In this epistle we are introduced for the first time to a person called Luke, who is referred to as a "beloved physician" (5:16). Around that single reference a tradition has developed about Luke that has little other biblical substantiation. Let me say that there is much to admire in Colossians—indeed, I have always loved this brief work—but there is nothing in it that convinces me, or most New Testament scholars, that it is Pauline, so I include it in the post-Pauline category.

The epistle to the Ephesians I have loved even more. Ephesians is the epistle in which mysticism seems to enter the Christian story, with God's plan being to unify all things in Christ. It is in this epistle that Christians are instructed that they are to speak the truth in love. Ephesians calls its readers into a new understanding of Christian maturity rather than allowing them to remain in a perpetual state of childlike dependency, as so much religious teaching seems to do. In its still sexist language it none-theless exhorts us all to "attain the unity of the faith" that we might arrive at "mature manhood," which the author defines as "the measure of the stature of the fullness of Christ" (4:13). We are also directed in this epistle not to let "the sun go down on our wrath" (4:26), which has always seemed like good advice to me.

Finally, in Ephesians we have the account of what it means to "put on the whole armor of God, that we might stand against ev-erything that evil might throw our way" (6:13). In this memorable passage the author urges his readers to gird their loins with truth, to put on the breastplate of righteousness, to have their feet soled with the equipment of the gospel of peace and to take the shield of faith, the helmet of salvation and the sword of the spirit, which this author defines as the "Word of God." Since when Ephesians was written the New Testament had not yet come to be identified as the "Word of God," this author was probably referring to the scriptures of the Jewish people.

Ephesians is a powerful letter. One theory about its origin was that after Paul's death, when his epistles were gathered together into a single collection, the decision was made to send them with a cover letter to a number of churches. What we today call the epistle to the Ephesians is believed by many to have been that cover letter. The word "Ephesus" as the designation never ap-pears in this letter. Indeed, the salutation is a general one: "To the saints who are also faithful in Christ Jesus" (1:1). One of the churches, however, to which this collection was sent was obvi-ously located in Ephesus. Maybe it was even true that Ephesus was the first church to receive this collection and that is how this epistle got its name. We will never know for sure, but we do know that Ephesians has blessed the lives of many Christians and because it has, whether it is an authentic letter of Paul or not, it deserves its place in the canon of sacred writings of the Chris-tian community. It remains one of my favorite books of the New Testament.

Of these three early post-Pauline epistles, Colossians and Ephesians have always been regarded as the most substantive and even as the most profound; and, despite their inauthentic Pauline claims, they probably do deserve to be part of what we call "sacred scripture." Perhaps authenticity is not nearly as important as it seems. Paul's seven authentic letters are the only books in the New Testament that now appear to have been written by the person their title suggests, a fact that includes all the gospels. Given the worth that all of these books bring to us, being able to know the actual author does not determine the value of the work.

PART X

The Synoptic Gospels

CHAPTER 42

Exploring Mark

The Original Gospel

Some years ago when I was on a tour with the publication of my book *Rescuing the Bible from Fundamentalism*, I appeared on a late-night talk show with host Tom Snyder, who was broadcasting at that time out of a studio in Burbank, California. In the interview I mentioned that the gospels were generally dated between 70 and 100 CE. Tom, a lapsed Roman Catholic, bestirred himself and said: "Now wait a minute, Bishop. If the gospels were written that late, none of them could have been written by eyewitnesses." I responded: "That is correct, Tom." "But that is not what the nuns taught me in parochial school," he said. "What did they tell you?" I inquired. "They said that the disciples followed Jesus around and wrote down everything he said, and that is how the gospels came into being." Amused at how naive an otherwise educated and worldly-wise person could be about religious matters, I asked: "Tom, did the nuns tell you that the disciples used spiral notebooks and ballpoint pens?"

It was wonderful to see a new realization sweep across my host's face. So I begin this study of Mark and the gospels with some biblical facts.

The gospels are not eyewitness accounts. They are the product of the second and, in John's case, perhaps even the third generation of Christians. All of the gospels were originally written in Greek, not Aramaic, the only language in which both Jesus and his disciples were fluent. The gospels were written with no punctuation marks, no chapters, no verses, no sentences, no capital letters—not even with a space between the words. All of these things were imposed on these texts long after their origins. In order to study the Bible appropriately we must start with these basic, rarely embraced realities.

There are still other things to be brought to our awareness. The "common knowledge" that people assume and think of as having come from the Bible is not necessarily biblical. It may turn out to be nothing more than the result of an ever-expanding process of storytelling. For example, there are no camels in the biblical story of the wise men, no stable in which Jesus was born and no animals present in that non-existent stable. Many people are incredulous when they hear these things for the first time. Most of our knowledge of the Christmas story appears to have come from attending and/or participating in Christmas pageants, not from reading the gospels themselves. With this brief introduction to some of the problems a serious study of the gospels must confront, I turn now to the gospel of Mark.

I date Mark shortly after the fall of Jerusalem to the Roman army in 70 CE. I see in Mark several hints that support this as its time of writing. In chapter 13, known as "the little apocalypse," the words seem to describe the pain endured by the residents of that holy city during that catastrophe. The people are urged to flee into the hills of Judea and even to Galilee. In the story of the transfiguration of Jesus in chapter 9, Jesus is portrayed as having replaced the Temple as the meeting place between God and human life, for the shekinah, the light of God that once was thought to have enveloped the Temple, now is made to shine on Jesus. That story makes no sense unless the Temple is no more.

I see in the name of the traitor, Judas, another reason to date Mark shortly after the 70 CE fall of Jerusalem. This one takes some explaining, so listen closely. Since the idea that the traitor was one of the twelve and one whose name was Judas was not known to Paul, I look for the reason that these details entered the passion story. The name Judas was identical with the name of the entire Jewish nation; Judas, as we saw earlier, is nothing but the Greek spelling of Judah. Following the catastrophic defeat of the Jews at the hands of the Romans in the Jewish-Roman War (66–73), there was a sharp rise in the hatred of the Jewish people on the part of the Romans for provoking this war with their rebellion in the first place. At the same time, circumstances fed Jewish hatred of the Romans: The defeat of the Jews was bitter. It had resulted in the destruction of the holy city of Jerusalem, the leveling of the Temple and the disappearance of the Jewish state from maps of the world.

In the midst of all that animosity, the Roman authorities were intent on punishing the Jews for foolishly inaugurating the war. Rome was non-discriminating when it came to Jews. A Jew was a Jew to them, so the disciples of Jesus, the great majority of whom were Jewish, had to share this pain with the Temple leaders and the Orthodox Jews, who had, in fact, provoked the hostilities. The Jewish followers of Jesus sought a way to separate themselves in the minds of the Romans from the Orthodox party and the militant zealots whose aggressive behavior had made the war inevitable. What better way to do that than to give to the traitor and anti-hero of the Christian movement the same name as the Jewish state and to make the Orthodox Jews the ones responsible for the death of Jesus? The people the Romans hated were the same people who were responsible for the death of our founder, they said. It was a clever ploy, and I don't think it could have happened until after 70, when the Romans began to pour into and to level the city of Jerusalem. So I see in Mark's introduction of a traitor named Judas another hint that this book was written shortly after Jerusalem fell in 70 CE.[1]

When we come to read Mark's gospel the primary thing that the text reveals is that the Jewish scriptures had already been

---

1   I developed this point much more fully in my book *Jesus for the Non-Religious*. See bibliography for details.

wrapped around the memory of Jesus, showing evidence of the synagogue in gospel development. Mark reveals this linkage in the first verse of his gospel when he announces that this is "the gospel of Jesus Christ as it is written in the prophets." From that beginning Mark's correlation between the story of Jesus and the narrative found in the Hebrew scriptures becomes so intertwined that no one can ultimately separate them. Stories about events in the lives of Jewish heroes like Moses, Elijah, Joseph, Samuel, David and various prophets show up vaguely disguised as stories about Jesus.

Mark also sees Jesus primarily in terms of his being a God-infused, but nonetheless fully human life. In his opening story about Jesus being baptized by John, Mark asserts that this was the moment when the power of God in the form of the Holy Spirit entered into the human Jesus, and only then was he acclaimed to be God's son. Next Mark moves on to tell the story of Jesus being tempted in the wilderness for forty days, but he gives no content to those temptations. That was destined to come in the later gospels, where Mark was expanded with developing stories in which Jesus was made to appear to have relived much of the history of the Jewish people, including a period of time wandering in the wilderness. Increasingly the early Christians saw in the Hebrew scriptures the anticipation of the messiah's life and when they became convinced that Jesus was that expected messiah, they began to interpret these scriptures as anticipatory of their day and of Jesus' messiahship. These data once again point clearly to the fact that the original setting for gospel development was in the synagogue.

Another clue that reveals the synagogue as the place in which the story of Jesus was remembered is the fact that the gospel of Mark is organized around the liturgical year of the Jews. Mark provides an appropriate story about Jesus designed to be read at each of the great Jewish liturgical observances of the year. One cannot see this organizing principle, however, if one is not familiar with that liturgical pattern, which was relived annually by the Jews. So let me file, almost by title, the major events in the annual liturgical cycle of the Jewish people—or, to put it in Christian language, "the church year"—and then I will proceed to place Mark's gospel onto this cycle.

The first great Jewish liturgical observance was Passover, celebrated on the fourteenth and fifteenth days of the month of Nisan, the first month in the Jewish year, according to the book of Leviticus (23:23–24).[2] This would come in our calendar in late March to mid April.

Fifty days later came Shavuot or Pentecost, the day on which the Jews recalled the giving of the law by God to Moses on Mount Sinai. This would come in our calendar in late May or early June.

Four months further into the Jewish year, on the first day of the seventh month of Tishri, roughly mid to late September, would come Rosh Hashanah, called Jewish New Year, observed with prayers for the coming of the Kingdom of God at the end of time and a call to repentance.

Ten days later (still in Tishri) came Yom Kippur, the Day of Atonement. It was marked with solemnity and penitence, with sacrifices and scapegoats.

Between the fifteenth and twenty-second days of Tishri, in our calendar in late October, came the Jewish harvest festival, an eight-day celebration known as Sukkoth, but also called Booths or Tabernacles.

In the month of Kislev, roughly December, came another eight-day celebration known as Dedication, but familiar to most of us today as Hanukkah. It was a celebration of the return of light in the dead of winter.

Then, after the months of January and February came and went, Passover was celebrated once more, usually in late March or early April, and the whole cycle started over again.[3]

---

2   This text from Leviticus indicates that Rosh Hashanah is to be celebrated on the first day of the seventh month. By inference this means that Nisan is the first month of the Jewish calendar and thus Passover, observed on 14–15 Nisan, is the first celebration of the Jewish year.

3   There were some other minor days in the Jewish calendar, such as Purim and the Ninth of Ab, to which I referred in my chapter on Esther and Lamentations. They were not, however, major observances in first-century synagogue life.

As I develop the correlation between the events in Mark's gospel and the worship life of the synagogue, I trust it will become clear that Mark was written as a liturgical book to be read in the synagogue, with its purpose being to reveal Jesus as the fulfillment of the law and the prophets. Neither Mark nor any of the other gospels is a history book. The gospels are rather interpretive pieces designed to incorporate the memory of Jesus into the ongoing life of the synagogue. If you, my readers, are like me, then once this key unlocks the story, the gospel of Mark will never be the same.

CHAPTER 43

Mark's Use of Synagogue Worship Patterns

I n the previous chapter I outlined the Jewish liturgical year. Now I want to place Mark's gospel against that liturgical background and watch the insights develop.

As we have seen, all Christians are "spiritual Semites." Judaism is the womb in which Christianity was conceived and the faith tradition in which Christianity was nurtured until the church and the synagogue parted company in a rather unpleasant manner around the year 88 CE. Embrace that date if you will. The Christian movement did not separate itself from Judaism until some fifty-eight years after the crucifixion of Jesus! This means that the foundation of at least the first three gospels, Mark, Matthew and Luke, was laid prior to the time the Christians separated from the synagogue. This means that for almost three generations disciples of Jesus and Orthodox Jews worshiped side by side and Sabbath by Sabbath.

As we have seen, the disciples of Jesus at this time were not called Christians but "followers of the way." They were regarded by the Orthodox power center of Judaism as a group of "Jewish revisionists" who were dedicated to incorporating Jesus into the ongoing Jewish story in the same way that prophets like Isaiah,

Amos and Micah had themselves once been incorporated, with their words subsequently being added to the sacred story of the Jews.

This close interconnection with Judaism undergirds my thesis that the primary place the stories of Jesus were remembered and recalled during the oral period of Christian history was in the synagogue at Sabbath day worship services. In that liturgy, first the Torah and then the prophets would be read, interspersed with psalms. Next, the assembled worshipers would be solicited for their comments on the scripture readings. In this manner the disciples of Jesus recalled events and related some of the teachings they had associated with Jesus' life to the sacred words that had just been read. Soon those scriptures began to be understood by these disciples not only as pointing to Jesus but even as having been fulfilled in Jesus. Inevitably these remembered Jesus stories were also then incorporated into the annual cycle of feasts and fasts regularly observed in the synagogue. Ultimately, these memories and practices formed a consistent and set body of material that was told and retold around the cycle of the Jewish liturgical year. It was this practice that has quite obviously shaped the message we find today in the gospel of Mark.

With this order established in Mark's gospel, it was destined to dominate both Matthew and Luke, since both of these gospel writers used Mark as the basis of their own volumes. This meant that they inevitably adopted the same liturgical frame of reference that Mark had first used. Even with Mark as their common shared source, however, both Matthew and Luke differed greatly, since they reflected two very different worldviews, about which we will become conversant when we get to those gospels. Still, the first three gospels had in their common Marcan background so many similarities that the three of them came to be thought of together and were called the "synoptic gospels." Matthew has in fact incorporated about ninety percent of Mark into his narrative, most of it almost verbatim. Luke, a bit less dependent on Mark, has still included about fifty percent of Mark's content in his narrative. More important, both Matthew and Luke have adopted Mark's outline and his story line, which was the telling of the Jesus narrative against the background of a one-year cycle of synagogue liturgical observances. That is why each of these gospels presents Jesus' public ministry as a one-year phenomenon—not because that ministry was one year in duration (we have no idea how long it was), but because the story of his public life, from his baptism to his crucifixion, was told against the background of a one-year synagogue cycle. This becomes quite apparent as we lay Mark's gospel out across this liturgical grid.

The climax of Mark is the story of the passion and crucifixion of Jesus. So impressive is this moment in understanding the meaning of Jesus that Mark devotes almost forty percent of his gospel to the last week in the life of Jesus. Of Mark's sixteen separate chapters, the first ten are dedicated to the life of Jesus from his baptism up to his entry into Jerusalem on Palm Sunday, just five days prior to Good Friday and just seven days prior to the story of the resurrection. That last week in Jesus' life then consumes the final six chapters in Mark. Mark's focus, contrary to modern church practice, is far more on the crucifixion than it is on the resurrection. Today Easter draws the bigger crowds of worshipers to the church than does Good Friday. In this first gospel, however, we need to note that Mark dedicates one hundred and five verses of his text to the story of the cross, while his coverage of Easter is relegated to only eight verses.

The first and most obvious fact that arises out of this story of the crucifixion of Jesus is that it is told against the background of the Jewish observance of the Passover celebration. Jesus had been interpreted some fifteen years earlier by Paul, writing to the Corinthians, as the new "paschal lamb, who has been sacrificed for us" (I Cor. 5:7). People have assumed for centuries that Mark was stating as a matter of history that the crucifixion had occurred during the Passover season. I believe it is far more probable that the Passover had itself been used in the synagogue by the followers of Jesus to interpret the death of Jesus as the new paschal lamb, and that this later usage is what pulled the two observances together.[1] It was not history so much as it was liturgy.

Once we have connected the crucifixion with the Passover observance, we roll Mark's text backward across the synagogue's liturgical year. An amazing confluence emerges.

The Jewish celebration of Dedication, or Hanukkah, came in the dead of winter, about three months prior to the Passover. This holy day had been enjoined on the Jews during the period of the Maccabees to celebrate the return of the true light of God to the Temple after a period of desecration. The story in Mark's gospel that falls exactly at the time of that celebration is the account of Jesus' transfiguration (9:2–10). In Mark's narrative the light of God falls not on the Temple, as it did in the Feast of Dedication, but on Jesus first and then on Moses and Elijah, the heroes of the old Jewish story, transfiguring all three of them. This transfiguration story further suggests that Moses, a symbol for the law, and Elijah, a symbol for the prophets, had been subsumed into the meaning of Jesus, who is now being interpreted as the new Temple. Liturgically it reveals that Jesus has replaced the Temple, an idea that will be expressed again and again in the gospel tradition.[2] Surely that could not have developed if the Temple were still standing.

If we keep rolling Mark backward across the liturgical year of the synagogue, we arrive next at the Jewish feast called Sukkoth, or Tabernacles, which was an eight-day celebration of the harvest—the Jewish Thanksgiving celebration, we might say. Here Mark, in the exact place it needed to be, tells us a Jesus story about Sukkoth and the harvest (4:3–9). It is the parable of the sower, who sowed his seed on four different kinds of soil, which

---

1   Those data necessary to make this case very clear are beyond the scope of this book, but for those who might be interested I outline them in detail in my book *Liberating the Gospels: Reading the Bible with Jewish Eyes*. There I look at the body of data in the gospels suggesting that the crucifixion occurred not in the spring, but rather in the fall of the year.

2   See John's story of Jesus claiming that he could raise the Temple in three days (7:19–21), an account in which he is speaking not of the Temple, but of his own body.

then yielded four different types of harvest. This is followed by Jesus' explanation of that parable. Indeed, this chapter not only has a clear harvest theme, but it also contains sufficient material to cover the eight days of Sukkoth.

Rolling Mark further backward, we come next to Yom Kippur, the Day of Atonement, observed some five days before Sukkoth begins. We discover in the second and third chapters of Mark a series of healing, cleansing stories, including the call of Levi into discipleship from the unclean world of being a tax collector for the Gentile conquerors (2:13–14). These were perfect Jesus stories to carry the meaning of Yom Kippur. Once again, Mark's order fits the synagogue's liturgical year. Finally, we come to the beginning of Mark's narrative, which relates the story of John the Baptist (1:1–11), corresponding to the next Jewish holiday: Rosh Hashanah, the New Year. The Jews observed that day liturgically by blowing the shofar (a ram's-horn trumpet), gathering the people, announcing that the Kingdom of God was at hand and urging the people to prepare for the coming of that kingdom by repenting. Here, Mark's gospel, both ingeniously and obviously, casts John the Baptist in the role of being a human shofar, whose call gathers the people. Then John, in the role of the one who prepares the way of the Lord, announces that the Kingdom of God is dawning in the life of this Jesus and he urges people to prepare for his coming with repentance. It is a clear Rosh Hashanah message.

The generally unrecognized organizing principle in this first gospel reveals that Mark has crafted Jesus stories to be used in the synagogue, so that his followers could relate Jesus' life to synagogue worship from Rosh Hashanah to Passover. Have you ever wondered why Mark is shorter than Matthew or Luke? The reason is clear! Mark covered only six and a half months of the liturgical year. Have you ever wondered why Matthew and Luke both felt the need to expand Mark, which both of them did? It was because both Matthew and Luke wanted to stretch Mark by providing Jesus stories to cover the other five and a half months of the year. First, grasp the concept. Then we will fill in the details.

CHAPTER 44

Mark's First Narrative of the Crucifixion

A Passover Format

The first account of Jesus' crucifixion to be written achieved its shape and form in Mark's gospel, which means it was written some forty years after the fact. It is found in Mark 14:17–15:47. We noted earlier that all Paul told us in I Corinthians about the crucifixion was one line: "Jesus died for our sins in accordance with the scriptures" (15:3). Did Paul record no narrative details of that event because there were no narrative details at the time he was writing? That is quite probable, since Mark tells us that when Jesus was arrested, *all*—not some, but *all*—the disciples "took flight and fled" (14:50). If this is true, and I see no reason for Mark to have related an embarrassing abandonment if it were not true, this would mean that Jesus in all probability died alone, without any eyewitnesses. This would, of course, have made the details of the crucifixion impossible to record, since no one witnessed the event.

That would be a shattering insight to many, because we have so literalized the crucifixion details we have in Mark's gospel that we assume them all to be history. When we look closely, however, we note that we are told not just what Jesus said from the cross, but what Jesus and the high priest said to each other and even what Jesus and the crowd said to each other. One must wonder who was present in each of these deliberations and later even at the cross to record all of these words of conversation. The overwhelming probability is that the familiar details of the cross are not the result of historical memory at all, but are rather liturgical interpretations of who it was who died on the cross and what his death meant to believers. A quick analysis of the details from this earliest narrative reveals that the story of the crucifixion that Mark told was drawn not from the memory of eyewitnesses at all, but from the scriptures of the Jewish people, primarily Psalm 22 and Isaiah 53. That means that this crucifixion narrative is interpretive material, not eyewitness reporting. Embrace the fact that even this central story of the final events in Jesus' life now looks like the work of an interpretive imagination more than it looks like the work of a historian. One has only to read the two Hebrew scripture sources on which Mark's story of the cross is based to conclude that it was written to conform to the images found there.

From Psalm 22, Mark drew some of the most familiar elements of his story. The cry of dereliction, "My God, my God, why have you forsaken me?" (15:34), which he places on the lips of the dying Jesus is actually lifted from the first verse of Psalm 22. Next Mark refers to the attitude of the mocking crowd, "shaking their heads" and stating that, "since he trusted in God, let God deliver him" (Mark 15:29, 30). Mark has incorporated this almost verbatim into his narrative from Psalm 22:8. The notion of Jesus' disjointed bones connected with the process of crucifixion generally is found in Psalm 22:14. The reality of Jesus' thirst (15:23, 36) is taken from Psalm 22:15. The piercing of his hands and feet in the crucifixion itself (15:25) finds a reference in Psalm 22:16. The story of the soldiers' parting his garments and casting lots for his robe (15:24) is lifted directly from Psalm 22:18. When we see that the words used to describe the crucifixion are drawn from a work written at least four hundred years before the event it surely becomes obvious that this is not eyewitness reporting, but rather interpretive portrait-painting.

Mark's dependency on Isaiah 53 is equally intense. Isaiah 53 is part of a portrait that the writer we call II Isaiah painted of a figure he called simply the "Servant," or the "Suffering Servant," which we have previously encountered in our walk through the Bible. Mark has simply incorporated the narrative of II Isaiah's "Servant" into his portrait of the Christ. So Mark's picture of Jesus is of the one who was "despised and rejected," a "man of sorrows and one acquainted with grief." These words are direct quotations from Isaiah 53:3. These Isaiah images do not stop there. Mark goes on to describe Jesus as being "wounded for our transgressions" and "bruised for our iniquities," images once again lifted almost verbatim from Isaiah 53:5. The "Servant" in Isaiah, like Jesus in Mark, "is silent before his accuser" (15:5, Isa. 53:7–8), and of Isaiah's "Servant" it was said that "with his stripes we are healed" (Isa. 53:5), which Mark turned into the story of the scourging of Jesus (15:14). This language was destined later to inform the Christian idea of Jesus in the substitutionary theory of the atonement. That was, however, not what it meant when Mark first borrowed it from II Isaiah.

This identification becomes even more exact when we read in Isaiah that the "Servant" will be numbered among the transgressors (53:12), which in time gave rise to the story first introduced by Mark of Jesus being crucified between two thieves (15:27). It is noteworthy that the role of the thieves grows as each succeeding gospel is written.[1] Isaiah also stated that this "Servant" would, in his death, "make his grave with the rich" (53:9), a line that eventually led to Mark's story of Jesus being buried in the tomb of Joseph of Arimathea, who was "a ruler of the Jews" and thus a person of means (15:42). This Joseph story, once it entered the

---

1   Compare Mark 15:27 with Matt. 27:38, 44 and Luke 23:32, 39–43.

tradition, grew with each successive gospel just as the story of the two thieves did, until Joseph was finally joined by Nicodemus in John's gospel.[2]

As much as this knowledge flies in the face of a familiar literalism, which has been carved in stone for us in such artifacts of our worship as the passion accounts set to music by J. S. Bach and the devotional practice known as the Stations of the Cross,[3] and in such ecclesiastical habits as sermons binding together the "seven last words," the truth is that Mark's story of the crucifixion is not the remembered history of an eyewitness at all, but is rather a second-generation interpretation of Jesus' death shaped by biblical sources that had fed Jewish messianic expectations through the ages. So our first step in understanding the familiar story of the cross is to free our minds from any assumption that we are reading history. What we are reading is the interpretation of Jesus' death as his Jewish disciples had come to understand it in the light of the Passover and the messianic expectations of the prophets. That is why none of this material was known to Paul. It had not yet been developed when Paul wrote.

The second step in this eye-opening process is to notice that this first narrative story of the cross was itself actually crafted by Mark to fit practices learned in the synagogue. Current studies of first-century Judaism inform us that the Jews observed Passover in a setting with their extended families gathered for about three hours. Included in this three-hour period were these elements: the family gathering, various games played to enhance the holiday spirit and the Passover meal itself, which included feeding on the "body of the lamb of God," as well as on foods that symbolized their past, such as bitter herbs and unleavened bread, reminders of their life in slavery and their hasty exodus from Egypt. Following the meal the youngest boy in the extended family would say

---

2   Compare Mark 15:42–47 with Matt. 27:57–61, Luke 23:50–56 and John 19:38–42.

3   Pictures of scenes from the passion placed in churches from the Middle Ages on so that worshipers could walk through the story of the crucifixion meditatively. Much of the content of the "stations" is not biblical or is a blending of the four gospel stories.

to the senior patriarch of the family, "Father, why is this night different from all other nights?" which would give the head of the household the chance to relate the story of the exodus and thus to recount the moment of the birth of the Jewish nation. The meal would then conclude with the singing of a hymn, and any extended family members who did not live in this house would depart into the night for their own homes.

Church historians and liturgical scholars have discovered some evidence that by the latter years of the second century CE, Christians were observing the passion of Jesus by stretching the three-hour Passover celebration of the Jews into a twenty-four-hour vigil. The question is: When did that vigil practice begin? I think the evidence in Mark's story of the passion is that it began very early, certainly prior to the writing of this first gospel, for the outline of a twenty-four-hour vigil is in the text of Mark's passion narrative itself. If we look at Mark's story of the last day in Jesus' life (14:17–15:47) and study the text carefully, we can see that twenty-four-hour outline.

Mark's story starts at sundown on what we now call Maundy Thursday and it runs to sundown on what we now call Good Friday. Let me point out the time markers that are in the text of Mark's gospel itself. Mark 14:17 has Jesus arrive with the twelve disciples at a house in Jerusalem to eat the Passover meal. The time was, says Mark, "when it was evening" (14:17)—that is, at sundown, or approximately at 6:00 P.M. Mark has earlier given us the details of the preparation that the disciple band had undergone to ready a place for this meal to be eaten together that night (14:12–16). After the supper is described, Mark says the evening ended with the singing of a hymn and Jesus and his disciples went out into the night (14:26). If the Passover normally lasted three hours, it is thus now about 9:00 P.M. The first segments of the twenty-four-hour vigil had been completed.

Jesus and his disciples then went to the Garden of Gethsemane (14:32ff) where, after choosing Peter, James and John to accompany him, Jesus discovered that they were not able, without falling asleep, to watch with him "one," "two," or "three" hours, which would carry the vigil through the second segment. It was now midnight. In 14:43 Mark then relates the act of betrayal, which took place, he says, at midnight, making the darkest deed in history occur at the darkest moment of the night. It is dramatically powerful, but hardly historically accurate.

Following that midnight arrest comes the trial before the high priest and the chief priest, which is told by Mark in 14:53–65 and which carries us to 3:00 A.M. The next watch of the night, the one between 3:00 A.M. and 6:00 A.M., is called "cockcrow." Into these three hours Mark has placed the story of Peter's threefold denial (14:66–72), presumably one denial for each hour of that watch until the cock crowed and, says Mark, the broken Peter wept.

Then the text says "as soon as it was morning" (15:1), which means it was now about 6:00 A.M. This is the time to which Mark has assigned the story of the trial before Pilate (15:1–14). Here we meet the enigmatic figure of Barabbas and we watch the torture by the soldiers unfold, complete with the "kingly" symbols of a purple robe to announce Jesus' royalty and a crown of thorns to be placed upon his head. Mark then informs us (15:35) that it was the third hour when they crucified him, or 9:00 A.M. The drama of the cross reaches its crescendo when, in verse 33, the text says that darkness covered the earth from the sixth hour until the ninth hour, or from noon to 3:00 P.M., when Jesus uttered his cry of dereliction and died. When we arrive at Mark 15:42, we are told of his burial before "evening came," or about 6:00 P.M. For the Jews, the Sabbath started at sundown on Friday, not at midnight. The fact that they did not have time to complete the burial process before the Sabbath began is Mark's segue to explain just why it was that the women had to come with embalming spices at dawn on the first day of the week, which sets the stage for his Easter story. Mark has told the story of the passion in eight three-hour segments to carry the readers from sundown on Thursday to sundown on Friday.

Vestiges of the twenty-four-hour vigil still exist in liturgical churches today. The climax of Holy Week begins with the Maundy Thursday service commemorating the establishment of the Eucharist. This is frequently followed by a ceremony called the stripping of the altar, which leaves it bare and tomblike. The sacrament, representing the body of Jesus, is then placed into the ambry and worshipers are invited to keep watch through the night. Sometimes churches organize the vigil to make certain that some members are always present. On Good Friday, the elements are distributed from the reserved sacrament, since the somberness of the day precludes a "celebration" of the Eucharist. Next comes a three-hour service, with worshipers observing that time when darkness was covering the earth between noon and 3:00 P.M. Then Jesus' "rest" in the tomb is marked beginning at sundown (or 6:00 P.M.) on Friday and extending through "holy Saturday," until the fires are lit that evening at the first "mass of Easter." The tradition is ancient. The Easter vigil was observed, I am now convinced, before the first gospel was written. Mark did not create it; Mark observed it and wrote his gospel account to help people observe it—indeed, to act it out.

It was the liturgical life of the synagogue, rather than the remembered life of Jesus, that so clearly organized Mark's gospel. He in turn set the example for Matthew and Luke, who followed that pattern. As we turn to consider those two gospels, we will see how both expanded and lengthened Mark, but neither ever challenged his organizing principle, which was and is the annual cycle of the liturgical life of the synagogue.

CHAPTER 45

Matthew

The Most Jewish Gospel

The second gospel to be written was Matthew, which made its debut a decade or so after Mark. I would date it in the 82–85 CE range. Matthew's gospel was heavily dependent on Mark, incorporating quotations from that earlier source almost verbatim. One has only to read a book called *Gospel Parallels*[1] to become aware of exactly how much was copied and, perhaps more important, what things in Mark were deemed unworthy of inclusion in Matthew. It also becomes clear that Matthew bent Mark's message toward a more traditional Jewish perspective.

Who was Matthew? An early church tradition that linked this gospel to Levi Matthew, the tax collector, is today generally discredited. This gospel was written originally in Greek, indeed a better Greek than that which appears in Mark. A Jewish follower of Jesus who had earlier sold his services as a tax collector to the alien, and by Jewish standards "unclean" Gentiles, as Levi Matthew had, would hardly have been expected to have the educational and scriptural background that is revealed in this book.

1   See bibliography for details.

This gospel also displays a rather sophisticated theological perspective, probably second only to that of John among the gospel writers. We have no reason to believe that any of the twelve disciples of Jesus were educated or learned men, and this includes one called Levi Matthew.

From internal evidence we can discern that the author appears to be the leader of a synagogue that followed the liturgical patterns and observed the high holy days of the ongoing Jewish tradition that we have previously discussed. Whoever the author was, he had a deep knowledge of and appreciation for the Jewish scriptures. He also shared in the historical Jewish expectation that the messiah would come to and for the Jews. When we analyze some aspects of Matthew's editing of the text of Mark's gospel, we discover that he is prone to remove from Mark things that might offend the Jews. Some scholars have even suggested that he wrote an autobiographical note into his text when he told the brief parable of the householder (13:51–52). Here we find these words: "Every scribe who has been trained for the kingdom of heaven is like a householder who brings out of his treasure what is new and what is old." The author of the second gospel was clearly dedicated to preserving what was old.

Matthew at the same time adds a number of things to the developing Christian tradition that we have not found anywhere before he wrote his gospel. To become aware of Matthew's unique contributions, we need to note that this is the first gospel to introduce a genealogy of Jesus (1:1–17). That genealogy is unusual in many ways. It begins with Abraham and journeys through the high points of Jewish history to King David, then through the kings of the House of David to the Babylonian exile and finally to the life of Jesus. When we come to Luke's gospel later, we will discover that he too adds a genealogy, but it will be quite different from Matthew's, and their differences cannot be reconciled. Was the father of Joseph named Jacob, as Matthew asserts (1:16), or Heli (Eli), as Luke contends (3:23)? Did Jesus' line flow through the royal lineage of kings from David to Solomon to Rehoboam, as Matthew states (1:6–11), or did it avoid royalty altogether by going from King David to Nathan and skipping all of the Judean kings, as Luke states (3:31)? Luke's genealogy also includes many more generations than Matthew's. They cannot both be accurate. The consensus of the scholars is that neither is accurate![2]

Matthew is also the first person to introduce any account of Jesus' miraculous birth into the developing tradition (1:18–25). Luke, writing a decade more or less after Matthew, also tells us a virgin birth story, but once again it is quite different from the one in Matthew (Luke 1:26–38, 2:1–14). Only in Matthew do we have an account of a star in the east and magi who followed that star bringing gifts of gold, frankincense and myrrh to the Christ child (2:1–6). Only Matthew involves King Herod in the birth narrative, both by having him give the magi directions to Bethlehem and later by developing the account of Herod sending his soldiers to slaughter all the Jewish boy babies in a vain attempt to wipe out this presumed threat to his throne (2:7–18). Only Matthew has the holy family flee to Egypt to escape the murderous wrath of Herod and then return to their home in Bethlehem after Herod's death (2:13–15). Later, God was said to have warned Joseph in a dream about the continuing danger represented by Herod's son, who was now on the throne, and directed him to take the child to the safety of Galilee in order for Jesus to grow up in the village of Nazareth (2:19–23). In each of these episodes in Matthew's birth story, he makes the claim that these maneuvers occurred "in order to fulfill the scriptures," by which he always meant the messianic expectations of the Jewish scriptures. Why was Jesus born in Bethlehem? Matthew says it was to fulfill the expectations of Micah (5:2) that the messiah must be born in the city of David's birth in order to demonstrate that he was the direct heir to David's throne. Why was Jesus born of a virgin? It was, says Matthew, to fulfill a text from Isaiah (7:14), which we have already noted does not have the word "virgin" in it. Why did Herod

---

2   There are other distinctions between the two genealogies, such as Matthew includes four women. Luke begins with Adam not Abraham, but this is enough to establish the point.

slaughter the male babies of Bethlehem? It was, says Matthew, to fulfill a text in Jeremiah (31:15) that spoke of Rachel weeping for her children who were lost. Why did Mary, Joseph and the child flee to Egypt? It was, says Matthew, to fulfill the words of Hosea (11:1) that "out of Egypt have I called my son." Why did Jesus move to and grow up in Nazareth? It was, says Matthew, to fulfill a prophecy that he would be called a Nazarene, but in this case we have no idea which prophetic text it was to which Matthew was referring!

Were any of these particular texts being properly used by this author? If we are speaking literally, not one of them was. Indeed, they are not even close! Micah was referring to a Davidic messiah coming out of Bethlehem who would restore the fortunes of the Jews. In all probability Jesus was born in Nazareth. The first gospel, Mark, assumes that. In Isaiah 7:14 the prophet was referring to a birth in the royal family that would be a sign that Jerusalem would not fall to the foreign armies of Kings Pekah and Resin that were surrounding the holy city as Isaiah wrote. He was certainly not referring to an event seven hundred plus years in the future. Jeremiah was referring to Rachel, the tribal mother of the Northern Kingdom, weeping for her children who were lost to the Assyrians when those foes conquered the Northern Kingdom in 721 BCE. Hosea was referring to the exodus in which God called his people out of slavery in Egypt, not to a trip of safety engineered by Joseph for Jesus centuries later. Finally, we know of no expectation that the messiah would be related to Nazareth. The fact is that Matthew quoted scripture in such a way as to make it serve his own interpretive agenda.

Matthew was also the first gospel writer to give detailed content to the story of the temptations in the wilderness (4:1–11).[3] Mark had said only that Jesus was in the wilderness for forty days being tempted (1:12–13). Matthew not only spells out the

---

3   Many scholars think that this content is from the so-called Q document— more on that in a later chapter—because the details are similar to the content related in Luke. Luke, however, reverses the second and third temptations, which raises still other questions.

content of the three temptations, but he also records Jesus' response to each.

To the surprise of many when they first hear it said, Matthew is the only gospel to record Jesus delivering the Sermon on the Mount (5–7). Luke scatters some of the Sermon on the Mount material throughout his gospel, but only Matthew pulls it together in the form that we know best.

Parables unique to Matthew include the parable of the weeds (13:24–30) and its interpretation (13:36–43); the parable of the hidden treasure and the pearl of great price (13:44–46); the parable of the net (13:47–50); the parable of the unmerciful servant (18:23–25); the parable of the wise and foolish maidens (25:1–13), and the parable of the judgment, where the sheep are separated from the goats (25:31–46).

When we come to the narrative of the final events in Jesus' life, Matthew alone adds the unique notes that the betrayal by Judas was for thirty pieces of silver (26:15) and that Judas hurled that money back into the Temple when he repented of his deed. Matthew alone tells us that Judas then went and hanged himself (27:5). Matthew is also the first gospel writer to give us narrative details about Jesus appearing to the disciples in Galilee following the resurrection (28:16–20). He said, for example, that this appearance occurred on a mountaintop, and he added the first occasion on which the risen Jesus was quoted as saying anything to anyone. Those words, you may recall, are what we now call the Great Commission: "Go into all the world!" There is no Pentecost moment in Matthew, but only the promise that Jesus is "Emmanuel" (1:23), which means "God with us." "Lo, I am with you always" (28:20) is as close to the coming of the Holy Spirit as Matthew gets.

It is necessary to absorb these special Matthean touches before we can begin to put this gospel into an interpretive context. For now, I ask you simply to embrace Matthew's special contributions to the developing Christian story. Try to isolate Matthew's point of view as it is revealed in his additions to the story. Then we can begin the process of penetrating the mind of this writer of the second gospel in order to discern just how he perceived Jesus.

CHAPTER 46

Matthew's Interpretive Secret

Matthew's gospel has always fascinated me more than the others. It is not the most profound of the gospels, but it does open interpretive eyes for me more widely than the others. The doorway into this perception is found in the process of being able to ask the right questions. Matthew is the "Jewish gospel" par excellence, and if one does not understand what it means to be a Jewish gospel, one will never understand this book. Two biblical characters are taken by Matthew from the Jewish scriptures and used as symbols around which to weave his story of Jesus. I will look at both of them in an effort to demonstrate that Matthew is deeply dependent on his audience having a sufficient understanding of Judaism to recognize his allusions both to Jewish history and to Jewish scripture.

The first of these Jewish characters is Joseph, the patriarch whose story is told in Genesis 37–50. This is the Joseph of the coat of many colors, the firstborn son of Jacob by his favorite wife Rachel. In our earlier trek through the Old Testament, we noted the deep and historic division between Judah, the dominant tribe in the south, and the Northern Kingdom of which Joseph was the principle ancestor. Recall that the tribes of Ephraim and

Manasseh, both sons of this same Joseph, were dominant in both population and acreage in that separate part of the Hebrew nation.

One agenda that drove Matthew's gospel was to present Jesus as the messianic life that was capable of binding up this long and deep division between the northern Jews and the tribe of Judah. When we read Matthew knowing this background, we can watch just how he does it. Matthew opens his gospel with a seventeen-verse genealogy in which he traces the lineage of Jesus through King David and the Jewish world that centered in Jerusalem, with all the named personages being members of the tribe of Judah. In this genealogy he clearly roots Jesus in the Southern Kingdom. Jesus was a son of the tribe of Judah as the heir of David.

Then Matthew introduces into the developing tradition the story of Jesus' miraculous birth and, in the process, confronts us with a new character, whom he is going to portray as Jesus' earthly father. The name of this character is Joseph, a man who has never before been mentioned anywhere in Christian writing. In the new story of Jesus' birth to a "virgin," there is a clear need for someone to play the role of "earthly father" and to give the child the protection that only a man could give in that fiercely patriarchal society. By having someone named Joseph—after the great patriarch—name this child, thus claiming him as his own, Matthew counters the rumors of illegitimacy that were swirling around from ninth-decade critics of the Christian movement. Thus Matthew, by making Jesus heir to David's throne and giving him an earthly father and protector named Joseph, has bound Jewish history together in the person of Jesus.

Next look at the portrait of Joseph as Matthew painted him. Everything we know biographically and biblically about this Joseph we learn in Matthew's birth narrative, where we are told three things. First, Joseph has a father named Jacob (1:16). Second, God speaks to him only in dreams (1:20, 2:13, 2:19, and 2:22). Third, his role in the drama of salvation is to save the child of promise from death by taking him down to Egypt (2:13–16).

Now go back to the story of the patriarch Joseph in the book of Genesis (37–50) and read that narrative. There you will discover three things about that older Joseph. First, he has a father named Jacob (37:2). Second, he is constantly associated with dreams (37:5–11) and was even called the dreamer by his brothers (37:19); indeed, he is noted primarily as the interpreter of dreams (40:1–19), and even rides into political power in Egypt based on that gift (41). Third, his role in the drama of salvation is to save the people of the covenant from death by taking them down to Egypt (46).

Is this simply coincidence, or are we beginning to discern how the Jewish scriptures were used to interpret the Jesus experience? Matthew was not writing a biography of Jesus; he was interpreting Jesus in the light of the Jewish scriptures. Literalism is never the way to read any Jewish story. Literalism is, in fact, a late-developing Gentile heresy. To make Jesus simultaneously a son of Judah and a son of Joseph was something Matthew's Jewish readers would have understood.

The second shadowy figure from the Hebrew scriptures around which Matthew weaves the story of Jesus is Moses. Moses was the founder of the Jewish nation, the giver of the law, or Torah, and the ultimate hero of Judaism. Moses makes his first appearance in Matthew's birth narrative in the account of the wicked King Herod, who slaughtered the male babies in Bethlehem in a vain attempt to remove a potential pretender to his throne (2:16–18). Every Jewish reader of Matthew's gospel would have recognized that account as a Moses story. When Moses was born, a wicked king called the pharaoh decreed that all the Jewish boy babies were to be destroyed so that his power would not be threatened (Exod. 1:8–22). To save their son from this fate, Moses' parents put him in a basket on the River Nile where, according to that story, he was rescued by the pharaoh's daughter. Matthew in these early verses of his gospel was signaling to his Jewish readers that he was interpreting Jesus under the popular messianic image of "the new Moses." This theme is picked up later in the birth narrative when Matthew quotes Hosea as saying, "Out of Egypt have I called my Son" (2:15). This was once again a clear reference to Moses, but used by Matthew to mark Jesus' return from his flight to Egypt, to which he and his parents had fled to avoid Herod.

Matthew next interprets the baptism of Jesus in such a way as to frame it as an analogy to Moses' crossing of the Red Sea, where he had separated the waters so that the people could walk through the sea on dry land. Once again Jewish readers would have recognized this theme, for splitting the waters was a regular occurrence in the Jewish scriptures. Moses did it at the Red Sea (Exod. 14:21ff); Joshua did it at the Jordan River (Josh. 3:11–13). Both Elijah and Elisha also split the waters of the Jordan River on their way to and from the place of Elijah's departure in a fiery chariot (II Kings 2:8, 14). Now Matthew brings Jesus, in the first story of his adult life, to the Jordan River for baptism (3:1–10). In this narrative he was clearly seeking to say that the God presence we believe we have met in Jesus is even greater than the God presence our ancestors met in Moses. It was a stunning claim. How did he develop this theme? At the baptism, Jesus steps into the waters of the Jordan River, but he does not split these waters. That had been done so many times that it represented nothing special. Jesus rather splits the heavens, which we are told in the creation story is "the firmament," which separates the waters above from the waters below (Gen. 1:7). Jesus thus splits the heavenly waters, which then fall on him as the Holy Spirit, for that is what "living water" means in the Hebrew scriptures (see Zech. 14:8).

What did Moses do after his "baptism" in the Red Sea? The Torah says he wandered in the wilderness for forty years trying to determine what it meant for Israel to be the "chosen people" (Exod. 10:35). What did Matthew have Jesus do after his "Red Sea" experience in the Jordan River? He wandered in the wilderness for forty days trying to determine what it means to be the designated messiah (4:1).

While Moses was in the wilderness, he had three critical experiences. The first involved a shortage of food, and it was solved with manna from heaven (Exod. 16:31). The second was when a shortage of water forced Moses to "put God to the test" by striking a rock and demanding that water flow from it (Exod. 17:5). The third occurred when his people in his absence turned away from God and began to worship a golden calf as "the god who brought them out of Egypt" (Exod. 32:46).

Matthew, as noted previously, is the first gospel writer to give content to the temptations that Jesus had to endure in the wilderness. Let us examine that content. The first temptation involved the shortage of food: "Turn these stones into bread, Jesus" (4:3–4). The second had to do with putting God to the test: "Cast yourself off the pinnacle of the Temple, Jesus. He will give his angels charge over you" (4:5–7). The third temptation had to do with worshiping something other than God: "Bow down before me, Jesus, and I will give you all the kingdoms of this world" (4:8–10).

Once more, does anyone think this is coincidental? Or are we beginning to see Matthew's gospel as interpretive writing designed to show that Jesus relived the messianic image of being the new Moses by having Moses stories from the Hebrew scriptures wrapped around him. Matthew's Jewish audience would immediately have understood the interpretive tools he was employing.

The most distinguishing marks of Matthew's gospel begin to form a pattern. The baptism story with the heavens parting is a Red Sea story. The temptations are shaped by the Moses narrative. Then comes the powerful and uniquely Matthean portrait of Jesus giving the Sermon on the Mount. That discourse, Matthew's special creation, enables him to portray Jesus as the new Moses on a new mountain, giving a new interpretation of the Torah. In this literary creation, Matthew has Jesus compare Moses to himself: "You have heard it said of old—but I say unto you" (5:21, 27, 33). Jesus thus reinterprets Moses, driving the external law of Moses toward the internal level of motivation. Moses is quite clearly one of the great interpretive clues to Matthew's gospel. One has to read this book with Jewish eyes.

CHAPTER 47

Matthew and the Liturgical Year of the Synagogue

Earlier, when examining the gospel of Mark, I sought to demonstrate that it was the liturgical life of the synagogue that formed the organizing principle in that first gospel. What Mark had done, I suggested, was to provide Jesus stories appropriate to the synagogue celebrations from Rosh Hashanah (the John the Baptist story) to Passover (the crucifixion story). Rosh Hashanah, however, comes in the autumn and Passover comes in the early spring, so the gospel of Mark covered only six and a half months of the year, leaving out the five and a half months that, in the Jewish calendar, separate Passover from Rosh Hashanah (April–September). There was, therefore, a desire after Mark's gospel appeared to fill in that blank space with additional Jesus material, which soon became an imperative need. Within about a decade, Matthew wrote the first expansion of Mark and aimed his story at the disciples of Jesus who worshiped in rather traditional Jewish synagogues. Recall once again that the split between the church and the synagogue would not occur until near the end of the ninth decade, so when Mark and Matthew were written, they and their readers were still in the traditional synagogue.

When Matthew, like Mark, correlates the crucifixion with the Passover (Matt. 26–27), he signals that the core of Mark will remain intact in his gospel. Like Mark, Matthew has also correlated the transfiguration with the Festival of Dedication (Matt. 17:1–8); the harvest stories, including the parable of the sower, with the Festival of Sukkoth or Tabernacles (Matt. 13); and Jesus' teaching on fasting, cleansing demons and curing sicknesses with Yom Kippur (Matt. 12). When, however, Matthew comes to Mark's correlation of John the Baptist with Rosh Hashanah, he has a problem. The baptism of Jesus by John was the first event in Jesus' ministry according to Mark, but Matthew must cover five and a half months of Jesus' story before he comes to Rosh Hashanah. In Mark the baptism of Jesus had inaugurated his ministry, but Matthew could not save that story for five and a half months. How Matthew managed this dilemma is fascinating.

Matthew follows Mark by having the baptism of Jesus come as the first event in Jesus' adult life, so he uses this material early in his story. After the genealogy and the birth story, Matthew makes the John the Baptist story the third element. This means that it came long before the seventh Jewish month of Tishri, which is where Mark had introduced John the Baptist as his Rosh Hashanah content. So when Matthew gets to Rosh Hashanah in late September or early October, the John the Baptist story has already been related. So what does Matthew do? He uses a trick favored by the motion picture industry (think of Cecil B. DeMille!) and employs a flashback.

In chapter 11 of his gospel, at the time when Rosh Hashanah rolls around, Matthew reintroduces John the Baptist, now in prison, and has him send a messenger to Jesus. "Are you the one who is to come [that is, the messiah] or do we look for another?" (11:3), the messenger inquires. Jesus does not answer directly, but refers him to a passage in Isaiah that was regularly used in the synagogue at the observance of Rosh Hashanah. How will we know when the Kingdom of God is about to dawn? the prophet is asked. To this query, Isaiah responds: The signs will be that the blind will see, the deaf hear, the lame walk and the mute sing

(35:5–6). To this litany of signs Jesus adds other things that demonstrate his messianic claims: "The lepers are cleansed, the dead
are raised up and the poor have the gospel preached to them"
(Matt. 11:6). It is the Jewish Rosh Hashanah, or New Year, theme
being fully deployed. Matthew's Jewish audience would have understood. Then Jesus moves on to speak about John the Baptist in
glowing terms. It is a perfect Jesus story to be used in the observance of Rosh Hashanah.

There is one other Jewish festival that Mark, with his trun-
cated six-and-a-half-month format, had simply ignored. Fifty
days after Passover, the Jews celebrated Shavuot, or Pentecost.
This day, which usually falls in late May to early June, was designed to recall the Mount Sinai experience and to rejoice in the
Torah. Shavuot was normally observed in the first-century synagogue world with a twenty-four-hour vigil. The longest psalm
in the psalter, Psalm 119, was written to be used at this vigil,
as we saw earlier. It is both a hymn to the beauty and power of
the law and long enough to provide material for the entire vigil.
Psalm 119 opens with an eight-verse introduction, the first two
verses of which begin with the word "blessed." Then there are
eight segments of three stanzas each, designed for use at each of
the eight three-hour sections of the twenty-four-hour vigil. To
provide an appropriate Jesus story that demonstrates the theme
of Shavuot was the agenda that Matthew faced. Look now at
how he did it.

At exactly the right time in the year, assuming that Matthew
was stretching Mark's six and a half months out to twelve, we
find in Matthew 5–7 a discourse that we call the Sermon on the
Mount. Here, uniquely among the gospel writers, Matthew portrays Jesus as the new Moses. What most of us are not aware of,
however, is that Matthew patterns this sermon after the Shavuot
Psalm 119. He opens with an eight-verse introduction in which
each verse, not just the first two, begins with the word "blessed."
We now call these eight "blesseds" the Beatitudes. Then in the
rest of the sermon, Matthew provides a commentary on each
of these beatitudes, in reverse order from eight to one, which in

effect supplies the Christian content for the eight three-hour segments of this twenty-four-hour vigil. It is a perfect fit!

Covering Shavuot also completes the last festival of the synagogue year. To provide Jesus material to carry the worshipers from Passover, where Mark told the story of the crucifixion, to Rosh Hashanah, where he told the story of Jesus' baptism, Matthew has to front-load Mark. Look again at exactly how he does it. The new items of the genealogy and the birth story fill up the first two chapters. Then in chapter 3 he uses the story of John the Baptist baptizing Jesus to introduce Jesus to the public just as Mark did, but he expands that story by including some of the content of John's preaching. In chapter 4, he takes Mark's two-verse account of the temptations in the wilderness and includes in it the content and full description of the three temptations and of Jesus' response to each. Then he adds the Sermon on the Mount in chapters 5–7. When Matthew gets to chapter 13, he has finally caught up with where Mark was in chapter 4. From that point on, the two gospels track very closely together.

As we have seen in this chapter, Matthew's motive for expanding Mark's content was to give the worshiping disciples a sufficient supply of Jesus stories to enable them to cover the entire synagogue year. The New Testament is quite exciting as soon as one dismisses the literal approach to these texts and begins to discover the uniqueness of each gospel. Now continuing our attempt to discover the particular interpretation that each gospel writer sought to convey, we move on to the gospel of Luke.

CHAPTER 48

Luke

Moving Toward the Gentile World

B y the time the third gospel, known as Luke, was written, history had moved to the last years of the ninth decade CE at the earliest and quite possibly to the early years of the tenth decade. The Christian movement had journeyed beyond its earlier traumas and tensions and was now concerned with making a case for its legitimacy in the Roman Empire. I date Luke between 89 and 93, though there is debate on both ends.

This gospel reflects Christianity's transition out of Judaism and toward the Gentile world. The community for which it was written appears to have been made up primarily of dispersed Jews who no longer followed their traditions in a rigid pattern and, as a consequence, were beginning to attract a rising tide of converts from the Gentile world. These Gentile proselytes, as they came to be called, had little dedication to or interest in the cultic practices of circumcision, kosher dietary rules and unfamiliar liturgical practices, such as the twenty-four-hour vigil around Shavuot and the eight-day celebrations of both Sukkoth and Dedication. They were not interested in losing the meaning of these holy days, but they clearly were eager to shrink the time it took to observe them and to reduce the festivals' place of importance and the hold they had once had on their lives.

The author of Luke is unknown, but tradition has always identified this book with Luke the physician, who accompanied Paul and was mentioned in two of the post-Pauline epistles (Col. 4:14, II Tim. 4:11). What we do know about the author of the gospel of Luke, beyond the fact that the same person clearly wrote the book of Acts as Volume II of his gospel, is that in all probability he was born a Gentile and had been drawn into the ethical monotheism that marked Judaism. He appears to have actually converted to Judaism and to have joined the synagogue, and through that synagogue he later moved into Christianity. He may well have been one of Paul's converts; at least he clearly identifies himself with Paul's point of view and he champions it in both the gospel and the book of Acts.

The internal data that point us to these conclusions are plentiful. First, there is the Jesus genealogy in Luke chapter 3, to which we have previously referred. Here Luke carries the ancestry of Jesus back not just to Abraham, the father of the Jewish nation, but to Adam, who would have been understood in the worldview of that day as the father of the whole human race, including the Gentiles. Luke does not tie Jesus to King David's royal line, an idea that would have had little interest for his Gentile readers. Instead, Luke's ancestral line flows from David to a son named Nathan, who is mentioned in the Bible only one other time (I Sam. 5:14) and is certainly not a significant figure. So we wonder why Luke settled on this name. Perhaps a clue is found in the moral and upright nature of the hero of the story of David and Bathsheba, a prophet named Nathan, about whom I have written earlier. In other places, Luke appears to borrow names from Old Testament characters if those older personages suit the message he is trying to communicate, so the connection with Nathan, the prophet, might be a good guess. We also know that Luke was not impressed with either royalty or magi, as they both are deemphasized in the Lucan corpus.[1]

In other notes that may give us insight into Luke's values, we observe that this is the first gospel, and thus the first place in the Bible, ever to mention the Samaritans, and Luke does so with sensitivity and inclusiveness. Only Luke, for example, tells us the parable of the good Samaritan (10:25ff). That is just one more indication that Luke's community of believers has moved beyond the Jewish point of view. Later, in the book of Acts (chapter 2), Luke emphasizes anew the universal theme in his narrative when he suggests that the Holy Spirit fell on the entire gathered Christian community. He is quite pointed in noting that Pentecost was a worldwide event in which the Spirit fell not only on the Jews, but on all the peoples of the world. Clearly Luke envisioned a Christianity loosed from the ethnic limits of Judaism and propelled into being a universal faith.

We note also that the author of this gospel makes no claim to having been an eyewitness to the story of Jesus, but rather mentions the research that he has done, which enabled him to produce this work. He says in his preamble that "many have undertaken to complete a narrative of the things which have been accomplished among us just as they were delivered to us, by those who from the beginning were eye witnesses and ministers of the word" (1:1–5). We can now be certain that Mark was one of these sources, since Luke reproduces in his gospel about half of Mark. Many scholars also suggest that Luke and Matthew both had a common source made up of a collection of Jesus sayings from which they both quote frequently and almost identically. This popular hypothesis requires the existence of a now-lost book to which the title Q has been attached. There are some other scholars, a minority to be sure, who dismiss the Q hypothesis and assert instead that Luke also had Matthew in front of him when he wrote and that, while he preferred Mark, he did use a number

---

[1]   First note that kings become shepherds in Luke's story and then read Luke's treatment of Simon Magus, the magician, in Acts 8:9ff. Luke apparently did not care for magi either.

of Matthew's additions to Mark. The use of those additions, say these theorists, is what created the similarities between Luke and Matthew that are attributed to Q. While the majority of scholars still follow the Q hypothesis, I for one have never been convinced of it. It is not important to enter that debate here; I merely state it as a way of keeping the argument open.[2]

Luke also introduces a number of things into the developing Christian story that have not to our knowledge been there before. The first one is the account of the birth of John the Baptist (Luke 1). It is a fascinating story from many angles, but it is clearly not history. It reminds me of a song popular in my teenage years that claimed, "Anything you can do, I can do better." John is born to a post-menopausal mother. That is a wonder, but it pales into insignificance in the light of the story of Jesus being born to a virgin. When the birth of John occurs, the neighbors gather to celebrate. When Jesus is born, however, it is not neighbors, but angels who come crashing through the midnight sky to celebrate his arrival. Clearly, when Luke wrote, there was still some tension between the followers of Jesus and the followers of John the Baptist. That is why there is such a concentrated effort in all the gospels to assert that John the Baptist, who was clearly the first of the two on the scene, knew that he was subservient to Jesus: "He must increase, I must decrease" (John 3:30). Luke pushes this to the extreme by having the fetus of John the Baptist in the womb of Elizabeth leap to salute the fetus of Jesus in the womb of Mary (1:39–45). In this narrative, Luke appears to have borrowed a story from Genesis and applied it to his narrative (see Gen. 25:20ff). In both stories, a baby leaps in the womb of its mother. In the Genesis story, it is Rebekah, Isaac's wife, who is pregnant with twins. As these twins struggle in Rebekah's womb, she seeks the counsel of an oracle to determine the meaning of this leaping, only to learn from the oracle that the older son (Esau) would ultimately serve the younger son (Jacob).

---

2   I am convinced by the argument offered by the late English New Testament scholar Michael D. Goulder against the Q hypothesis in the preface to his two-volume work on Luke, entitled *Luke: A New Paradigm*. See bibliography for details.

In Luke's story the babies are not twins, but Luke does make them kin—perhaps cousins—but the meaning is the same: The older boy, John, will serve the younger boy, Jesus.

The custom of taking material from familiar Old Testament sources, such as the book of Genesis, to tell the Jesus story is discernible in other places. In Luke's narrative about the birth of John, he says that the Baptist's parents, Zechariah and Elizabeth, conceived him when both were beyond the child-bearing age. That motif was clearly borrowed from the story of Abraham and Sarah, who were well into their old age (Sarah was said to be ninety) when Isaac was born (Gen. 17–18). The names of John the Baptist's parents were also, in all probability, plucked from Old Testament sources. Luke portrays John the Baptist not as Elijah, but as "the voice crying in the wilderness" (3:4), a phrase that comes from the book of Malachi. The immediate predecessor to the book of Malachi in the Bible was the book of Zechariah, so Luke uses that name for the father or immediate predecessor of John the Baptist. Identifying the source of the name Elizabeth for John's mother is more difficult. There is only one other Elizabeth in the Bible, and she is the wife of Aaron, the brother of Moses, and the sister-in-law of Miriam. As sisters-in-law, Elizabeth (written as Elisheba in Hebrew) and Miriam (written as Mary in Greek), their children therefore would be first cousins. Only Luke among the gospel writers implies kinship between Jesus and John, and he accomplishes this by his creative use of names drawn from the story of Moses and his siblings. There is no historical evidence except proximity in time that would suggest Jesus and John the Baptist were in any way related.

As we look more deeply into Luke's unique way of telling the Jesus story, we will see again and again that Luke's purpose is to interpret Jesus in the light of the Hebrew scriptures, not to re-create him historically. Unless we understand this clearly we will never be able to hear the powerful message of Luke. This new vision also introduces into the study of the Bible a playful kind of speculation that leads us deeper and deeper into scripture's truth. As our consideration of Luke moves on, that will become more obvious.

CHAPTER 49

Luke's Vision of
Universalism

In this final segment on Luke, the third gospel, I want to illustrate once again, and hopefully to establish firmly in the
minds of my readers, the major thesis that each of these first
three gospels is organized on the basis of the annual liturgical cycle of the synagogue in which Christianity lived in its first
generations as a movement within Judaism. These gospels, in
order to be understood properly, then must be read from a Jewish
perspective. The later Greek-thinking period of Christianity,
which shaped the creeds in the fourth century and informs Christian doctrine to this day, gave us a very different and, I believe,
distorting lens through which to read the synoptic narratives.

To enter Luke in this new way I want to do two things. First,
I will take a story from Luke's gospel that is moved by Luke to a
new and strange location and seek to explain why. Second, I will
probe Luke's entire corpus for what I believe is his central interpretive clue, drawn from the Hebrew scriptures and the traditions
of the Jews, and show how Luke uses this clue to paint his portrait of Jesus. I hope this twofold approach will give us a different
way to read and to understand this magnificent gospel.

The misplaced story in Luke is the account of the woman
washing the feet of Jesus in a public place. In both Mark (14:3–9)

and Matthew (26:6–13) this story is located in the last week of Jesus' life, just prior to the crucifixion. In both of those earlier gospels Jesus proclaims, appropriately in that setting, that she has anointed him for burial. Luke, however, has moved this story into the earlier Galilean phase of Jesus' ministry, far removed from the final events of his life (7:36–50).

Another reality of this story is that Luke has heightened the sensuous, sexual nature of this act and the perceived evil represented by this woman. There is no sense of scandal in this story in either Mark or Matthew, but the story reeks with scandal in Luke. Only in Luke is this woman identified as "a woman of the street," a euphemism for a prostitute. Only in Luke does this woman intimately fondle his feet, washing them with her tears and drying them with her hair. This woman was unclean by the standards of her day and her physical touching of Jesus rendered him unclean as well. Luke records that even Jesus' host, who is identified as a Pharisee, casts moral judgment upon him. A prophet, this Pharisee asserts, would know what kind of woman this is and would not allow this outrageous behavior. Since Jesus does allow it, the Pharisee implies, Jesus could not possibly be a prophet.

When we locate this story in the text of Luke's gospel, we discover that it comes immediately after the author, like Matthew before him, has reintroduced John the Baptist (7:18ff) in a scene where Jesus claims for himself the messianic power outlined in Isaiah, echoing the words that formed the Rosh Hashanah– Jewish New Year call to prepare for the in-breaking of the kingdom of God. Jesus answers John's question about whether he is "the one that should come" (7:20) by pointing to the messianic acts—the blind see, the deaf hear, the lame walk and the mute sing.

We next observe that shortly after this bizarre story of the woman of the street washing Jesus' feet comes the Sukkoth harvest parable of the sower who sowed his seed on four different kinds of soil (8:5ff). We note that in Luke's version of this parable, it is greatly shortened from its form in Mark and Matthew, and we remember that in those earlier and more traditional gospels, the harvest festival was eight days in length. Luke's community had moved some distance from the agricultural cycle and found that eight-day celebrations did not fit well into their lifestyle. They were more like modern Americans, who move most holidays to Monday to create a long weekend. In that moment the theme of the holiday is not lost, but the way it is observed is certainly curtailed.

In any event the Jewish liturgical observance that falls between Rosh Hashanah and Sukkoth is Yom Kippur, the Day of Atonement, where the sins of the people are cleansed and taken away liturgically. What Luke has so obviously done is to turn the account of the woman's washing of Jesus' feet into a Yom Kippur story, and that is why he has changed its location and the tone of the story. Jesus in this narrative is portrayed as willingly submitting to a process that has the power to render him unclean. He has entered the world of evil, only to reveal that it has no power over him. Like the scapegoat of Yom Kippur, he has taken away the sins of this woman, transformed her, made her whole and in the process thrown off the judgment of Simon the Pharisee, who was host at the dinner. It is a perfect narrative for Yom Kippur and reveals once again how Luke was guided by the flow of worship in the synagogue and how he used his material adroitly to accomplish not the task of a historian to get the facts, but the task of an interpreter of the power of Jesus—power to create wholeness, to set aside barriers and to call people into a new humanity. I find this a freeing, exciting insight into the author of this gospel.

Next we seek to find in Luke the primary interpretive clue that he has used to communicate the Jesus experience for himself and the community of dispersed Jews and increasing numbers of Gentile proselytes for whom he writes. This study will inevitably carry us beyond the limits of the gospel of Luke and into this author's second volume, which we know as the book of Acts. There is a sense in which Luke's understanding of the life of Jesus does not reach its climax in the crucifixion and resurrection, but in the later ascension and Pentecost experiences, which Luke hints at in the gospel but does not really relate until the first two chapters of the book of Acts. So come with me now on a scavenger hunt for clues hidden in the corpus of Luke's work, which I will seek to assemble in order to unlock his meaning.

In the Jewish tradition the law was identified with Moses, while the Jewish hero primarily associated with the prophets was Elijah. In Jewish messianic expectation there were suggestions that the messiah would be both a new Moses and a new Elijah. Later, the Elijah focus began to be downgraded, and this was expressed in the idea that Elijah must return before the messiah, to prepare the way. Both of these understandings were present in early Christianity. The equality of Moses and Elijah was expressed in the story of the transfiguration of Jesus, introduced by Mark and repeated by both Matthew and Luke as their way of relating Jesus to the Festival of Dedication.

The idea of Elijah as the forerunner was certainly present in Mark, who identified John the Baptist as the new Elijah emerging out of the wilderness to urge upon the people preparations for the coming of the messiah. That messiah, in Mark's mind, was Jesus of Nazareth. Matthew accepted this understanding, if anything heightening it.

That is not so with Luke. He identifies John the Baptist not with Elijah, but with the unnamed voice drawn by Malachi. People wondered, says Luke, if John was the Christ/messiah (Luke 3:15). John denied it and asserted that his role was only to prepare the way of the Lord. When Herod arrested John, says Luke, Jesus emerged onto center stage (3:20). Later, when John the Baptist from jail reentered the Jesus story, Jesus was made to define him overtly with the nameless voice found in Malachi (Luke 7:27, Mal. 3:1). John the Baptist had come in "the Spirit of Elijah," but for Luke he was not the new Elijah. Luke wanted to save that image so that he could apply it to Jesus himself.

Next we look at the two miracle stories that are told in Luke alone. They must, therefore, have some purpose in the way Luke was developing his story. The first one is the story of Jesus rais-

ing from the dead the only son of a widow in the village of Nain
(7:11–17). Where did Luke get this story? There is a very similar
account in the first book of Kings (I Kings 17:24) in which the
prophet Elijah raises from the dead the only son of a widow.
Luke, it seems, was building his case for interpreting Jesus as the
new Elijah.

The second miracle story unique to Luke's gospel is the account of the cleansing of ten lepers, and only one of them, a foreigner and a Samaritan, returned to give thanks (17:11–22). This
story has many similarities with a narrative once again in the
Elijah-Elisha cycle of stories—an account in which Elisha heals
a foreigner, Naaman the Syrian, of his leprosy (II Kings 5:1–27).
Luke had earlier referred to that story when he had Jesus remind
his audience that God's concern reaches beyond the boundaries
of Judaism's tribal mentality (4:24–30). This further connection
with the Old Testament tells us that Luke is clearly drawing on
the Elijah-Elisha material to tell his Jesus story. The prophetic
movement called the Jews beyond their boundaries into the wider
world. That was the theme that resonated with Luke's community of Christians, who lived at the place where the various
peoples of the world came together.

The climax of Luke's story is related in Acts 1, where we are
told of Jesus' ascension into heaven, and in Acts 2, where we are
told that he had poured out the Holy Spirit at Pentecost on the
gathered community. Neither is a literal story, a fact about which
we should be quite pleased, for in a space age we know that the
way to approach God is not to rise into the sky. That will get one
either into orbit or, by ultimately escaping the laws of gravity,
into the infinity of space. Neither image is spiritually edifying.
Well, if they are not to be understood literally, what do these accounts mean? They are quite simply Elijah stories magnified and
retold about Jesus in such a way as to make a claim for the ultimate validity of Jesus' life as being a transformative experience
of the presence of God.

If one turns to II Kings 2, one reads the ancient account of
the ascension of Elijah. It is a dramatic story filled with symbols.

I relate it briefly here. Elijah, nearing the end of his life, is on a final journey with his designated successor Elisha into the wilderness, where the transition in leadership will take place. They are talking about final things, and people along the way make it clear that their rendezvous is to be with death. They come to the Jordan River and cannot get across. Elijah sweeps his mantle across the river and it splits just as the Red Sea did in the past, so they walk across on dry land. The God who was present in Moses, implies this connection with the Red Sea account, is clearly present in Elijah.

When they arrive at their final destination Elisha makes a kind of death-bed request of Elijah: Master, he says, if I am going to be your successor I will need to be endowed with a double portion of your spirit. To this request Elijah responds, in effect: I do not know if that is within my capacity to give, but if you see me ascending into the sky, then you will know that your request has been granted (II Kings 2:9ff).

At that moment, according to this story, out of the sky comes a magical fiery chariot drawn by magical fiery horses. This chariot swoops down out of the clouds and lands exactly at the place where Elijah and Elisha are standing, just as if this were a regular stop on a bus route! Elijah hops on board and waves good-bye. God sends a whirlwind behind the chariot to propel it upward and Elisha sees that happen. He knows he has been endowed with a double portion of Elijah's enormous but still human spirit.

Elisha then picks up Elijah's mantle, which is all that remains of his master, wraps it around his shoulders and begins his journey back to his people. He comes to the Jordan River and cannot get across until he remembers that he now has "Elijah power," so he sweeps Elijah's mantle across the river and the waters split once more, in Red Sea fashion, and he walks across on dry land. The same God who had been present in the life of Moses and Elijah is now present in Elisha. Upon his return, this reality is validated as a group, known as "the sons of the prophets," proclaims that now "the Spirit of Elijah rests upon Elisha" (II Kings 12:15).

Luke, portraying Jesus as the "new Elijah," takes that story, magnifies it and retells it about Jesus. Jesus and his disciples walk out to the rendezvous point of Jesus' departure. The new Elijah needs no magical chariot drawn by fiery horses. He rises into the sky under his own power. He does not give to a single disciple a double portion of his human spirit, but he pours out on all the gathered community of his followers the infinite power of the Holy Spirit, sufficient to last through all the ages. Luke takes the fire from the chariot and horses and turns it into tongues of fire that dance on the heads of the gathered followers (Acts 2:1–3). He takes the whirlwind that propelled Elijah heavenward and turns it into the "mighty rushing wind" that filled the entire room (2:2).

Finally, Luke spelled out his experience with Jesus. It was to break the barriers that separate us from one another. When the Spirit of God fell on the gathered people, they were lifted into a new human community, where they spoke in the languages that the hearers understood.

Luke's Jesus, who could bring Jew and Samaritan, Jew and Gentile together, could now, through the church, draw the entire world into a new sense of what it means to be human.

This is how Luke climaxes his gospel and opens the theme of the book of Acts. We will next look briefly at the remainder of the book of Acts and watch how the theme of universalism is developed there.

CHAPTER 50

Acts

The Spirit That Embraces the World and Drives Toward Wholeness

After its dramatic opening chapters the book of Acts becomes something of a travelogue, the account of the journey of this Jesus movement. It was designed by Luke to bring fulfillment to the words he puts into Jesus' mouth at the very beginning of the book: "You shall be my witnesses in Jerusalem, in all Judea and Samaria, and to the ends of the earth" (1:8). Luke is intent upon portraying the Jesus movement as one that started humbly in the hills of a remote Galilee and then moved through Samaria on its way to Jerusalem, where Luke records its first climax in the crucifixion of Jesus. Asserting that the death of Jesus was not the end of this movement, he then proceeds to tell the story of how the movement began to spread from Jerusalem until it reached its second climax in the capital of the known world, the city of Rome.

This author has his story move in only one direction; never in Luke's narrative does the story return to a place from which it has departed. One illustration of this becomes visible when the angelic messengers of the resurrection in Luke's narrative do not order the disciples to return to Galilee, as they do in both Mark and Matthew, but rather ask them "not to depart from Jerusalem, but to wait for the promise of the Father" (1:4). To signal the beginning of the next phase of his story, Luke repeats the words of the promise originally stated earlier in his gospel by John the Baptist that, while John has baptized with water, the disciples of Jesus will be baptized by the Holy Spirit and in the power of that Spirit a worldwide mission will be inaugurated.

Then in quick succession, Luke brings the appearances of the risen Christ to an abrupt end, removes Jesus physically from the earth in the act of ascension and depicts the inauguration of the Christian church with the outpouring of the Holy Spirit on the gathered community in which the people of the world discover a new sense of oneness. The reader is not allowed to miss the world-wide significance of this latter story, for Luke lists the nations of the world to whom the gospel is now proclaimed. That list says that those gathered at that time included "Parthians, Medes, Elamites, and residents of Mesopotamia, Judea and Cappadocia, Pontus and Asia, Phrygia and Pamphilia, Egypt and parts of Libya belonging to Cyrene and visitors from Rome, both Jews and proselytes, Cretans and Arabs" (2:9–11). Given the knowledge of geography available in that day, this is a rather impressive list.

Luke uses the device of sermons that he places on the lips of Peter (1:15–20, 2:14–36, 3:12–26, 4:8–12) and Stephen (7:2–56) to communicate his message. Jesus is the fulfillment of the Jewish scriptures, and Luke's story announces that God has made Jesus, whom "you crucified and killed," both Lord and Christ—that is, both a divine presence and the expected messiah of the Jews. In the process, we are given a view of how Luke perceived the early Christian movement. With the election of Matthias to replace Judas Iscariot, a story that only Luke tells (1:22–26), the Christian church was to be patterned after Israel with twelve tribes or leaders. The followers of Jesus devoted themselves to "the apostles' teaching and fellowship, to the breaking of bread and the prayers" (2:43). They were portrayed as being capable of both signs and wonders since the Spirit dwelled within them, and they held all things in common (2:44, 5:1–11). They attended the Temple "day by day" and in the privacy of their homes they conducted the Eucharist by breaking bread together (2:46). Peter was always cast as the leader according to Luke; though sometimes accompanied by John, Peter was clearly the spokesperson for the Christian movement.

Next Luke introduces the first account of tension with the leaders of Judaism in the persons of Caiaphas, John and Alexander, together with all of the members of the high-priestly family. That conflict came to a resolution, according to the book of Acts, in the words of a leader of the Pharisees named Gamaliel, who urged the rulers to wait upon the test of time. "If this movement is of God," he said, "you cannot stop it and if it is not of God, it will fail without assistance from you" (5:33–42). With this sage advice Gamaliel prevailed and we watch as this tension between church and synagogue begins to fade. This is part of the process we use to date the book of Acts, for the author is describing life in the early church just after the followers of Jesus were expelled from the synagogue after 88 CE and before the year 100.

That original tension, however, was replaced by one within the movement of the followers of Jesus themselves and the book of Acts now turns its attention to this battle. It was between the strict constructionist Jewish Christians on one side and the newly converted Hellenist or Greek Christians on the other. The book of Acts will pivot on this conflict. Peter was the champion of the strict Jewish point of view, which argued that Jesus did not set aside the Torah, but rather fulfilled it. This meant that the power of Jewish law was still to be observed in Christian circles, including the rituals of circumcision, kosher dietary laws and the Sabbath worship traditions. This group also asserted that the only doorway open to Greek converts to Christianity was to become Jews first and then Christians. Paul is introduced in this book as the one who would ultimately become the champion of the Gentile Christian movement. Stephen enters the story as one of the newly chosen deacons who would expand the Christian community's leadership in order to enable them better to care for the needs of the Hellenists.

According to the book of Acts, Paul began his career as a defender of the full power of the Torah and as a persecutor of those who would relativize its claims. The narrative in the book of Acts pauses to allow the tensions in the Christian community to build by introducing another deacon named Philip, who also presses the boundaries of the Torah. Philip baptized an Ethiopian eunuch, an act which violated the way the strict construction-ists interpreted the law on two levels. First, the Ethiopian was a Gentile who was brought by his baptism directly into the Chris-tian movement with no journey through Judaism. Second, as a eunuch, this Ethiopian was a direct challenge to the literal truth of the Torah, for Deuteronomy could not be more specific on this issue: "He whose testicles are crushed or whose male member is cut off should not enter the assembly of the Lord" (Deut. 23:1).

Next, Luke moves to relate the story of Paul's conversion on the road to Damascus, after which Paul is baptized, has his blind-ness ended and begins his missionary career. From Paul's writings we have already learned about the conflict he had with those he called "the Judaizers" and his showdown with Peter, their spokes-person (Gal. 1). By the time Luke wrote the book of Acts, how-ever, that tension was more a part of history than it was currently alive and real. Luke even explains how it was overcome by telling the story of how Peter had been converted to Paul's perspective. This dramatic tale will form the end of the Peter section of Acts (10:9–16), to which we now turn, and open the Paul section.

Peter's conversion took place on a rooftop at noon where, Luke says, he was engaged in prayer (10:9ff). Being hungry, Luke tells us, he fell into a trance and saw the heavens opened, from which a great sheet descended, laden with creatures—animals, reptiles and birds that were edible, but not kosher, perhaps including both pigs and shellfish. A heavenly voice invited Peter to ease his hunger by rising, killing and eating. Peter declined, saying in effect, I have never eaten anything common or unclean. To which the voice from heaven pro-claimed, "Peter, what God has cleansed, you must not call common" (10:15). This vision was repeated, according to the book of Acts, three times before Peter got the message and went to the home of an "upright and God-fearing Gentile" named Cornelius, and baptized him and his whole family. That was the moment, says Luke, when the Holy Spirit fell on the Gentiles. The words of Peter then became the new mantra for the Christian movement: "Truly I perceive that God shows no partiality, but in every nation anyone who fears God and does what is right is acceptable to him" (10:34–35).

The issue at stake in this battle was whether or not Christianity would become a universal movement. It was Peter himself, the champion of the strict constructionists, who forged the new way forward. Peter thus is portrayed not only as the one who launched the Christian movement, but also as the life through which the boundary between Jew and Gentile was breached and as the one in whom the new vision of universalism was born. His work having been completed, Peter fades away and Paul now moves front and center. It is ultimately on the shoulders of Paul that the inclusive character of Christianity would be formed, one that would, as Paul says in Galatians, embrace "Jew and Greek, male and female, bond and free" (3:28).

So Luke turns to the story of Paul and through the vehicle of his life tells how Christianity reached Rome or what the King James Version calls the "uttermost parts of the earth," which seems far more dramatic than the RSV's "to the ends of the earth (Acts 1:8). The tribal boundary that separated the Jews from the Gentiles was enormous. As intense as this battle was inside Christianity, it would not be either the last or the bitterest fight that would mark Christianity in its journey toward universalism. There would be other tensions and conflicts before Christians were able to see women, people of color, adherents of other religions, homosexual persons, mentally ill persons and even left-handed persons as fully human. There would also be others in history who would play the role of Peter and ease the Christian movement into its calling to bring abundant life to all. Only then could the invitation of Jesus, "Come unto me, all ye," be fully heard. The book of Acts chronicles the story of Christianity's walk into what it was created to be. Today we continue to write our chapter in this same ongoing narrative.

CHAPTER 51

Paul and Early Christians as Viewed Through Acts

W hen the book of Acts moves beyond the conflict that set Jewish Christians against Greek Christians, it is ready to chronicle the story of how Christianity became a universal human religion. From the capital of Judaism to the capital of the Roman Empire is the story line that this book follows. The hero of this expansionist phase of the Christian movement is Saul of Tarsus, whom we know as Paul the apostle. We have previously examined both the autobiographical details and the content of Paul's epistles, but now in the book of Acts Luke fleshes out the portrait of his life and his personality as others experienced him. How much of this portrait is historical and how much is the product of Luke's fertile imagination is often hard to determine. Luke writes the book of Acts some thirty to forty years, or two generations, after the death of Paul, and legends about heroes do tend to grow after the heroes have died. This fate may well have befallen Paul in the book of Acts.

Acts does give us, however, the only cohesive picture we have of Paul's adventurous missionary journeys, a picture that correlates well with corroborative details in the Pauline epistles. This sense of historicity is strengthened when Acts shifts dramatically from the pronoun "they" to the pronoun "we" (16:19), and continues this pattern for some time. It is as if the author of Acts found a diary of the journeys of Paul written by one of Paul's companions and simply incorporated this diary into his larger work. These "we" sections of Acts are accorded by many, but certainly not by all, New Testament scholars a place of greater significance and greater authority than any other part of this book, so I simply call these passages to our attention and further study.

When I try to glimpse the portrait of the Paul of history as we have received it from ancient times, I always find the "personal notes" dropped almost accidentally into the text of the book of Acts to be enormously helpful. These notes offer a kind of unplanned access into the person of Paul. I think, for example, of that tale in Acts about an event that occurred on Paul's first missionary journey, during which he was the number-two person to Barnabas on the missionary team. In this story, the two missionaries were in the city of Lystra (14:6ff) and were mistaken for Gods visiting from Mount Olympus. The people, looking at the two of them, began to refer to Barnabas as Zeus, the king of the Gods, and to Paul as Hermes, the messenger God. In the cultural patterns of that day the tradition defined Zeus as tall and commanding in stature. Barnabas, then, must have himself been a person of imposing size to have been mistaken for Zeus. Hermes, the messenger God, was portrayed as small and wiry and constantly speaking. For Paul to have been thought of as Hermes, he must have been similar in stature and above all talkative. Clearly Paul elicited that kind of image in the minds of his hearers. Paul is described in one other second-century apocalyptic source as thin, with dark connecting eyebrows stretched across the entirety of his face.[1] There is some similarity in these two descriptions.

In Acts 13:13–15 Barnabas and Paul are said to travel to the town of Perga in Pamphylia and then on to Antioch of Pisidia. In the rest of that chapter, the liturgical practice of the first-century synagogue was described, presumably just by chance, giving

---

[1]   The Apocryphal Acts of Paul and Thecla from the book by this title edited by Jan Bremmer. See bibliography for details.

us the best insight we have into how the synagogue functioned on the Sabbath at that time. There we learn of the priority of the reading of the books of the Torah, which were attributed to Moses, how the readings from the prophets were organized and how members of the congregation were invited to do what preachers call "bring a message." It was at this point, as I have suggested before, that the disciples of Jesus began the process of demonstrating that the Jewish scriptures pointed to Jesus in almost every verse. By the time the gospels were written, this interpretative pattern was both assumed and operative. The author of Acts relates the details of Paul's sermon in 13:16–41 and provides us with dramatic insights into the way Christians employed the Jewish scriptures and the way that Christianity emerged in the synagogue.

The book of Acts also chronicles in some detail the hostility that broke out over Paul and his teaching on the part of the Orthodox Jewish world. On his journeys, in whatever city he visited, Paul, forever a committed Jew, always went to the synagogue first. In these synagogues outside the Jewish homeland, there were three distinct groups gathered for worship: the Orthodox, traditional Jews who believed that the entire truth of God was embodied in the Torah and who were not, therefore, prepared to welcome any deviations from or additions to the traditional text; the liberal-leaning Jews now dispersed from their homeland and more and more interacting with their Gentile neighbors, and finally those known as "Gentile proselytes," the people drawn to the synagogue by the ethical monotheism of Judaism, but unwilling to adopt the Jewish cultic practices.

Paul's message appealed first to these Gentile proselytes and second, but quite significantly, to the liberal Jews of the Diaspora. Paul drew, however, little more than hostility from those identified as the Orthodox party, for whom any change threatened their security. So this latter group was the primary source of the hostility toward Paul, which plagued him everywhere he went. Acts 15 describes a council of church leaders gathered to deal with this tension. According to this Acts account, a compromise was worked out by James, the Lord's brother, who at that time appeared to have headed the Jerusalem community of Jewish believers in Jesus. In this compromise, Paul was given carte blanche to continue his work among the Gentiles and was assured that his converts did not have to comply with Jewish ritual practices, except in three details: abstain from eating meat that had been offered to idols, abstain from unchastity and abstain from blood from any animal that had been strangled and was thus not ceremonially clean. Whether the details of this council are accurate is hard to say, but it did serve to set the Christian movement free from the constraints of the defining Jewish rituals and to legitimize the separation from Judaism, which had originally given birth to Christianity.

When Paul and Barnabas prepared for their second journey, a dispute broke out between them, leading to a split up of this team. The issue, according to Acts, was whether to take John Mark (generally called simply Mark) with them. Mark appears to have abandoned them on their first missionary journey in order to return home. Paul was unwilling to have Mark go again with him, so Paul and Barnabas parted company and Paul became then the senior member of a second missionary team, choosing Silas to accompany him. Barnabas then took Mark with him and in this manner the movement spread.

On this second tour (16:1–10) we learn that Paul had a dream of a Macedonian imploring him to come to Macedonia. Paul obeyed the vision and Christianity moved into what is now Europe. Paul had adventures in Greece, including a debate in Athens that he clearly did not win. Paul's direction was now set and he turned his efforts toward the vast Gentile world. This turning further aroused the hostility of the Orthodox party of Jews.

Paul promised to return to Jerusalem to bring money for the relief of the Jewish followers of Jesus, so he made a final trip to this holy city (21:1ff). There his condemnation on the part of the Orthodox party of Judaism caused him to appeal their guilty verdict to Rome under his privilege as a Roman citizen. This resulted in his subsequent journey to Rome by ship, a narrative that makes up the bulk of the remainder of Luke's second book. On both the trip to Jerusalem and the trip to Rome, the book of Acts becomes an exciting adventure story. On one occasion, Paul began a sermon at midnight and preached so long that a young man named Eutychus, who was sitting in a window, went to sleep and fell to the floor as if dead. Paul revived him, but the admonition against long sermons found a scriptural basis (20:7–12)! On his trip to Rome, we read of storms, shipwrecks at sea, the bite of a poisonous viper and many other adventures (Acts 27). In the final chapter the story of Paul's arrival in Rome is told (28:16), and soon thereafter the book of Acts closes rather abruptly, saying that Paul lived in that city at his own expense for two years under very loose arrangements, welcoming all who came to him (28:30).

While the story of Paul's death is not told, Luke's purpose has been achieved. The Christian message traveled from Galilee to Jerusalem to Rome and was now planted firmly in that capital of the known world. As we say, "The rest is history." Is Acts an accurate account? We can never be sure. The Christian church did, however, move with Paul into all the world.

PART XI

The Pastoral Epistles, Hebrews and the General Epistles

CHAPTER 52

I and II Timothy and Titus

"We Have the Truth!"

Thus far, as we have explored the origins of the various books of the New Testament, we have not yet come across that familiar form of human religion that asserts: "We have the truth! If you disagree with us, the truth is not in you. It is our God-given duty to define truth, defend truth and impose truth." Up until this point in the biblical story, the Christian movement has basked in the wonder of the Christ experience, sought words that could convey the power of that experience to others and dealt with conflict only in the attempt by believers to clarify what this Christ experience really meant. Since, however, religious systems almost always devolve into security-giving systems in which "my understanding of God" is assumed to be the same as God, we should not be surprised to discover this negativity making its appearance within the Christian movement. When we turn to the pastoral epistles, the ones we have named I and II Timothy and Titus, our wait comes to an end. This suggestion that any person can possess "ultimate truth" in his or her propositional statements permeates almost every verse of these particular writings. This attitude is so apparent that it actually helps us to date these works. That, in turn, forms the data that make us absolutely certain Paul is not the author of any of these epistles.

The pastoral epistles are clearly the product of a later period of church history, when missionaries, prophets and teachers have been replaced by hierarchical and authoritative figures called bishops, priests or presbyters and deacons—all institutional functionaries. Even more, the office of a senior bishop, elder, or archbishop has had time to develop. The primary task of this official, it seems, is to impose order on the life of the various congregations in a given geographical region and to guarantee conformity in both their worship and their teaching. From other sources, we can identify this ecclesiastical structure as reflecting the period in church history no earlier than 90 CE and possibly as late as 120 CE.

While these dates alone rule out Pauline authorship, they also make us aware that enough time has passed so that Paul is regarded as a respected, but not a controversial figure. In these works, Paul is portrayed as a revered elder statesman-apostle pos-sessing great authority—indeed, such authority that the words of these epistles were thought to be buttressed by the claim that they had been written in his name. Timothy and Titus, the younger companions of the historical Paul—men who were named in Paul's own authentic letters (Timothy in Romans, I and II Cor-inthians, Philippians and I Thessalonians, and Titus in II Corin-thians and Galatians)—have been transformed into symbols of the next generation of Christian leaders who listen eagerly to the elder Paul's advice. While the Paul of history could write his ode to love in I Corinthians 13 and speak about his own conversion in Romans 8:38–39, the Paul of the pastoral epistles is interested only in order, "sound" teaching, proper obedience and the need to drive away erroneous and false teaching. In the pastoral epis-tles "orthodoxy" has been defined in inflexible ways.

In content, the pastorals are quite similar to the five letters of Ignatius of Antioch, written between 110 and 113 CE while he was on his way to his own martyrdom. They reflect similar church structures and lines of authority and issue similar warnings against false teachers, once again demonstrating that the pastoral epistles are the products of about the same time and history. The chief function of a bishop in both of these sources is to defend the faith and to establish orthodoxy, a word that means simply "right thinking." Words like "doctrine" and "teaching" are a major concern of these books that clearly favor the developing church doctrinal order that would later be referred to as "Christian orthodoxy" or "Catholic teaching."

It is also apparent in these writings that something is threatening this sound doctrine. Historians have identified the enemy as a group of Christians who called themselves Gnostics.[1] The pastoral epistles exhort younger leaders to protect the "true faith" by confronting evil, rebuking or silencing these false teachers who are disparaged as imposters, unbelievers and deceivers (II Tim. 3:10ff). The battle grew quite hostile with words like "stupid," "unprofitable" and "futile" being used (II Tim. 2:23). God-given authority was claimed for established church leaders. These leaders alone were authorized to determine what constitutes "true doctrine" and they alone had the power to ordain new leaders, who, in order to qualify for ordination, had to take vows to be faithful to the established tradition. Those who, in a previous generation, had themselves been "revisionists" in the synagogue were now determined to allow no "revisionists" in the church. The language of the pastorals is replete with familiar religious hostility. Titus 1:13 refers to Cretans as "liars, evil beasts and lazy gluttons." I Timothy calls those opposed to sound doctrine "immoral persons, sodomites, kidnapers, liars and perjurers" (1:10). II Timothy says that these enemies of Christian truth engage in "godless chatter" and likens their talk to "gangrene" (2:16).

---

1   Gnostics were people who claimed to possess secret knowledge or even special revelatory insights. They thus challenged orthodox authority on the basis of this source of truth, which lay outside hierarchical control. With the discovery of authentic gnostic writings at Nag Hammadi, they do not look nearly so evil or threatening as some of their critics portrayed them as being. I think I could make the case that many elements found in the Protestant Reformation represent a revival of Gnosticism.

Church fights can frequently be anything but Christian! By this time in church history the disciples of Jesus seem to have moved rather far from Jesus' admonition to "love your enemies"! Yet in the midst of this rather rampant hostility we are startled to find familiar and treasured passages, words that have enriched our vocabulary and are frequently repeated, but about whose origin we have generally had no clue. I refer to such phrases as: "A little wine is good for your stomach" (I Tim. 5:23); "The love of money is the root of all evil" (I Tim. 6:10); "We brought nothing into this world and it is certain that we can carry nothing out" (I Tim. 6:7). Christianity so often blends good and evil.

Someone once said that Christianity probably would not have survived had it not become institutionalized and that it might not continue to survive because it did become institutionalized. Institutions, certainly including the Christian church, always subvert truth to institutional needs. That is why the various factions within Christianity have developed irrational power claims such as, "My pope is infallible," or "My Bible is inerrant," or "There is only one true church, and it is mine" or "No one comes to the Father except through my church or my faith tradition."

These assertions always arise in religious movements when the decision is made that the wonder, truth and mystery of God can in fact be captured inside human words that originated inside human minds. God and my understanding of God become the same. The power needs of religious institutions become identified with the truth of God and the well-being of church leaders. This mentality almost inevitably produces religious wars and religious persecution, resulting in atrocities such as the Inquisition and other incredible cruelties that we Christian people have inflicted on our victims over the centuries. It also finds expression in the rudeness frequently seen in religious debate.

Two stories will serve to make this point clear and to reveal why I have no great appreciation for the pastoral epistles, which not only introduced but also attempted to justify these attitudes and helped to make them part of the life of institutional Christianity.

I have been on a number of book tours to Australia. In the Anglican Archdiocese of Sydney, Christianity has been captured by a Northern Irish Protestant fundamentalism of an eighteenth-century variety and frozen in time in the South Pacific. The Bible to that group of Christians has to be read literally, women cannot be ordained or have authority over men and homosexuality is an abomination! So my arrival there appeared to frighten Sydney's Anglican leaders and had regularly resulted in a "call to arms" against one who might (they seemed to suggest) be the Antichrist. When in the 1990s I went on a lecture tour for my book *Resurrection: Myth or Reality?* these leaders quickly wrote and published a fundamentalist paperback rebuttal that hit the bookstands the day my plane landed. In addition to that, they devoted a number of pages in their archdiocesan newspaper *The Southern Cross* to arming their people with the "facts" necessary to resist the onslaught of this non-fundamentalist, and thus non-true-believing Christian. Finally, they appointed a "truth squad" headed by one of their bishops, Paul Barnett, to follow me around Australia to "correct my errors" publicly, lest the people be corrupted. They contacted any radio or television station on which I was scheduled to appear to demand "equal time" for "the truth." One noonday TV program decided to book us together rather than accede to their "equal time" request. The conversation went well, at least from my point of view, until Paul Barnett exploded with the words, "Jack, you're nothing but a Gnostic." I responded, "Paul, the wonderful thing about that charge is that ninety-nine percent of our Australian viewers do not know whether you have just insulted me or complimented me." I apparently bothered Paul Barnett as much as the Gnostics had bothered the authors of the pastoral epistles.

The second story happened in a public lecture in western North Carolina some years ago. The pastor and some members of a "Community Bible Church" expressed great alarm about the fact that I had been invited to do a lecture series in that town, so they planned, unbeknownst to me, a public counterattack.

In the question and answer session following the lecture I

recognized a man who was holding his hand high. He was perhaps the fourth questioner who spoke on that night. When the microphone got to him, he said "Bishop Spong, I'm sick." I immediately responded that nothing we were doing that night was more important than his health and asked what we could do for him. "You don't understand," he replied, "I'm sick of you!" and then he began to rehearse the familiar line about those who, in his opinion, defiled the inerrant word of God by looking at the scriptures in a non-fundamentalist way. After listening to him for a few minutes, I interrupted him to ask the audience if they would like for this man to be allowed, in the name of fairness, to address the whole audience. They shouted back with loud denials, and the man took his coat and departed. It is of interest to me that in my life I have received sixteen death threats. None came from an atheist! None came from a Buddhist! All of them came from those who claimed to possess "the true faith" or to be "born-again Bible-believing Christians." It is amazing that rude and even potentially murderous behavior can so easily be justified with appeals to God. The scriptures may well point to the reality of a transcendent God. The scriptures, however, do not, cannot and will not ever capture the truth of God. It is into that limitless truth of God that we walk. The one essential prerequisite for being on this journey is that each of us must relinquish the popular religious fiction that we already, in our religious systems, possess that truth.

Ultimate truth can never be fully captured in propositional statements made in human history by time-warped and time-bound human words. To claim that it can be is to admit to idolatry. The destructive idea that truth is contained in any religious form was first introduced to the Christian movement by the pastoral epistles. Christianity has been compromised by this strange idea from that day to this.

CHAPTER 53

The Epistle to the Hebrews

We do not know who wrote the epistle to the Hebrews. We do not know the date of its composition. We do not know to whom it was actually written. What do we know? We are clear that it was not authored by Paul. Though we call it an epistle, it was certainly not written as a letter. Its format is much more that of an address, a lecture or a sermon. The "Hebrews" to whom this work is addressed do not appear to be Hebrews, at least not in a religious sense. They were, rather, Jewish Christians—that is, people of Jewish background who had become followers of Jesus. They had roamed far from the strict orthodoxy of traditional Judaism, but they were still deeply familiar with and committed to Jewish liturgical practices. They were Hellenized, having breathed deeply of the Greek culture that had spread over the known world from the time of the conquest by the Macedonians in the fourth century BCE under the leadership, first, of King Philip II and, later, of his son Alexander the Great. This letter to the Hebrews was written in Greek, the language of the empire, not Aramaic, the language of traditional Judaism. It nonetheless reveals a deep and significant connection to the Hebrew scriptures. It is noteworthy, though, that whenever the epistle to the Hebrews quotes these scriptures, it does so from the Septuagint, the Greek translation of the Old Testament. Where these Greek-speaking, dispersed Hebrews lived when they received this book cannot be determined. The guesses as to the time of its writing range from the late 60s CE at the earliest to about 140 CE at the latest. The weight of opinion, however, would fix the date no earlier than the late 80s and no later than 100 CE. The epistle of Clement, a well-known piece of early Christian writing that is generally dated in the middle years of the tenth decade, does in fact quote the book of Hebrews. This should provide us with an outer limit, but the proposed date of Clement is itself also widely debated, with most scholars gravitating to around 96 CE. All we can really do is to peruse the text of this book and learn whatever we can from its content about both its author and its audience.

The atmosphere reflected in the epistle to the Hebrews is tense. The text speaks of those who are in danger of drifting away (2:1). It mentions those who have fled for refuge (6:18). It urges its hearers to hold fast to their confession of hope without wavering (10:23). It refers to those who have the need of endurance (10:36). It urges perseverance in the task set before them (12:1). Finally, it assures its readers that since Jesus Christ is the same "yesterday, today and forever," their hearts should be strengthened by grace (13:8–9).

Many scholars suggest that this level of tension in the Christian community reflects the persecution under the Emperor Diocletian, which ravaged the nascent church between 81 and 96, making the latter years of this reign our best guess for the date of the composition of this book.

The recipients of this treatise seem to reflect one particular constituency in the evolving Christian church. While Christianity was born in a Jewish womb as a Jewish movement within the synagogue, it turned, primarily under the influence of Paul and Paul's followers, including the author of Luke/Acts and Paul's younger associates Timothy and Titus, into being more and more a Gentile religion. This fact served to make it harder and harder for some of the earliest disciples of Jesus, who were traditional Jews, to continue to live and worship inside the Christian movement. That is a reality that has been replicated again and again in religious history. Growth always marginalizes the original members of a particular tradition, who feel left behind and thus not part of the present consensus. The recipients of the book of Hebrews appear to have felt that they no longer fitted into what Christianity was becoming. They were beginning to pull away from their Christian convictions and were even, it appears, tempted to return to the Judaism of their childhood. The author of this book sought to dissuade them from this step by attempting to demonstrate the superiority of Christianity to traditional Judaism. The way this author chose to do that is quite telling.

To understand Hebrews we must return to the material about Yom Kippur, the Day of Atonement, that we have previously introduced. The book we call Hebrews makes no sense until we read it in terms of that significant holy day in the life of the synagogue. So at the risk of being repetitive, let me bring Yom Kippur back into our awareness with some new details. The liturgy of Yom Kippur focused on two animals that were brought to the high priest. Both animals had to reflect what the Jewish people yearned to be, physically perfect in body and morally perfect in mind and spirit. These animals were gone over scrupulously by the high priest until he was assured that they were perfect physical specimens; they could have no scratches, blemishes, scars or broken bones. They were deemed to be morally perfect by their nature, since they lived below the level of human freedom and were thus incapable of choosing to do evil.

One of these animals was then slaughtered in a sacrificial, liturgical manner and its blood was smeared on the mercy seat of God in the Temple's Holy of Holies. This blood was believed to possess cleansing power. Through the blood of this offering to God, the people believed they could now stand before God at least on this one day, despite their sinfulness. They came to God, they said, through the blood of the sacrificed creature that washed their sins away. In the latter half of the book of Isaiah (40–55) this animal is clearly identified as a sacrificial lamb, but that is not clear from the book of Leviticus (23:26–32).

The second animal, referred to in Leviticus as a goat, was then brought into the assembly of the people and placed before the high priest who, taking the goat's horns, began to confess the sins of the people. Those sins were thus said to come out of the people and to land on the head and back of this goat, making it the bearer of the people's sins. This animal was then banished from the assembly and run into the wilderness, leaving the people symbolically cleansed from their sins. This goat was called "the scapegoat," for it bore the sins of the people and vicariously endured the fate the people had earned for themselves.

There is no doubt that the liturgy of Yom Kippur was instrumental in interpreting the Jesus experience among the earliest Jewish Christians. Echoes of this connection are found again and again in the New Testament. Paul, as we noted previously, uses this Yom Kippur formula when he wrote in I Corinthians that Jesus (like the sacrificial animal of Yom Kippur) died "for our sins in accordance with the scriptures" (15:3). Mark makes reference to this liturgical understanding when he writes that Jesus, like the Yom Kippur sacrifice, gave his life as a "ransom" for many (10:45). When John the Baptist saw Jesus for the first time in the Fourth Gospel, he called him "the lamb of God who takes away the sins of the world" (John 1:29), a phrase lifted almost verbatim from the Yom Kippur liturgy.

The author of the letter to the Hebrews was thus apparently writing to discouraged Jewish Christians, who no longer felt at home in the predominantly Gentile worshiping communities, hoping to prevent their return to the fold of Judaism. One cannot go back, the author argues, to the ineffective Yom Kippur sacrifice, which has to be repeated annually because it affects nothing permanently. Yom Kippur, he contends, only expresses a yearning for change; it does not itself create change. The sacrifice of Jesus on the cross, he argues, did in fact break the power of sin that made those sacrifices necessary in the first place. We can now enter the presence of God, the author of Hebrews argues, with all our warts and shortcomings visible, for in the cross of Calvary the love of God accepted the offering of the new lamb of God, embraced us in our sinfulness and transformed us. So, he concluded, if one leaves the Christian faith to return to Judaism, one is actually leaving the sacrifice that made all future sacrifices unnecessary in favor of a sacrifice that must be repeated annually. Jesus was the perfect offering for which God yearned, while the Yom Kippur animals were only a symbol of the eternal human yearning to be whole. It is to our ears a strange argument, but it must have resonated with the audience to whom it was first addressed.

The author of Hebrews also likens the priesthood of Jesus, not to the high priests of Jewish worship, but to the eternal priesthood of a figure named Melchizedek mentioned in the book of Genesis (Heb. 6:19–20, Gen. 14:18). Melchizedek's priesthood, it was said, was without beginning or ending. Perhaps this is the place where the idea of pre-existence first entered the Christian story. In this paradigm, the Christ is at one and the same time both the new sacrifice and the sacrificing high priest. It was an argument based on ancient worship patterns, but it must have impressed some contemporary leaders since this book was quickly incorporated into the canon of Christian scriptures. Yet, as the church became more and more Gentile, the power of this argument faded. Today it sounds like another version of the old religious cliché: "My God is superior to your God!" In its day, however, it stated the essential Christian claim that all people can come into the presence of God just as they are, because the love of God seen in Jesus embraces them all—which is, I believe, the one irreducible Christian claim. The epistle to the Hebrews ultimately proclaims that there are no boundaries on the love of God. That is a worthy message, even when couched in an archaic form.

CHAPTER 54

The General Epistles

James, I and II Peter and Jude

When we come near the end of the New Testament, we run into four small books that bear the names of well-known figures in the gospel tradition. They are James and I Peter, each of which consists of five chapters; then II Peter with three chapters, and finally Jude with only one.

James is, in many ways, a counterpoint to the main thrust of the New Testament, particularly to Paul, and was traditionally thought to be the work of James, the brother of the Lord, though that assertion is widely dismissed today. This book does, however, emerge out of the community of Jewish Christians with which James was identified. At one point, James, the Lord's brother, seemed to have represented a strong option regarding what it meant to be Christian. The epistle of James seeks to present a later form of that early argument and it serves today to balance Paul's overwhelming theology of grace. Martin Luther, clearly a direct theological descendant of Paul, called this epistle an "epistle of straw" and tried to have it expunged from the New Testament. Obviously, he failed! The epistle of James asserts that faith is insufficient without works; indeed, it says that without works faith is dead (2:17).

Like the epistle to the Hebrews, the epistle of James is more a treatise or a sermon than it is a letter, arising out of the earliest Jewish Christian strand of pre-Pauline Christianity. In its one hundred and eight verses, it contains sixty imperative statements about how the gospel is to be lived. It has some echoes in it of the Sermon on the Mount and is steeped in ethical prescriptions. For this epistle "ethics" means the demands of the law or the Torah, while for Paul "ethics" means the fruit of the Spirit. Therein are set the battle lines for the oldest fight in Christian history. We have seen this fight now from three angles. Paul's take on it was in Galatians, then we saw it in the book of Acts, now it appears in counterpoint to Paul in one epistle to James.

This epistle is generally dated in the last decade of the first century, between 90 and 100 CE. While James, the Lord's brother, is clearly not its author, the epistle does support the point of view that James appears to have held. Even that, however, is not certain, for most of what we know about James comes from Paul in Galatians or from Luke in the book of Acts, and neither source would be anywhere near objective. I find the epistle of James to be of value, but not of great value. It has, in fact, inspired charitable work among the poor, and that is its major claim to belonging in the New Testament.

I Peter was written probably late in the first century. Its message is conveyed in elegant Greek that Simon Peter, the fisherman from Galilee, could never have mastered. It is clearly not written by the head of the apostles. Its purpose was to encourage Christians undergoing persecution, probably in the region of the world that we today call Turkey. It purports to have been written from Rome at the time of the persecutions under Nero, when Peter was supposedly crucified upside down. This epistle has thus been used to buttress the Vatican's claims that Peter became the first bishop of Rome and thus the first pope and that Christianity, therefore, had to be run from Rome. Of course, there have been other such claims in history. Constantine thought the Christian church should be run from Constantinople. The Mormons thought it should be run from Salt Lake City. The Religious Science movement thought it should be run from Boston. We ought never to confuse institutional power claims with the gospel.

There are, nonetheless, some things in the epistle we call I Peter that merit mention. The text seems to oppose the physicality of the bodily resurrection and to identify Jesus' resurrection with what later came to be called "the ascension," rather than with a resuscitated body. This would line the author of this book up with Paul and place him in opposition to Luke. This fact causes me to date I Peter prior to Luke, or at least prior to the time when Luke's gospel gained ascendancy in the mid-90s.

It is from I Peter that the creedal phrase "He descended into hell" evolved. The word "hell" originally meant not a place of torment, but something more like Sheol or Gehenna, simply the abode of the dead. I Peter suggests that, between the crucifixion and the resurrection, Jesus went and preached to "the souls in prison" (3:19). This text was thus used to support an argument that Christianity developed, seeking to give access to salvation to those who lived before Jesus while still maintaining the authority to make exclusive claims for the ultimacy of this new faith system. Human sensitivity always seems to find a way to lessen the horror of hostile theological rules. Creeds that many seem to believe "dropped from the sky complete with footnotes" in fact reveal a remarkable ability to adapt to new realities and new sensitivities.

II Peter, as we noted earlier, was probably the last-written book to be included in the New Testament. It is generally dated in the first half of the second century, perhaps around 135 CE. This book was not written by Peter either. None of the author claims made for any of these books will stand up to any real scrutiny, a fact that has been known in Christian academic circles for at least two hundred years. II Peter actually quotes from the epistle of Jude, which we know was not written until well after the turn of the first century. It also refers to Paul's letters as if they are not only bound together in a single volume, but are already regarded as "scripture" equal in authority to any other part of the sacred text. These attitudes once again reflect a point of view and indeed a practice that did not develop until the second century. In today's world II Peter is, I fear, little noticed and seldom quoted. That is probably what it deserves, because like some of the lesser prophets, it speaks almost not at all about the concerns of today's world.

Jude is the final of the non-Johannine general epistles. It claims to have been written by Jude or Judas, also one of the brothers of Jesus. There is no suggestion that the Judas who was supposedly the traitor is the author of this book, but the naming does open us to consider the meaning of the fact that, on some of the New Testament's lists of the twelve, there are two apostles named Judas, one of whom is thought of as good. Luke calls this good Judas simply the son of James (Luke 6:16) and lists him alongside Judas Iscariot as one of the twelve. John, who never gives us a list of the twelve, does, however, refer to one called Judas, who is "not Iscariot" (John 14:22). It is Mark's gospel, once again, that refers to a Judas who is the brother of Jesus (6:3). Tradition has tried to associate one of these figures with the epistle of Jude. To identify any biblical character with the authorship of this book is by any measure a stretch. Jude is a late-first-century work written well past the life span of any of the New Testament characters, a fact revealed quite clearly in its text.

The epistle of Jude is a treatise that reflects a time similar to that of the pastorals Timothy and Titus. It assumes that Christianity is now a fully worked out, even codified faith system. It speaks of a Christianity that can be and in fact has been articulated in a recognizable creedal form. It even refers to Christianity as "the faith which was once for all delivered to the saints" (1:3). It seems to assume that Christianity dropped from heaven in a set of propositional beliefs. Some "systematic theology" books today still appear to believe that this is true. The authors of these books talk of "the deposit of faith," which reminds me more of a cow patty than it does of a living relationship with God. This attitude is part of what created the kind of religion in general, and the kind of Christianity in particular, that has fueled the darkest side of our history, including such tragic events as the Crusades, the Inquisition and the activity we call forced conversion. When I wrote my book *The Sins of Scripture* this text from Jude was one of what I called "the terrible texts of the Bible." It earned that designation by the fact that it has been used throughout history to justify a variety of life-killing prejudices and even the continued degradation of our environment. The book of Jude has, in my opinion, few saving graces, but one of them might be the benediction with which the book closes (1:24–25). In an adapted form, these verses have entered the liturgies of many churches.

Not all parts of the Bible are equally holy. Some of the epistles we have looked at in this brief unit do not come close to some other parts of the New Testament in either integrity or power. They are, however, "in the book" and so, to complete our journey through the Bible, I include them. I urge you to read them once. It will not take more than ten minutes. Then you will have done it and you will never have to do it again; for some parts of the Bible, once is enough.

PART XII

The Johannine Corpus

CHAPTER 55

Introducing the Johannine Material

The last series of books that must be considered to complete our study of the Bible's origins and meanings is referred to as "the Johannine literature." It consists of five separate pieces: the gospel of John; the three epistles, I, II and III John, and the Revelation of John. There was a time when people generally assumed that these five books were all the products of the same author. That point of view has long been abandoned in academic circles. There are connections that bind the Johannine material together, to be sure. I John and the gospel of John are quite similar in content, style and word usage, sufficient to cause some scholars to assume common authorship. Others suggest that the author of the first epistle of John was writing a treatise on the gospel, from which he quoted liberally, and that this accounts for the similarities. There are more questions about II and III John, the texts of which claim as their author one who was known as "the Elder." Almost no one today believes that the book of Revelation and the gospel of John are products of the same person.

There appears to have been a school of Christian thought near the end of the first century organized around a man known as John the Elder, who himself may have been a disciple of John Zebedee, which opens us to the possibility that these five books are the products of different members of that Johannine school. If that is so, it would account for the similarity found in these works as well as for the obvious differences. Although one can only speculate about first-century authors, this proposition makes more sense to me than anything else and I have adopted it until further study offers a better possibility.

Without doubt the crown jewel of the Johannine literature in the Bible is the gospel of John, frequently called simply the "Fourth Gospel." It is clearly the last of the gospels to have been written. It is dramatically different from the synoptic gospels, Mark, Matthew and Luke, which are deeply interdependent and thus can be studied together. John's gospel, however, has exercised a large and even a disproportionate influence on the development of the Christian creeds and the doctrines that define "orthodoxy" in the Western Christian church. It is probably the favorite gospel of most of the people who sit in the pews of our churches, if they had to choose a favorite. It contains many passages with which church people are deeply familiar. The so-called prologue, a hymn of praise to the Logos, translated as "Word" in most English Bibles, has been the most frequently used part of the New Testament in Christian liturgies. Passages from John are assigned reading in almost every Christian funeral—"In my Father's house are many mansions" (John 14:12) being the most familiar funeral line.

The Fourth Gospel has created unforgettable characters that dot the landscape of the Christian imagination. One thinks of doubting Thomas, the Samaritan woman by the well, Lazarus who was raised from the dead, Mary Magdalene alone and weeping at the tomb on Easter Day, Nicodemus who comes to Jesus by night, and the man born blind who is the hero of a long and detailed narrative. All of these figures are made vivid in our imaginations through the literary genius of the author of the Fourth Gospel. With the exceptions of Mary Magdalene and Thomas, they are not mentioned in any other gospel, and yet Magdalene and Thomas stand out in John in a way quite different from their portraits in the synoptic accounts.

Was the author of the Fourth Gospel familiar with the earlier gospels? Certainly there was a common body of tradition from which each of the gospel writers drew. John reveals a familiarity with the story line followed by the synoptics. All four gospels begin the story of the adult Jesus by relating him to the figure of John the Baptist. In Mark, Matthew and Luke, John the Baptist actually baptizes Jesus. The gospel of John introduces John the Baptist in this proper place, but the Baptist only bears witness that Jesus is the messiah; he never baptizes Jesus. All of the gospels conclude their narratives with a triumphal entry that we associate today with Palm Sunday. The passion story of each has the account of a betrayal, arrest, crucifixion and resurrection. In Mark, Matthew and Luke, however, the only time Jesus journeys from Galilee to Jerusalem is at the time of the crucifixion, while in John Jesus goes back and forth between Galilee and Jerusalem on several occasions. Mark, Matthew and Luke treat the public ministry of Jesus as something that is told over a one-year period; John suggests that the public ministry of Jesus was up to three years in duration. We can find references that appear to point to a rather specific connection between both Mark and Luke and the Fourth Gospel that suggests a possible dependence on these two as sources for John's writing, but that linkage is harder to establish with Matthew.

Yet despite all these similarities and connections, there are some very real differences between John and the other three gospels. There is no story in John of Jesus' miraculous or virgin birth. On two occasions (1:45 and 6:42) John's gospel refers to Jesus as "the son of Joseph." Jesus delivers no parables in John. The teaching of Jesus in the Fourth Gospel comes in long, somewhat convoluted theological discourses. John records no agony in the Garden of Gethsemane, but rather has Jesus walk resolutely toward his crucifixion, which he expects to be his moment of glorification. The high-priestly prayer in John 17 appears to be John's version of Jesus' prayer "Let this cup pass from me" found in the synoptics. There is no account of the Last Supper in John; instead we read the story of Jesus washing the feet of his disciples. John denies that the Last Supper was the Passover, while the earlier three gospels claim that it was. John is the only gospel writer who places the mother of Jesus at the foot of the cross to watch the crucifixion. Miracles present in the three synoptic gospels are turned into "signs" in John. The resurrection of Jesus in John is quite physical, sufficient to have Thomas be invited to touch the print of the nails in Jesus' hands and feet and to thrust his hand into the wound in Jesus' side, a wound that only John describes. In these resurrection details John is closer to Luke and in opposition to Paul. Indeed, the differences between the Fourth Gospel and the earlier three are so significant that a harmonization of the gospel tradition into a single narrative about Jesus is almost impossible. Mark presents us with a fully human Jesus upon whom God's Spirit was poured at his baptism, making him a God-infused but still human life, while John suggests that Jesus was the pre-existent word of God, enfleshed in the life of Jesus. The Jesus of Mark can emit from the cross the plaintive human wail, "My God, why have you forsaken me?" (15:34). The Jesus of John ends his life with the pronouncement, "It is finished" (19:30), which replicates the original creation story and portrays Jesus as the author of the New Creation. For John, Jesus is never separated from God: "The Father and I are one," John's Jesus says (10:30).

When the fellows at the Jesus Seminar were doing their work aimed at determining the authenticity of the words of Jesus recorded in the four gospels, they concluded that less than twenty percent of the words attributed to Jesus in the entire gospel tradition were actually spoken by him, which of course means that more than eighty percent were not. It is of interest to note that in the gospel of John there is only one line attributed to Jesus that was deemed an authentic word of the Jesus of history (4:43), where he seems to assert that a prophet has no honor in his own country.[1] Yet even if that judgment is correct (and as a fellow in

---

1   Both of these assertions are taken from the Jesus Seminar's book *The Five Gospels*. See bibliography for details.

the Jesus Seminar, I find no reason to argue with that conclusion), I still concur in the opinion that John's gospel captures the essence of the Jesus experience more profoundly than any other part of the New Testament. So I think of John as the least literal, but the most profoundly true of the four canonical gospel writers. I will return to this claim as this study unfolds.

I doubt if there is any biblical book about which we could say that we have in the present, surviving text of that book the exact words that the original author actually wrote. Books hand-copied over a number of centuries lend themselves to the probability of having their words edited, added to and even deleted. The gospel of John is no different. There are three textual conclusions about John that have gained wide, if not universal support. One is that chapters 5 and 6 need to be reversed. In their present order, they make no contextual sense.[2] The second is that the beautiful story in chapter 8 of Jesus standing between the woman taken in the act of adultery and her accusers is not and never was part of the original text of John's gospel. The third is that chapter 21 is an appendix, an epilogue that was added later to the gospel and was not part of the original corpus. I will assume in this unit the truth of each of these three textual insights.

With this introduction, I turn now to look at the Johannine corpus, first the gospel, then the epistles and finally the Revelation of John.

---

2   C. H. Dodd is the strongest voice against this. See bibliography for details.

CHAPTER 56

The Gospel of John

Not a Literal Book

If I had to give my readers one clue and one clue only that would unlock the Fourth Gospel and allow its honesty and wonder to flow forth, it would be that the author is constantly poking fun at anyone who would take his message literally, misunderstand his use of symbols or attempt to literalize the words he has attributed to Jesus. Can any of us imagine for one moment an itinerant prophet named John the Baptist literally saying the first time he meets Jesus, "Behold, the Lamb of God that takes away the sin of the world," and then claiming for this Jesus the status of a pre-existent divine being? Yet that is what John the Baptist does in the first chapter of John (1:29–30). That text sets a pattern that this gospel writer will follow, but it is just the beginning.

In the second chapter, we find equally enigmatic words. Here we are told that at a wedding party Jesus actually changes water into wine so that the party can go on! Can any of us imagine a set of circumstances in which that narrative would be taken literally? Medieval alchemists spent centuries trying to turn iron into gold and failed. Given the price of good wine today, perhaps they would have been more successful if they had followed Jesus' example and tried to turn water into wine. Surely John did not think of this as a literal story, with its suggestion that Jesus' freshly fermented beverage was so superior to that which was served originally that it violated the social norm of the day, which was to serve the "good stuff" first and then, when the guests were well drunk, to bring out the "screw-top gallon bottles." So we need to ask just what it was that John was seeking to communicate when he opened his second chapter with this story and called it "the first sign" of Jesus' public ministry that "manifested forth his glory" (2:11). Perhaps this author dropped another clue that these words are not to be taken literally when he began this particular narrative with the words "On the third day," since these words, echoing the third day of the crucifixion/resurrection story, would be deeply infused with meaning in the company of believers to whom they were addressed.

In the next episode described by John, Jesus is in Jerusalem and there he drives the money-changers out of the Temple. In the earlier gospels, this story of the cleansing of the Temple is the provocative final act that leads directly to the crucifixion. John, however, places it at the beginning of Jesus' public ministry. John's first readers would know that John was using this episode not to describe something that had happened, but to make a messianic claim.

Continuing the same theme in chapter 3, John has Jesus say to a man named Nicodemus, "Unless you are born anew, you cannot see the Kingdom of God" (3:5).[1] Nicodemus is baffled because he hears these words literally and wonders how it is possible for a grown man to be born anew when he is old. "Can I climb back into my mother's womb and be born a second time?" he asks (3:4). Literalism makes no sense, but John is not writing a literal story.

_____

1   The word translated here "anew" or sometimes "again" can also mean "from above." It is one of a series of expressions John uses with double meanings. Others include "lifted up," "it is finished" and "rise again." The word "blind" is also used in two senses, one physical and the other a type of spiritual blindness. Oscar Cullman develops the meaning of these words or signs in his book *Early Christian Worship*. See bibliography for details.

In the fourth chapter of John, the author has Jesus speaking to a Samaritan woman at Jacob's well about water. The conversation began when he asked the woman to give him a drink from the well. When she demurred and retreated into the boundary that separated Jew from Samaritan, Jesus said to her, "If you knew who it was that is asking you for a drink, you would have asked him and he would have given you living water" (4:10). The woman looked at him with the blank stare of literalism and said, in effect, "Man, you don't even have a bucket!" The Jesus of John's gospel then says, "Whoever drinks of the water I give will never thirst again" (4:14). The woman, still trapped in the prison of literalism, responds, in effect, "That is great. Give me your water and I will never have to come again to this well. That would make my life easier."

As if that were not sufficient warning that this book is not to be read literally, John continues his theme when he relates the story of Jesus' disciples returning and interrupting this private conversation. They then urge Jesus to eat. To this urging, however, John's Jesus responds by saying, "I have food to eat of which you do not know" (4:32). The disciples, still captive to a literal mind-set through which they hear his words, say to one another: "Has anyone brought him food?" (4:33).

In the sixth chapter of John, Jesus is made to place his message into Eucharistic language and then to watch as his words are once again heard as if they were intended to be literal. Here Jesus says: "He who eats my flesh and drinks my blood abides in me" (6:56). The literal-minded disciples are repelled by what seems to them to be a reference to cannibalism, and some begin to draw back and to cease following him.

Time after time, the author of the Fourth Gospel asserts that this book is an interpretive book, not a literal one. It is a symbolic book, not a historical book or a biographical story. To read the Fourth Gospel with literal eyes is to miss the essence of its message. Yet throughout Christian history, this book has been read with literal eyes and this literal misreading has been used to buttress the case for orthodoxy, binding creeds and the rationally incomprehensible ecclesiastical doctrines that stand at the heart of what people assume is essential Christianity.

One other unique aspect found in John alone is the fact that Jesus, time and again, is quoted as calling himself by the name that, according to the book of Exodus, God revealed to Moses as God's own at the burning bush. Tell them, God said to Moses on that occasion, that "I AM" sent you (Exod. 3:13–14). So John now has Jesus say, "Before Abraham was, I AM!" (8:58), and "When you have lifted up the Son, then you will know I AM" (8:28). There is no "he" in this final statement—"I AM he"—despite the fact that the translators add one because they do not understand what this gospel writer is trying to say. At the time of Jesus' arrest in the dark of night in the Valley of Kidron (18:1–8), John portrays Jesus as approaching the band of soldiers and Temple police led by Judas and asking, "Whom do you seek?" They respond, "Jesus of Nazareth." Jesus says, "I AM." Translators once again render that as "I am he." John's context, however, renders that translation inoperative, for John goes on to state: "When Jesus said to them, I AM, they drew back and fell to the ground." It would be strange behavior indeed if an armed guard confronting an unarmed political prisoner fell to the ground if he said "I am he." If, on the other hand John was portraying him as uttering and claiming the divine name "I AM" as they were about to arrest him, that would be quite another matter.

"I AM" is a key concept in the Fourth Gospel, repeated over and over again. John alone has Jesus say such things as these: I am the bread of life (6:35), I am the door (10:7), I am the light of the world (8:2), I am the vine (15:1), I am the good shepherd (10:11) and I am the resurrection (11:25). Jesus even asserts through his final "I AM" claim that he is the exclusive pathway to God (14:6), a statement that has been used throughout Christian history to justify the basest forms of religious imperialism and to fuel the most insensitive kind of missionary evangelism.

The fact is that John's gospel cannot be literalized if it is to be understood. It is a profound, even mystical, interpretation of the life of Jesus of Nazareth, written by a person deeply rooted in Palestinian Judaism, and its words are designed to lead John's readers beyond literal meaning into a life-giving relationship with God. History reveals what a high price has been paid because Christians have insisted on literalizing the words of this gospel. At the Council of Nicaea, a literalized understanding of John was used to justify the new orthodoxy of a man named Athanasius, a development that was destined to cloak the Christian story in a hierarchical authority system that became oppressive, insensitive and anything but life-giving.[2] When the shell of literalism is broken, however, the gospel of John enhances life, expands consciousness and calls us into a new relationship with the one whose deepest claim is to be a doorway into a new experience of that which is transcendent, holy and other. The call of John's Jesus is not into an engagement with a supernatural being, created in our image, who somehow lives above the sky and who, in the person of Jesus, appeared to masquerade as a human being. This is, of course, a caricature, but only a slight one. John's gospel is a work to be entered, a message to be breathed and a doorway into a life to be lived. It was not written to enable us to play religion's oldest game: "My God is better than your God."

I once was repelled by the Fourth Gospel because I related to it as if it were a literal document. When I broke out of that bondage, I found in John's words a real understanding not just of God and of Jesus, but of life itself. Someday, I hope to spell out that thought in detail. In the limits of this book, I must content myself with sketching in the briefest of forms a new vision of this gospel that all can see.

---

2   The assertion is well documented in *The Emergence of the Catholic Tradition* by Jaraslov Pelikan. See bibliography for details.

CHAPTER 57

The Raising of Lazarus and the Identity of the Beloved Disciple

W e began our study of John by identifying this book as a highly symbolic, interpretive account of Jesus of Nazareth. The author, we now know, created this book some sixty-five to seventy years after the events he is describing, which conclude with the end of Jesus' earthly life. To gain further insight into John's intentions, I turn now to two uniquely Johannine narratives, alluded to nowhere else in the Christian tradition. The first of these is the story of the raising of Lazarus from the dead (John 11) and the second is a series of stories through which the strange and enigmatic figure known only as "the beloved disciple" or "the disciple whom Jesus loved" comes into the tradition (13:23–21:25). In an interesting way these two apparently separate narratives are significantly interconnected.

Note first the dramatic place in his drama to which the author of the Fourth Gospel has assigned the story of the raising of Lazarus. That event is for John the catalyst that leads directly to the crucifixion. He then both compares and contrasts this

Lazarus story with the raising of Jesus from the dead, which will be the grand climax that concludes his gospel.

We begin our probe of this story by raising the question: Is it possible that the author of the Fourth Gospel ever entertained the idea that there was even a shred of historical data underlying his account of Jesus raising Lazarus from the grave? The answer to that question is simple. Not a chance! Consider these facts: Mary and Martha, two sisters who lived in Bethany, had been figures in the Christian memory for quite a while, even starring in an episode in the gospel of Luke (10:38ff). Nowhere in that earlier tradition, however, was it recorded that they had a brother named Lazarus, suggesting that John created Lazarus for his own literary purposes. Next in our supporting evidence is the fact that John describes the raising of Lazarus as an event that was quite public. Crowds, consisting of both the friends and enemies of Jesus, had gathered to mourn the passing of Lazarus. This was not a miraculous event done in private, the details of which might, in the course of time, be exaggerated. There were eyewitnesses galore. The lead-up to this story sets the stage for this event to be a source of great wonder. Jesus, we are told, postponed his journey to Bethany until the news came that Lazarus was actually dead. When he finally does arrive, the fourth day after Lazarus's death, the burial has been completed. Both Martha and Mary express their displeasure, berating Jesus for not coming earlier when, they suggest, he could perhaps have used his powers to restore Lazarus to health.

There is no hint in the Christian tradition that anyone anywhere had ever heard about this episode before. Embrace what that means. Here is a public event attended by a great crowd in which a man, dead for four days, has already been buried in a cave with a great stone covering its entrance. Jesus, the itinerant preacher, then proceeds to reverse this death, even though the corpse was already well into the decaying process. To accomplish the miracle this teacher, over the protests of the sisters of the dead man—"already he stinketh," the King James Version has Martha say (John 11:39, KJV)—orders the stone removed and calls

Lazarus to come forth. The mesmerized crowd then watches as the corpse of Lazarus, bound in the burial bands of cloth that secured both his hands and his feet and into which the burial spice of myrrh had been generously poured, comes staggering out of the cave. Jesus then orders the people to "unbind him and let him go." If this were history, can you imagine that it would have been possible to suppress the account so deeply that no hint of it would have appeared in any Christian circle or writing until John decided to reveal it some three generations later? No, the raising of Lazarus is not an event that occurred in history. Then how are we to read this story? What was its origin?

There is only one other figure named Lazarus who appears in the New Testament. He is a character in a parable that only Luke records (Luke 16:19ff). We call it the parable of Lazarus and the rich man, who in some translations is named Dives. This Lucan parable is about judgment. Lazarus, a beggar at the gate of the rich man, dies. So does the rich man, who apparently never "sees" this beggar. Lazarus is carried into the "bosom of Abraham" and the rich man is removed to the tortures of the condemned. In torment Dives asks Abraham to send Lazarus with water to ease his thirst. Abraham responds that one cannot get to Dives from where Lazarus is. Then Dives asks him to send Lazarus back to warn his living brothers to amend their lives, lest they too are sent to this place of torment. Abraham replies: "They have Moses and the prophets to warn them." If they do not listen to Moses and the prophets, "they will not listen even if one is raised from the dead." John, quite obviously, takes this Lucan parable, historicizes it and demonstrates its truth in the life of Jesus. The account of the raising of Lazarus in John's gospel does not create faith or even change behavior; it actually serves to make the crucifixion of Jesus inevitable. The character we call Lazarus is a literary creation of the author of the Fourth Gospel, based on a parable, which John uses to stand as a symbol for those who see God in Jesus, respond to that experience and move from their religious past into the new consciousness that becomes available in Jesus.

Moving on now to look at "the beloved disciple," we note several other crucial items in John's Lazarus narrative. First, this character called Lazarus is the only person whom the author of the Fourth Gospel says Jesus loved. The message that comes to Jesus from Mary and Martha, notifying him of their brother's illness and urging him to come quickly, is this: "Lord, he whom you love is ill" (11:3). The text also says, "Now Jesus loved Martha and her sister and Lazarus" (11:5). Later Jesus is portrayed as weeping as he makes his way to the tomb, causing the crowd to say, "See how *he loved him*" (11:36). If Jesus had a single "beloved disciple," this gospel never suggests that it could be anyone other than this literary character known as Lazarus.

Second, the designation "one of his disciples, whom Jesus loved," does not enter the Johannine narrative until after the story of the raising of Lazarus. Only then is the "beloved disciple" pictured as present at the Last Supper, "lying close to the heart of Jesus" (John 13:23). He is the one whom Peter implores to ask Jesus to identify the name of the traitor. We next confront the beloved disciple in John's text at the foot of the cross, where we hear the dying Jesus commend his mother to the care of this person (John 19:26ff). Could the mother of Jesus be a symbol for Judaism, the mother of Christianity, and could the beloved disciple be a symbol for one who sees the meaning of Jesus so deeply that he can carry Jesus' message into a new context in the Gentile world without losing "his mother" (Judaism) in the process? Rudolf Bultmann, probably the greatest New Testament scholar in the twentieth century, seems to think so; he has advanced this possibility in his monumental commentary entitled simply *The Gospel of John*.[1]

The next time "the disciple whom Jesus loved" is mentioned is in John's account of the Easter story (20:1–10). There we are told that he comes with Peter to the tomb that Mary Magdalene has reported to be empty, her suspicion being that the grave has been robbed, which would represent the final insult to the

---

[1]   See bibliography for details.

memory of Jesus. Peter and "the beloved disciple" run together. Peter, the older, the one who is rooted in the tradition of Judaism, runs more slowly. The beloved disciple, the one who will guide the Jesus' message into its universal future, is younger, so he runs more quickly and arrives at the tomb first. He does not go in, but pauses at the entrance. Judaism must enter the new place before the Christian movement can do so. The new tradition must be built on the old. It cannot be born except out of the old. Religion always evolves by transcending the limits of the past and giving birth to a new consciousness. So Peter, arriving later and presumably out of breath, enters the tomb. He sees the signs. The grave-clothes are neatly lying in place exactly where the head, the hands and the feet of the deceased Lord would have been. This resurrection is not to be like that of Lazarus, a resuscitation back to life in this world of one still bound by grave-clothes. This is a transformative experience in which death is transcended, limits are crossed and new life is achieved. "The disciple whom Jesus loved" then follows Peter into the tomb. Like Peter, he also sees, but he takes the vital next step—this seeing causes him to believe!

They both return home and that evening John's gospel tells us that Jesus appears to the other disciples except for Thomas. This raised Jesus is portrayed as being intensely physical, but at the same time beyond the body; we are told that he entered the house in which the disciples were hiding, despite the fact that the doors were shut and the windows were barred. Once inside, we are told, he breathed on them the life-giving breath of God. It was that same breath that had brought Adam into being at the first creation. This was the new creation and it was the beloved disciple who first stepped into it. The beloved disciple is clearly a symbol, not a person. He represents those lives in which the meaning of Jesus leaps the boundaries of yesterday's religious understanding. When Jesus appears to the disciples a week later with Thomas present, Thomas becomes the pivotal symbol to contrast those who believe because they see and those who do not see and yet who believe (20:29).

This beloved disciple is mentioned once more in the epilogue to John's gospel (21:7, 20ff). By the time this chapter was written and added to the text of the gospel, the literalizing process had already begun and John's symbol of "the beloved disciple" had been identified with a particular one of the twelve who had clearly died. The theory apparently had developed that this beloved disciple was supposed to live until Jesus' second coming. So his death had to be explained, and the epilogue seeks to do so. The point is then made that Jesus does come again every time another person enters the new life, the new consciousness that Jesus came to bring. Lazarus and the beloved disciple are one and the same, symbols of those raised to new life, those who in Christ are able to step beyond traditional religious thinking into a new consciousness.

CHAPTER 58

The Epilogue of John

The last chapter of John's gospel, known as the epilogue, as noted earlier, is not believed by most scholars to be part of the original text of this gospel. A careful reading of John 20, the next-to-last chapter, makes it clear that that was how the evangelist chose to end his story. Listen to his closing words: "Now Jesus did many other signs in the presence of the disciples that are not written in this book but these are written that you may believe, that Jesus is the Christ, and that believing you may have life in his name" (20:30–31). After that one expects no more. Yet chapter 21 has been added. It seems not to follow from or to fit in with anything said in chapter 20. The scene has shifted from Jerusalem to Galilee. A significant amount of time has elapsed. The disciples seem not motivated at all by the appearances of Jesus recorded in chapter 20. They have clearly passed the stage of mourning and have returned to their homes and picked up the pieces of their pre-Jesus lives. They have even gone back to the source of their livelihood as fishermen on the Sea of Galilee. One other aspect to this twenty-first chapter is that it replicates fairly closely the details of a particular Lucan narrative (see Luke 5:1–16), which Luke presents as a miracle story not of the risen Christ, but of the Galilean Jesus near the beginning of his public ministry. Despite these problems, I have always been attracted to this epilogue and it has played a major role in my understanding of the Easter event. I close my unit on the Fourth Gospel by describing how that connection came into being.

Earlier in my career, I made an extensive study of all of the resurrection narratives in the New Testament. This study resulted in the publication of a book entitled *Resurrection: Myth or Reality?* In that book, I tried to sort out the elements that seemed to culminate in the enormous power that was connected with the Easter moment. I asked of the gospel texts four questions: Who was it who stood in the center of the resurrection experience? Where were the disciples when the experience of resurrection dawned? When was the moment in time in which the meaning of resurrection broke through in the lives of the disciples? What was the context, the setting, in which the Easter experience emerged? I then began to explore the clues present in the New Testament that might lead to new conclusions about this central experience in our faith story.

As I worked through not only all of the specific resurrection texts, but also anything else that might throw light on the Easter experience, I came to these conclusions.

First, Peter is the crucial, central figure in the Easter story. Peter is singled out as the one who first "saw." Paul says, "He appeared first to Cephas" (I Cor. 15:5). Mark's gospel, the first, has the messenger say, "Go tell the disciples and Peter" (Mark 16:7). Luke has the disciples claim, "The Lord has risen and has appeared to Simon," that is to Peter (Luke 24:35). John portrays Peter as the first one who entered the tomb and saw its emptiness (John 20:1–10). In Matthew (10:46–52) and in other gospel texts (Mark 8:27–30, Luke 9:18–21) Peter is the one who makes the first confession at Caesarea Philippi. He is always listed first when the disciples are named (Mark 3:16, Matt. 10:2–4, Luke 6:14). In Luke's gospel, Jesus is quoted as saying to Peter, "When you are converted strengthen your brethren" (Luke 22:32), as if Peter would be the first one who would enable the others to see. The primacy of Peter in the entire gospel tradition seems to me to rest on the fact that he was the first one whose eyes were opened to see the meaning of both Jesus and his resurrection. Armed with that fact I then searched every Peter story in the gospels looking for resurrection clues. I believe that they are there, from the story of Peter after the feeding of the multitude in John, saying, "Lord, to whom shall we go, you have the word of eternal life?" (John 6:6–8), to Peter demanding to be washed all over when Jesus washes the feet of the disciples (John 13:9). All Peter stories ought to be read as resurrection stories, I concluded, for they show Peter's coming to faith very clearly. So I filed my first conclusion: Peter stood at the center of the resurrection tradition.

Second, I pursued the "where" question. The New Testament is divided by the competing claims for primacy in the resurrection tradition between Galilee and Jerusalem. Mark has the Easter messenger direct the disciples to return to Galilee with the promise that "there you will see him" (Mark 16:7). Matthew says that it was only in Galilee that the raised Christ ever appeared to the disciples (Matt. 28:16–20). Luke, however, counters this Galilean tradition by asserting that the appearance of the risen Christ occurred only in Jerusalem and its environs, thus overtly refuting the Galilean tradition (Luke 24). John supports Luke by insisting on the primacy of Jerusalem (John 20), but then to the end of John's gospel was attached the epilogue (John 21) that centers the resurrection squarely in Galilee. A deeper analysis of these competing texts reveals that the Galilee tradition was not only earlier, but it was more primitive and more original. It is noteworthy that all the Jesus sightings, the visions, the aspects of his bodily physicality, the feeling of his flesh and the touching of his wounds are associated with the later and clearly secondary Jerusalem tradition. So Galilee emerged from this study as the answer to the question about where the disciples were when the resurrection experience dawned. Building on that conclusion, I then looked at other stories that might also contain Easter references, from the disciples mistaking him for a ghost coming to them out of the darkness (Mark 6:49, Matt. 14:26), to Jesus walking on the water (Mark 6:45–52, Matt. 14:25–34, John 6:15–21), to the account of the transfiguration, which portrays him as translucent (Mark

9:2–8, Matt. 17:1–8, Luke 9:25–36). I noted that all of these were set in Galilee. My second conclusion was that it was while the disciples were in Galilee that whatever Easter was dawned on them.

I came next to the "when" question, where I confronted the familiar time symbol "three days." A study of the New Testament reveals that this symbol is wobbly at best. Paul says, "On the third day" (I Cor. 15:4). Mark also uses the phrase "on the third day" (9:31). Matthew and Luke change that time designation to "after three days" (Matt. 20:19, Luke 18:33), a variation that sounds similar, but clearly is not, for "on" and "after" do not result in the same day. According to a literal reading of the gospels, the time from burial on Good Friday to the empty tomb at dawn on Sunday morning is only thirty-six hours, or a day and a half. Mark has the resurrection messenger tell the women at the tomb that the disciples will see him in Galilee, in some resurrected form. Galilee is, however, a seven- to ten-day journey from Jerusalem, so this "seeing," whatever it was, could not possibly occur inside the literal "three days" symbol, whether it is "on the third day" or "after three days." Luke stretches the appearance stories over forty days, culminating with the account of the ascension (Acts 1:15). John has resurrection appearance stories occur in Jerusalem over a period of eight days, but in the Johannine epilogue the resurrection appearances appear to stretch out over months. These were the data that drove me to conclude that the phrase "three days" is not only a symbol, but one that was never intended to be a literal measure of time. That insight opened me to the possibility that the time between the crucifixion and the Easter experience needs to be expanded at least to months. My third conclusion thus became that I needed to destabilize and deliteralize the symbolic time-marker of three days and to extend the time between crucifixion and resurrection significantly.

Finally, when I searched for the context in which resurrection dawned, I found a key phrase in Luke: "He was known to us in the breaking of bread" (Luke 24:35). That valuable clue led me to look at all the feeding stories in the gospels for resurrection clues. So I examined the stories about the feeding of the multitude with a limited number of loaves and fishes, I examined the various accounts of the Last Supper, and I even looked at the parables of Jesus that focused on a great symbolic banquet. In each of these places I found elements of the interpretive meal in which the risen Jesus was experienced not only as present, but also as making himself known.

My study drove me to these conclusions: First, whatever Easter was, Peter stood at the center of it and was the first to "see," and he thus was the one who opened the eyes of the others so that they could also see. Second, Galilee was the original setting in which the meaning of Easter dawned, while the Jerusalem tradition was secondary. It was only in that late-developing Jerusalem tradition that the resurrection evolved into a supernaturalized story featuring a resuscitated body. Third, I concluded that the moment of Easter dawned slowly, over a period of months after the crucifixion. Finally, I became convinced that the common meal of the church was designed to be a liturgical reenactment of what the original resurrection experience was, so that a liturgical meal must have played a role in the beginning. With these conclusions in hand, I then returned to the gospels in search of a resurrection narrative that was based on these four principles.

I found it only in the epilogue to the Fourth Gospel, which I now regard as the most authentic, and perhaps even a reflection of the earliest, resurrection narrative in the New Testament. It is about Peter fighting his way through to a new understanding. It is set in Galilee. It clearly occurs sometime long after the crucifixion. It concludes by suggesting that it was during a beachside, early-morning Eucharist that the experience of their living Lord broke through first to Peter, then to the twelve.

The epilogue of John thus grew in significance for me. Further study opened me to the possibility that this narrative might well have been a version of an earlier tradition that floated freely during the oral period before finding two very different resting places, first in Luke as an early Galilean story and then in the epilogue of John as a resurrection narrative. My supposition is that someone, perhaps a member of the Johannine school, recognized the authenticity of this story and decided to attach it to the Fourth Gospel. That decision preserved, I believe, echoes of the earliest and most authentic memory of the dawning of Easter; at the same time, true to the Johannine principle, it was clear that this experience could never be literalized, for it was not bound inside either time or space. It is fitting that with this story the Fourth Gospel is drawn to its second conclusion, and that is why John says that "to know Jesus is eternal life" (John 17:3).

CHAPTER 59

The Johannine Epistles and the Book of Revelation

W e come now to the final chapter in our journey through the books of the Bible. We conclude with the final pieces of the Johannine literature: the three epistles that bear his name and the book of Revelation, also attributed to John. Since I treated the gospel in more detail and even mentioned these other Johannine pieces briefly in the introduction to the gospel, I will not spend much time on them in this final chapter.

This Johannine material is not necessarily the final work in time that makes up the New Testament. That honor, we have already suggested, probably goes to II Peter, which is quite clearly a mid-second-century work. The Johannine corpus, however, is dated at the end of the first century (95–100), which makes the gospel of John the last gospel to be written; moreover, the Johannine material has always been used as a counterweight to the synoptic gospels. So there is a sense in which the New Testament does not become whole or complete until the writings of John have been added to it. That is why I made the decision to treat John last. Throughout Christian history, the work of John has tended to dominate the life of the church. It was, more than any other book, the quoted authority behind the development of creeds, doctrines and dogmas. It was, as I noted earlier, the sole source quoted by Athanasius at the Council of Nicaea in 325 CE in his duel with a man named Arius, who incidentally buttressed his argument by quoting from all of the gospels. When that council backed Athanasius and dismissed Arius, the ascendancy of John in the development of traditional Christianity was clearly established. No less a person than Isaac Newton, writing in the seventeenth century, was learned enough to state that in his opinion the anti-Arius decision of that council was "the greatest mistake" made in Christian history.[1] It just may be that, because of the ferment in contemporary theology coupled with the critical insights of modern biblical scholarship, we are today in the process of rebalancing that traditional emphasis on John.

When we focus on the three epistles that bear John's name, only the first appears to be substantial, both in length and in content. It has five chapters, whereas II and III John have only one each. I John is a powerful treatise based significantly on the gospel and seems intent on drawing out that earlier text's ethical implications. Despite I John's similarity with the gospel I do not believe the authors are the same person, although that is still debated. There is, however, no debate about whether the writer of the gospel and the author of the second and third epistles of John are the same person. Both of these latter epistles claim to be written by one who is self-identified as "the Elder," and both reflect a time when there was a clearly defined body of truth that had to be defended and passed on. I think it is fair to say that if II and III John had not been included in the canon of the New Testament, not much of any great significance would have been lost to the church. It is interesting that no part of these latter two epistles that bear John's name is included in the various lectionaries for public readings at worship, a fact that speaks volumes about how these two books have been viewed historically.

That, however, is not the case with I John. This epistle has had a rich history. It is often quoted, often read and frequently the sub-

---

1   This reference comes out of the private correspondence of Sir Isaac Newton.

ject of sermons. I John is the primary place in the New Testament where God is specifically defined as "love." This author states that only the person who loves can truly be said to have been "born of God" (4:7). One cannot know God if one does not know love, this author argues (4:8). The presence of love, he states, is the ultimate manifestation of the presence of God. We love each other only with the love that God has given to us of God's own nature. The only way any of us can abide in God, he concludes, is by abiding in love (4:13ff). There is no fear in this love, he states, because "perfect love casts out fear" (4:18). To make this point very clear, this epistle states, "If anyone says, 'I love God' and hates his brother, he is a liar; for he who does not love his brother whom he has seen, cannot love God whom he has not seen" (4:20). The author's ultimate commandment to those to whom he writes is this: "The one who loves God, must love his or her brother and sister also" (4:21).

When I started this section on the New Testament I mentioned those who, because of the way the Bible has been used, would find it difficult to call this book "sacred scriptures." Now as I near the end I want to return to that theme, since this is the primary point made by the first epistle of John. The fact is that the anti-Semitism of the ages has been accompanied by the definition of Jews as those who fall outside the boundaries of the Christian definition of humanity. Only with that understanding could that negativity be expounded and expanded by some of the figures of Christian history—figures such as Irenaeus, Polycarp, John Chrysostom and even Martin Luther. In those writings, Jews were described as so subhuman as to be "unfit for life." Likewise, only by defining women, people of color and homosexual persons as less than fully human, as the church has done throughout history, could we dare to place them outside of God's all-encompassing love. The first epistle of John challenges this point of view with great power regardless of the group targeted, from Jews on, and this is why it is a treasured part of the sacred story.

The Bible closes its pages with the book of Revelation. It is a piece of apocalyptic or "end of the world" literature. Presumably that theme struck the leaders of the early church as the proper way to close the New Testament because they still expected the end of the world to be near. The book of Revelation has been a godsend to those who like to predict "doomsday." It is the favorite book of those who believe that events in modern history are the fulfillment of and can be explained as the living out of biblical prophecy. In my lifetime I have heard the beast of Revelation 13 identified with Adolf Hitler, Hideki Tojo, Joseph Stalin, Nikita Khrushchev and Saddam Hussein, just to name a few. My mother told me that Kaiser Wilhelm of Germany was called the beast of Revelation during World War I. While I am fascinated by the idea that the book of Revelation gives us great insight into early Christian writing, I personally have never found this book to be worthy of the study it would take to reveal its meaning and context. I have read it a number of times, but I have never been edified by it. It is all but nonsense to me. My good friend and greatly admired colleague Professor Elaine Pagels of Princeton University's religion faculty is now writing a book on Revelation. I shall read her work with delight when it is published, but I have never felt compelled personally to explore its words with any depth. I see this book as a dated piece of first-century literature and little more.

Despite this I can still say that one text from Revelation has always been among my favorites. Here the author, writing to the church of Laodicea, condemns that congregation for being neither "hot nor cold" but "lukewarm," regarding them thereby as "wretched, pitiable, poor, blind and naked" (3:15–17). As a bishop, I have known lukewarm congregations, religious bodies of human beings that stand for nothing and thus have no passionate commitment about much of anything. These churches will die of boredom long before they die of controversy. The love of God demands that we move beyond our limits, confront our prejudices and enter into transformed lives. That always means that controversy is part of the Christian life and should be embraced as part of the Christian vocation.

I began working on this volume about the origin and meaning of the various books of the Bible some four years ago. This study has required me to go back to my library to familiarize myself anew with every book included in the sacred text, even those that I had long ago dismissed as irrelevant. It has also kindled anew in me my longtime love affair with this book. For well over sixty-five years I have read this Bible daily, going cover to cover more than twenty-five times—yes, making it through both Leviticus and the who-begat-whoms. Some of its books I have read too many times to count. On many of its books I have spent more than a year in concentrated study. I am at this moment beginning my third year of study on the Fourth Gospel alone and will do two more years before I think about writing on it. Underneath the time-bound and time-warped words of the Bible, I still find in the words of this book a sense that all life is holy, that all life is loved and that each of us is called to be all that we are capable of being. Those are the biblical themes that I hope our world never loses.

I close this volume with the words that best capture my understanding of Jesus and remain today my favorite text of all. These words come from John's gospel (10:10): "I have come that they may have life and have it abundantly." Love which breaks down all barriers of separation and enhances all that we are is the life power that I find in Jesus. That is why I assert in Paul's words that "God" was in Jesus, and that is why he is and remains Christ for me.

Shalom!

BIBLIOGRAPHY

Acheson, Dean. *Present at the Creation: My Years in the State Department.* New York: Norton, 1969.

Albright, W. F. *Archaeology and the Religion of Israel.* Louisville, KY: Westminster John Knox Press, 2006 (originally published by Johns Hopkins Press, Baltimore, 1948).

———. *The Biblical Period from Abraham to Ezra.* Louisville, KY: Westminster John Knox Press, 2008.

Anderson, Bernard W. *Understanding the Old Testament.* Englewood Cliffs, NJ: Prentice Hall, 1986.

Barrett, C. K. *The Gospel According to St. John: An Introduction and Commentary on the Greek Text.* Philadelphia: Westminster Press, 1975.

Bremmer, Jan M. *The Apocryphal Acts of Paul and Thecla.* Kampen, The Netherlands: Kos Phares Press, 1996.

Brown, Raymond. *The Birth of the Messiah.* Garden City, NY: Doubleday, 1977.

———. *The Gospel According to John.* 2 vols. Garden City, NY: Doubleday, 1966–1970.

Bultmann, Rudolf. *The Gospel of John: A Commentary.* Translated by G. R. Beasley-Murray. Edited by R. W. N. Hoare and J. K. Riches. Philadelphia: Westminster Press, 1973.

Caird, G. B. *St. Luke.* Pelican Series. Baltimore: Penguin Books, 1963.

Childs, Brevard. *The Book of Exodus: A Critical Theological Commentary.* Philadelphia: Westminster Press, 1974.

Conzelman, Hans. *The Theology of St. Luke.* London: Faber & Faber, 1960.

Cox, Harvey. *The Secular City.* New York: Macmillan, 1966.

Crossan, John Dominic. *Jesus: A Revolutionary Biography*. San Francisco: HarperCollins, 2001.

Cullmann, Oscar. *Early Christian Worship*. Philadelphia: Westminster Press, 1953.

Darwin, Charles Robert. *On the Origin of Species by Means of Natural Selection*. Philadelphia: Univ. of Pennsylvania Press, 1959 (originally published in 1859).

Dodd, C. H. *The Epistle of Paul to the Romans*. London: Hodder & Stoughton, 1949.

———. *The Interpretation of the Fourth Gospel*. Cambridge, UK: Cambridge University Press, 1968.

Freke, Timothy, and Peter Gandy. *The Jesus Mysteries: Was the Original Jesus a Pagan God?* New York and London: Random House, 2001.

Fuller, Reginald. *The Formation of the Resurrection Narratives*. New York: Macmillan, 1971.

Funk, Robert, and Roy Hoover. *The Five Gospels: What Did Jesus Really Say?* New York: Macmillan, 1993.

Geering, Lloyd G. *Such Is Life: A Close Encounter with Ecclesiastes*. Santa Rosa, CA: Polebridge Press, 2010.

Goulder, Michael Douglas. *Luke: A New Paradigm*. Sheffield, UK: Sheffield Academic Press, 1989.

Grant, Robert M., ed. *Gnosticism: A Source Book of Heretical Writings in the Early Christian Period*. New York: Harper & Row, 1961.

Guilding, Ailene. *The Fourth Gospel and Jewish Worship: A Study of the Relationship of St. John's Gospel to the Ancient Jewish Lectionary System*. Oxford, UK: Clarendon Press, 1960.

Haenchen, Ernst. *The Acts of the Apostles: A Commentary*. Philadelphia: Westminster Press, 1971.

Harnack, Adolf. *The Mission and Expansion of Christianity in the First Three Centuries*. Translated by James Moffett. Freeport, NY: Books for Libraries Press, 1959.

Harpur, Tom. *The Pagan Christ*. Toronto: Thomas Allen, 2004.

Hawking, Stephen, and Leonard Mlodinow. *The Grand Design*. New York: Bantam Books, 2010.

Hoskyns, Sir Edwyn. *The Fourth Gospel*. London: Faber & Faber, 1947.

James, Fleming. *Personalities of the Old Testament*. New York: Scribner, 1955.

Josephus. *The Complete Works*. Translated by William Whiston. Grand Rapids, MI: Kregal Press, 1999.

Jung, Carl. *The Answer to Job*. London: Routledge & Kegan Paul, 1954.

Käsemann, Ernst. *The Testament of Jesus: A Study of the Gospel of John in the Light of Chapter 17.* Philadelphia: Fortress Press, 1968.

Kysar, Robert. *John: The Maverick Gospel.* Louisville, KY: Westminster John Knox Press, 2007.

Manson, T. W. *On Paul and John.* London: Macmillan, 1949.

Mantyn, J. Louis. *History and Theology in the Fourth Gospel.* New York: Harper & Row, 1968.

Meeks, Wayne. "The Man from Heaven in Johannine Sectarianism." *Journal of Biblical Literature* 91 (1972), no. 1: 44–72.

Nineham, D. H. *St. Mark.* Philadelphia: Westminster Press, 1977.

Nock, Arthur Darby. *St. Paul.* New York: Harper & Brothers, 1937.

Odenburg, Hugo. *The Fourth Gospel, Interpreted in Relation to Contemporaneous Religions.* Uppsala, Sweden: Almquist & Wiksells, 1929.

Olsson, B. *Structure and Meaning in the Fourth Gospel: A Text-Linguistic Analysis of John 2:1–11 and 4:1–41.* Lund, Sweden: Cuk & Gleerup, 1974.

Pagels, Elaine. *Beyond Belief.* New York: Random House, 2005.

———. *The Gnostic Gospels.* New York: Random House, 1979.

Pelikan, Jaroslav. *The Christian Tradition: A History of the Development of Doctrine,* 6 vols. Chicago: Univ. of Chicago Press, 1971. Special reference is to Vol. I, *The Emergence of the Catholic Tradition (100-600),* 1971.

Robinson, John A. T. *Honest to God.* Philadelphia: Westminster Press, 1963.

———. *The Human Face of God.* Philadelphia: Westminster Press, 1973.

Sanders, E. P. *Jesus and Judaism.* Philadelphia: Westminster Press, 1985.

Sandmel, Samuel. *The Genius of Paul.* New York: Farrar, Straus & Cudahy, 1958.

———. *Judaism and Christian Beginnings.* New York and Oxford: Oxford Univ. Press, 1979.

———. *We Jews and Jesus.* New York: Schocken Press, 1970.

Sanford, John. *Mystical Christianity: A Psychological Commentary on the Gospel of John.* New York: Crossroad, 1995.

Schnackenburg, Rudolf. *The Gospel of St. John.* 3 vols. New York: Crossroad, 1980–1983.

Spong, John Shelby. *Christpower.* Hawarth, NJ: St. Johan Press, 2008.

———. *Eternal Life: A New Vision—Beyond Religion, Beyond Theism, Beyond Heaven and Hell.* San Francisco: HarperCollins, 2009.

———. *Here I Stand: My Struggle for a Christianity of Integrity, Love and Equality.* San Francisco: HarperCollins, 2000.

———. *Jesus for the Non-Religious.* San Francisco: HarperCollins, 2007.

————. *Liberating the Gospels: Reading the Bible with Jewish Eyes.* San Francisco: HarperCollins, 1996.

————. *A New Christianity for a New World: Why Christianity Is Dying and How a New Faith Is Being Born.* San Francisco: HarperCollins, 2001.

————. *Rescuing the Bible from Fundamentalism: A Bishop Rethinks the Meaning of Scripture.* San Francisco: HarperCollins, 1991.

————. *The Sins of Scripture: Exploring the Bible's Texts of Hate to Reveal the God of Love.* San Francisco: HarperCollins, 2005.

————. *Why Christianity Must Change or Die: A Bishop Speaks to Believers in Exile.* San Francisco: HarperCollins, 1998.

Temple, William. *Readings in St. John's Gospel.* London: Macmillan, 1945.

Terrien, Samuel. *The Psalms and Their Meaning for Today.* Indianapolis and New York: Bobbs-Merrill, 1953.

Thompson, Francis. *The Complete Poetical Works of Francis Thompson.* New York: Modern Library, 1913.

Underhill, Evelyn. *The Mystical Way: A Psychological Study in Christian Origins.* London: J. M. Dent, 1913.

Von Hügel, Friedrich. In *Encyclopaedia Britannica*, 11th ed., s.v. "John the Apostle," and "The Gospel of St. John."

Von Rad, Gerhard. *Genesis.* Philadelphia: Westminster Press, 1972.

————. *Old Testament Theology.* New York: Harper & Row, 1965.

Webb, Val. *Like Catching Water in a Net: Human Attempts to Describe the Divine.* London: Continuum International, 2007.

————. *Stepping Out with the Sacred: Human Attempts to Engage the Divine.* New York and London: Continuum Press, 2010.

Wiesel, Elie. *Night.* New York: Bantam Books, 1982.

Other resources used include the following:

Book of Common Prayer, According to the Use of the Episcopal Church. New York: Church Hymnal Corp. and Seabury Press, 1979.

Gospel Parallels: A Synopsis of the First Three Gospels. New York: Thomas Nelson, 1949.

The HarperCollins Study Bible [NRSV]. Revised ed. Edited by Wayne Meeks. San Francisco: HarperOne, 2006.

The Hymnal of the Protestant Episcopal Church in the United States of America. New York: Church Pension Fund, 1940 and 1982.

The Interpreter's Bible. 12 vols. Edited by Nolan B. Harmon. Nashville: Abingdon Press, 1953.

The New Oxford Annotated Bible [RSV]. Edited by Herbert May and Bruce Metzger. New York: Oxford Univ. Press, 1973.